General Education
Development of G.
in Hong Kong, Taiwan and
Mainland China

MW01113336

This anthology brings together a distinguished group of general education scholars and teachers from Hong Kong, Taiwan, and mainland China, including some of the renowned general education experts in the region, such as Professor Huang Chun-chieh from National Taiwan University and Professor Hu Xianzhang from Qinghua University in Beijing.

With a comparative framework, the volume addresses three organizing questions of why, what and how. First, why has general education, a curricular movement started in the United States, taken center stage in today's undergraduate education in Hong Kong, Taiwan and mainland China? Second, what are the opportunities and challenges for general education across the region, in terms of program design, delivery and administration? Finally, how to execute an effective or successful general education program?

The book provides a comparative framework for assessing the status and development of general education in the region, promoting the philosophy and sound pedagogy of general education, and preparing for the pending transition to the new four-year program in Hong Kong. The 15 chapters in the collection are organized around four major themes of general education, including (1) concepts and objectives of general education; (2) curricular designs for general education; (3) pedagogical approaches to general education; and (4) strategies for general education assessment.

Xing Jun is Professor and Director of the General Education Centre at Hong Kong Polytechnic University. He is the author/editor of six refereed books and his most recent publication, *Service Learning in Asia: Curricular Models and Practices*, was published by Hong Kong University Press in 2010. As an internationally recognized scholar, Professor Xing is regularly invited as a speaker and consultant in the areas of curricular program design (baccalaureate core/general education), cross-cultural competency (diversity training) and civic education (service-learning).

Ng Pak-sheung is a historian and has been teaching at the General Education Centre, Hong Kong Polytechnic University since 2007. His areas of research cover political, social, military and minority studies with substantial emphasis on imperial China. In recent years, he has developed his research interest in general education in Hong Kong.

Cheng Chunyan received her MA in comparative literature from Beijing Language and Culture University. She is the author and co-author of a number of refereed journal articles and conference proceedings. Her research interest focuses on food and culture, particularly visual/cinematic representation of food in popular culture.

Routledge Research in Asian Education

This is an interdisciplinary series focusing on education in Asia. Open to established and emerging scholars with a focus on the region, it aims to inform readers of the latest research and contribute to the growth of scholarship on Asian education.

Books in the series include:

General Education and the Development of Global Citizenship in Hong Kong, Taiwan and Mainland China
Not merely icing on the cake
Edited by Xing Jun, Ng Pak-sheung and Cheng Chunyan

General Education and the Development of Global Citizenship in Hong Kong, Taiwan and Mainland China

Not merely icing on the cake

Edited by Xing Jun, Ng Pak-sheung and Cheng Chunyan

Routledge
Taylor & Francis Group

LONDON AND NEW YORK

First published 2013 by Routledge

2 Park Square, Milton Park, Abingdon, Oxfordshire OX14 4RN
711 Third Avenue, New York, NY 10017

Routledge is an imprint of the Taylor & Francis Group, an informa business

First issued in paperback 2018

British Library Cataloguing in Publication Data
A catalogue record for this book is available from the British Library

Library of Congress Cataloging in Publication Data
General education and the development of global citizenship in Hong
Kong, Taiwan and mainland China: not merely icing on the cake / Edited
by Xing Jun, Ng Pak-sheung, Cheng Chunyan.
    pages cm -- (Routledge research in Asian education)
    Includes bibliographical references and index.
    1. General education--China--Hong Kong. 2. General education--
Taiwan. 3. General education--China. 4. Education, Higher--China--
Hong Kong. 5. Education, Higher--Taiwan. 6. Education, Higher--
China. I. Xing, Jun, editor of compilation.
    LC988.C6G46 2013   370.11'10951--dc23
    2012017738

ISBN: 978-0-415-62397-1 (hbk)
ISBN: 978-1-138-70111-3 (pbk)

Typeset in Galliard
by Bookcraft Ltd, Stroud, Gloucestershire

Contents

List of illustrations

Figures

Tables

Appendices

Notes on contributors

John Freeman Babson is a Senior Lecturer at the General Education Center at The Hong Kong Polytechnic University. Dr. Babson earned his MS and PhD degrees at the University of Hawai'i at Mānoa in high energy physics, doing research in neutrino physics and astronomy. He has lived, studied or worked in five different cultures: New York, Korea, Hawai'i, Japan and Hong Kong. A former US Army officer, he is intensely interested in the world and how it works, in particular people (culture and psychology) and nature (physics, chemistry, biology and ecology). Currently he teaches astronomy, ecology, and Chinese technology and environmental history, and has written a textbook for one of his courses.

Cao Li is Professor of English, Director of the Centre for the Studies of European and American Literatures and deputy director of liberal education at Tsinghua University, Beijing, People's Republic of China. She has a PhD in English from the University of Cambridge. She is the author, editor and co-editor of a number of books and papers on liberal education and English and American literature. She is currently completing a book on Cambridge critics and their impact and significance in China.

Cheng Chunyan received her MA in comparative literature from Beijing Foreign Language and Culture University. She is the author or co-author of a number of refereed journal articles and conference proceedings. Her research interest focuses on food and culture, particularly visual/cinematic representation of food in popular culture.

Fan Ka-wai received his PhD from the Chinese University of Hong Kong in 1997. He is an Associate Professor at the Chinese Civilisation Center, City University of Hong Kong. His research interests include Chinese history, history of Chinese medicine and internet resources on Chinese studies. His most recent publications include: *Physicians and Patients in Medieval China* (Shanghai: Fudan University Press, 2010) and *A Guide to Chinese Medicine on the Internet* (New York and London: Routledge, 2008).

Feng Huimin is a Professor in the School of Education Science of Wuhan University, People's Republic of China. She has a PhD in law from Wuhan University. Her publications include *Universities General Education in*

China (2004), *On the Concept of Educational Equity of the Communist Party of China* (2009), *Higher Educational Quality and Educational Innovation* (2008). She has also published a number of occasional papers, for example, *A Report of Investigation and Analysis on General Education in Wuhan University* (2003), *On General Education in Higher Education Institutions of Mainland China* (2006), *A New Trend and Enlightenment of Core Curriculum Reformation in Harvard University* (2008), *On the Binding Constraint and Countermeasures to Promote the Development of General Education in Mainland Universities* (2007), *Some Ideals to Improve the Quality of General Education in Universities* (2009).

Hedley Freake is a Professor of Nutritional Sciences at the University of Connecticut. His research uses molecular techniques to address nutritional issues, currently pertaining to zinc homeostasis and action. He teaches courses ranging from Food Culture and Society, intended for first-year students, to Nutrition and Gene Expression for advanced graduate students. Dr. Freake chaired the university's General Education Oversight Committee at a time when a new general education program was being instituted and has been extensively involved in faculty governance of the curriculum. He spent 2009/10 based at Hong Kong Polytechnic University, working as part of the Fulbright team on developing general education programs in Hong Kong universities.

Hu Xianzhang is Professor at Tsinghua University, Beijing, People's Republic of China. He graduated from Tsinghua University in 1963, specializing in optical instruments. He was Vice-President of the University Council and Dean of the School of Humanities and Social Sciences. He is now senior advisor of the National Steering Committee for Cultural Quality Education. Professor Hu has published a number of books and dozens of papers and articles on higher education and university culture.

Huang Chun-chieh, PhD (1980, University of Washington, Seattle, USA), used to serve as Advisor to the Confucian Ethics Team of Singapore, Visiting Professor of the University of Washington and President (now Honorary President) of the Chinese Association for General Education. He is currently the Distinguished Professor of History, Dean of the Institute for Advanced Studies in Humanities and Social Sciences, National Taiwan University and a Research Fellow of the Institute of Chinese Literature and Philosophy, Academia Sinica, Taiwan. He was the President (2010–11) of the Society for Cultural Interaction in East Asia based at Kansai University, Japan. Professor Huang is the author of three books in English, including *Taiwan in Transformation: 1895–2005* (Transaction Publishers, 2006), *Mencian Hermeneutics: A History of Interpretations in China* (Transaction Publishers, 2001) and *Humanism in East Asian Confucian Context* (Bielefeld: Transcript Verlag, 2010). His most recent books in Chinese include *Confucian Classics and Their Ideas in the Cultural Interaction in East Asia* (National Taiwan University Press, 2010). His personal website is: http://huang.cc.ntu.edu.tw

Lai Kwok Hung is currently the Senior Student Affairs Officer and the Adjunct Assistant Professor of the Curriculum and Instruction Department of the Hong Kong Institute of Education. In addition to professional involvement, Dr. Lai was also an elected member of the District Council and chair of numerous government and district organizations for over 22 years. Dr. Lai received his first degree in Social Science (Social Work) at the Chinese University of Hong Kong, and his MSocSc and PhD at the University of Hong Kong, specializing in Criminology (Sociology). He has published widely, with articles in refereed journals, books, book chapters and newspaper articles and has presented papers at international conferences in student affairs, civic education, service-learning, juvenile delinquency and youth issues. He has been invited to be the reviewer of a special issue on service-learning for the journal *New Horizons in Education* and speaker or chairmanship of parallel sessions for various international conferences and symposiums.

Leung Mei Yee is Programme Director of the General Education Foundation Programme, Associate Director of University General Education and Associate Director of the Baldwin Cheng Research Centre for General Education at the Chinese University of Hong Kong. She is an alumna of the university as an undergraduate, and received a Maîtrise d'Histoire degree and a Doctorat en Histoire degree from the Université de Paris I, Panthéon-Sorbonne. Currently, she is working on several research projects related to quality assurance, students' learning and curriculum development in general education, and is a regular contributor to *University General Education Bulletin* (《大學通識報》) and other Chinese-language journals.

Li Manli is a Professor in the Institute of Education, Tsinghua University, Beijing, People's Republic of China. She has a PhD in Education from Peking University. Her teaching and research focuses on higher education and human resources education. She has published *General Education: An Interpretation of the Idea of the University* (Tsinghua University Press, 1999). She is also a chapter contributor ("The Concept of General Education in China") to *Knowledge across Cultures: A Contribution to Dialogue among Civilizations*, edited by Ruth Hayhoe and Julia Pan (University of Hong Kong, 2001). She has translated *General Education in a Free Society* (the Harvard Committee "Red Book," 1945) into Chinese, published by Peking University Press in 2010. She conducted a research project on liberal education and engineering education excellence supported by the US Fulbright program, as a visiting scholar in the Center for International Studies, MIT, in 2007/8.

Liang Jia-chi is an Associate Professor in the College of General Studies at Yuan Ze University, Taiwan. She received her PhD from the University of Texas at Austin in 2002 (Science Education Program). Her main research interests include science education, curriculum and instruction and teacher education.

Lin Mei-chin is the Director and Professor of the Graduate Institute of Educational Leadership and Development at Fu Jen Catholic University, Taiwan. She was the Dean of the Holistic Education Center at the university from August 2008 to January 2012. She received her PhD in Higher Education Management from the University of Missouri at Columbia in 1997. Her previous publications include "Need Orientation of Teacher Professional Growth Activities and Its Operation" (2006), "The Use of the Developmental Teacher Mentoring System to Develop Strategies for the Educational Practicum" (2007), "The Study of the Relationships between Curriculum Implementation and Learning Gains in the Course of Introduction to University Studies" (2009), "The Study of Student Attainments in the Course of Philosophy of Life Immersing Service-Learning Activities" (2009), "The Unchangeable School's Identity, Ways of Dealing with a Constantly Changing Environment and Conducting Changes for Educational Leaders" (2010). Her book on *Organizational Changes of the School: Reform and Balance Needs of the Organization, Leader and Members* was published in 2007. Her current research interests include teacher leadership, organizational leadership and changes, teacher development, general education and student attainments.

Ng Pak-sheung received his doctoral degree from the University of Arizona. His areas of research cover political, social, military and minority studies with substantial emphasis on the Tang and Song dynasties. His current research interest is general education in Hong Kong.

Shi Jinghuan is a Professor in the Institute of Education, Tsinghua University, Beijing, People's Republic of China, where she serves as executive director. Before this position she was a vice-dean of the Department of Education at Beijing Normal University. Her teaching and research focus on higher education and comparative education. Her research involves the examination of the college student experience and the history of higher education. She conducted a research project at the University of Maryland supported by the US Fulbright program.

Song Shanggui is Dean and Professor in the School of Education and Psychology at the University of Jinan, People's Republic of China. He received his PhD in education from Huazhong University of Science and Technology. He is working on general education and management systems in higher education. His most recent books include: *University Credits System Theory and Practice* (2006) and *University General Education Theory and Model* (2007), published by the China Ocean University Press. His work has appeared in the *International Journal of Psychology*, *Psychological Science*, *Educational Science*, the *Chinese Journal of Clinical Psychology*, the *Chinese Journal of Special Education* and the *Chinese Journal of Adult Education*.

Wang Lin-wen is a Professor in the College of General Studies at Yuan Ze University, Taiwan. He received his PhD from Case Western Reserve University, Cleveland in 1983, from the Department of Mechanical and

Aerospace Engineering. He is chief editor of the journal *Buddhism and Science*. His two books on the art and science aspects of I Ching were published in 2010 and 2011.

Wang Lixia is an Associate Professor in the Department of Mathematics in the Science School at Beijing University of Posts and Telecommunications, People's Republic of China, where she has been working since 2001. She has a PhD in history of mathematics from the Academy of Mathematics and Systems Science, Chinese Academy of Science; a master's degree in probability theory and mathematical statistics from Fudan University; and a bachelor's degree in computational mathematics from Wuhan University. Wang Lixia has published more than 20 academic papers. She is not only the translator of several articles and co-translator of two books in Chinese editions, but also the author, or co-author, of six textbooks.

Xing Jun is Professor and Director of the General Education Center at Hong Kong Polytechnic University. Professor Xing received his PhD in American Studies from the University of Minnesota, Twin Cities. Before assuming his present position in Hong Kong, Professor Xing was a faculty member and administrator for over 20 years in the United States. Professor Xing is the author/editor of six refereed English-language books and his most recent publication, *Service Learning in Asia: Curricular Models and Practices*, was published by Hong Kong University Press in 2010.

Xu Hui Xuan is an Assistant Professor in the Department of Curriculum and Instruction at the Hong Kong Institute of Education. She holds a doctorate from the Chinese University of Hong Kong (2007) and used to work at the Research Centre for General Education of the CUHK as a post-doctoral fellow. Her current research interests include general education curriculum design and development, curriculum leadership in general education, and adolescent identity development in service-learning. She is currently co-writing a book on theory and practice in university general education and working on a research project on adolescent identity development through service-learning in the Hong Kong context.

Foreword

Po Chung

General education (GE), or liberal arts education, is now firmly seen to be one of the keys to developing and nurturing civically responsible and economically productive citizens.

In my youth as an undergraduate in America, general education was mandatory. I was forced to take GE courses without realizing their merits. At that time, I didn't think these courses would be helpful for developing either my professional or personal competency. When I entered the real world of business after graduation, my first job was working as a toy buyer. My basic knowledge and skills in chemistry, physics, art appreciation, design, history, and social psychology that I learned during my undergraduate years and GE courses came into use almost every day. My exposure to other ways of learning that enabled me to express myself openly and honestly, without fear, and to have my ideas challenged on their merit by teachers and fellow students helped me to better understand my own values and appreciate other points of view. General education broadened and extended my experience and perspectives.

Later, when I set up DHL International Asia, I traveled throughout the region to build and develop the business. My knowledge of geography, various religions, cultural traditions and the diversity of ways people make a living and promote economic growth and prosperity contributed to my ability to find local leaders and employees who could help me grow DHL into the most global of global companies.

More recently, I realized that general education is a gift that keeps on giving. My early experience with general education and my use of this learning contributed enormously to the success and significance of my life and the lives of people who were affected by my thinking, behavior and leadership. Even after my retirement from DHL, my university GE exposure continues to motivate and enhance my desire for lifelong learning and attainment of life-fulfilling goals. It's clear to me now that my learning in GE courses continues to help me integrate, improve and manage my brain, body and behavior. I am constantly reminded of the value of my general education.

GE also enabled me to improve my ability to think outside of the box while also honing my skills at objectively evaluating my thinking and intuitive first impressions. These attributes are essential competencies for entrepreneurs, managers and service leaders in today's flat, globalized world. Further, general education is a well-developed model for promoting the development of critical thinking, problem-solving, effective communication, collaboration and positive social behaviour.

As a convert to the value of general education, I realize its importance and value in the business environment. This inspired my "evangelical" vision and passion to share the benefits of general education with Hong Kong, my home. Shortly thereafter, a priceless opportunity came: the Hong Kong government's Education Bureau and University Grants Committee (UGC) launched 3+3+4 education reform. Extending the university undergraduate degree from three years to four provided the perfect opportunity for me to promote the development of general education in Hong Kong. After evaluating different ways that I might help Hong Kong universities include general education in the new four-year degree, I decided to help create and fund the Fulbright Hong Kong General Education Program (FHKGEP).

FHKGEP was designed to promote and provide a platform for exchange between university scholars from the USA and their local counterparts. The program created a dialogue space for Hong Kong universities to exchange ideas, resources and experiences about how to localize the general education curriculum across the system while preserving individual university autonomy. I saw this as a timely and valuable investment that would help enable Hong Kong to increase and sustain its competitive advantage.

As I see general education being more widely included in Asia's curricula, I see it has precisely the same ability to bring our region the compelling benefits it brought to the United States. In short, to help universities deliver graduates who are critical and creative thinkers, problem-solvers, gifted communicators, team managers and ethical leaders. General education has the ability to develop and nurture civic responsibility and create communities of innovation. These are qualities that today's graduates and societies need to possess in order to thrive in this fiercely competitive and globalized world. They are also the competencies and values employers expect to find in the employees they hire to grow and expand their businesses today and manage them in the future. To maintain a competitive edge in the global market, it is crucial for university graduates in Hong Kong and elsewhere in Asia to be equipped with the character and care GE can deliver.

But I issue a cautionary note. General education pedagogy places great emphasis on the use of learning processes that require learners to practice putting knowledge, skills and values into action. As Hong Kong rolls out general education across its education system and Asian universities do so in selected universities and colleges in order to promote graduates attaining learning outcomes that benefit business, trade, commerce and society in general the ripe seed of general education is being sowed. However, be aware and be cautioned, the investment in general education will not yield its full benefits unless teachers and students are permitted to use and practice appropriate liberal education pedagogies. These include learning experiences and opportunities for dialogue that allow different opinions and values to coexist harmoniously in a safe learning environment – not only in the classrooms and halls of a university, but in the societies and halls of government within which a university carries out its purpose.

Acknowledgements

As co-editors, we want first to thank Hong Kong Polytechnic University for the learning and teaching development grant which provided seed money for the book. We would also like to acknowledge the camaraderie of our academic colleagues at the General Education Center (GEC), who provided both the inspiration and passion to complete a project that is so dear to our collective hearts! Our sincere thanks go to many other colleagues and friends who have helped with advice, encouragement and support every step along the way, particularly Poon Yuk-ling, who has provided the best secretarial, logistical and editorial support any scholar could ever wish for, and Christina Low, our commissioning editor from Routledge, whose enthusiasm, expertise and professionalism have guided us through the entire editorial and production process. Jaya Conser Lapham, Xing Jun's long-time American student and friend, has also assisted in research, editing and translation. Most importantly, we owe a huge debt of gratitude to every single one of our contributors, who has placed his or her trust and confidence in the project and responded to each of our inquiries, suggestions and requests for revisions with grace and generosity.

This book is the outcome of a remarkable collaborative effort: none of us could have done it alone. Editing a book with a group of scholars coming from several regions and diverse disciplines is a huge challenge. Both Ng Pak-sheung and Cheng Chunyan have served as effective coordinators between the contributors and the editorial team. In his typical gentlemanly manner, Ng Pak-sheung has nudged everybody along during this two-year-long journey. Cheng Chunyan's part of the editorship also includes English translation of the four Chinese-language chapters (Chapters 3, 5, 11 and 15). The introductory chapter is mostly Xing Jun's contribution, improved by Ng Pak-sheung's editorial suggestions. In the meantime, they have shared the editorial work for all the chapters in the collection.

Finally, responsibility for all omissions and inadequacies lies squarely with the co-editors.

Xing Jun, Hong Kong Polytechnic University
Ng Pak-sheung, Hong Kong Polytechnic University
Cheng Chunyan, Beijing Language and Culture University

1 General education and global citizenship

A comparative study in Hong Kong, Taiwan and mainland China

Xing Jun and Ng Pak-sheung

General education (GE), also known as the "common core" or the baccalaureate core, as a curricular movement, started in the United States in the 1920s. Over recent years, universities in the greater China area (Hong Kong, Taiwan and mainland China) have launched their own GE programs. Most of them have modeled their curricula after the American system, especially the so-called Harvard "core curriculum." As a relatively recent development in the greater China region, there has been little English-language scholarly publication on China-based practices and contexts of general education. Most of the published works on general education are monographs, teaching anthologies or guidebooks published in the United States, including series and booklets coming from the Association of American Colleges and Universities (AAC&U). Although these are significant works that have made contributions to the development of general education, there is an urgent need for a book that explores the specific local or indigenous practices and varied contexts of general education in Hong Kong, Taiwan and the Chinese mainland. Indeed, while sharing some common features, the concept, history, design, practices and administration of general education vary significantly from university to university and region to region because of their different social, cultural, and educational systems.

This anthology offers to help fill the gap by providing a comparative framework for assessing the status and development of general education in the area, and promoting critical pedagogy and best practices within general education, which is both reflective of international trends but also distinctive in its own local and regional characteristics, given the tremendous diversity both within and among Chinese societies. There are 15 chapters in the collection, written by a distinguished group of GE scholars and teachers from Hong Kong, Taiwan, mainland China and the United States. As disparate as they may seem, the essays collected here all address three organizing questions of why, what and how. First, why has general education, a curricular movement that began in the United States, taken center stage in today's undergraduate education in the greater China region? Second, what are the opportunities and challenges for general education across the region, in terms of program design, delivery and administration? Finally, how do we execute an effective and successful GE program for university faculty, administrators and students?

Why has general education taken center stage in today's undergraduate education?

The concept and core values of general education, as part of the liberal arts tradition, have been around for centuries. Over recent decades, however, general education has experienced a new spurt of interest and momentum in higher education. There are three major forces or larger trends that are driving this movement, including the knowledge-based global economy, an exploding number of interdisciplinary programs and a major paradigm shift in liberal arts education.

First, forces of globalization have reshaped the landscape in higher education for the greater China region over the last two decades, creating both opportunities and challenges for college students. When they graduate and enter the real world, they must have the cultural sensitivities and social skills, in addition to their professional training, to compete in a knowledge-based global economy. In response, Chinese institutions of higher education need to turn out thoughtful citizens instead of useful profit-seekers. "In contrast to the *consumer*," as William F. Pinar explains in his book on curriculum theory, "the *citizen* is capable of juxtaposing the private and the public, holding these separate, often dissonant domains together in creative tension, sometimes sacrificing the former for the sake of the latter."[1] For example, a number of Hong Kong universities have been working on a new integrated set of key attributes for their own graduates. Alongside professional competence, critical thinking, effective communication, innovative problem-solving, lifelong learning and ethical leadership are often cited among the given and desired key attributes for the GE curriculum. The "common core," in particular, is often seen as the key to provide students with those key competencies.

This new student profile is probably best captured by the dual citizenship concept put forward by the National Service Scheme of India. "Those who live in the 21st century will have dual citizenship," according to the document, "one, each person's national citizenship and the other the global citizenship. The former is a legal status represented by documents such as the passport while the other is more a set of personality traits, attitudes and values operating in the relationships with peoples of other cultures and conditions."[2] This concept of global citizenship represents a direct response to the phenomenon of globalization. As the report *The Global University* states, "Developing a global perspective enhances the development of the 'critical' skills that are at the heart of learning outcomes for all graduates: it is the very role of education to help students locate knowledge in the wider political, environment, social and economic contexts."[3] Indeed, given this context, universities, including those in the greater China region, are seeking ways to explore existing pedagogical theories and best practice in general education to internationalize their curriculum. Specifically, this concept of global citizenship should be fully embedded in the philosophy, objectives and design of every GE curriculum. In a sense, that mandate itself provides the very foundation for the general education reform movement in the greater China region.

Equally significant for institutions of higher education, pressing global problems challenge traditional disciplines and demand new forms of learning that reshape the boundaries of knowledge. Whether the issue is global warming, conflict resolution or health education, its solution often requires a truly interdisciplinary training that cuts across multiple academic fields. Indeed, history has taught us that knowledge creation often occurs at the interface of disciplines. In response to those rapidly changing dynamics, general education, with its strong emphasis on liberal arts, has taken an increasingly important role in undergraduate education. "The distribution model" in general education, for example, represents an attempt to equip students with those interdisciplinary training and perspectives. Indeed, the overall premise for this book is that higher education has to contribute to the public good by training more global citizens with a strong sense of civic responsibility and the multidisciplinary skills needed to participate as active citizens in an increasingly complex and interconnected world.

Finally, we clearly see a paradigm shift in liberal arts education. In his provocative and much-cited *Excellence without a Soul: Does Liberal Education Have a Future?* (first published under the title *Excellence without a Soul: How a Great University Forgot Education*), Harry Lewis, a long-time Harvard professor and former Dean of Harvard College, offered a scathing critique of the failure of American liberal arts education: "The great universities are respected and certainly prized in America, but the public regards with increasing scepticism the values they represent and their failure sometimes to represent any values at all." Interestingly, half-way across the world, Qian Xuesen (H. S. Tsien), father of China's space program, had equally harsh words for the quality of China's higher education. "Why do our schools always fail to nurture outstanding talents?" This is the question Qian asked on his deathbed in 2009. In response, 11 topnotch Chinese scholars issued an open letter to Yuan Guiren, Chinese Education Minister, urging him and their peers, "Let's face the 'Qian Xuesen question!'"

Not by accident, both critiques cited above call for a major paradigm shift in academia with regard to knowledge, the professions and the curriculum. First, there is an increasing realization in the world-wide academic community that a shift of emphasis must be made to the transformative rather than just the utilitarian value of knowledge in higher education. In addition, academicians need to shift back to viewing an academic career as a sacred calling, requiring a cultural outlook rather than mere technical expertise. Last, but certainly not least, there is the urgent need to return to the concept of whole-person education or, in our case, general education.

Taken together, all those factors listed above have changed the way we teach our students and have contributed to the popularity of the baccalaureate core or general education programs across Chinese universities in the region.

What are the promises and challenges for general education in the Greater China region?

In 2000, the Task Force on Higher Education and Society sponsored by the World Bank and UNESCO released a report on the prospects of higher education in developing countries in the twenty-first century, a whole chapter of which was devoted to explaining the importance of general education and calling for a broadly based GE program.[4] Indeed, due to their different social, cultural and political systems, while sharing some common experiences, the concept, content, system and practices of general education vary significantly among institutions of higher education in Taiwan, Hong Kong and the Chinese mainland. General education in Taiwan, for example, started in 1984 in response to a four to six credit general education mandate from the Ministry of Education, which was increased to eight credits in 1992. The entire development of general education over the past two decades in Taiwan was guided by four separate government policies. In the mainland, however, general education was not a widely accepted concept until recently, although "cultural value/quality education," a special version of general education which was a top-down government initiative, started officially in 1995. In addition, the execution of general education in mainland China was complicated and hindered by a number of unique challenges, including the traditional culture of examination-oriented education, the adoption of the Soviet-model of specialization in 1952, the lure of a new market economy over the past two decades and an increasing over-emphasis on professional training. As Sung Shanggui, the author of Chapter 3, says so clearly, although China has a long humanistic tradition going back to ancient times serious restraints have been placed on general education by the development of a unique Chinese university culture.

Similarly in Hong Kong, the status of GE programs also differs significantly among the eight UGC-supported schools. CUHK, for example, has one of the best-established GE programs, which began in 1963, while the rest started their GE course offerings in the early to mid-1990s. In this context, Hong Kong's government-mandated three+three+four reform (the pending change from a three-year British to a four-year North American-style college curriculum in Fall 2012) represents a bold step forward for secondary and university education in Hong Kong and a major investment in Hong Kong's future. It is perhaps one of the greatest educational experiments and enterprises of the twenty-first century. The design, delivery and administration of a significant GE program are one key requirement for the new four-year curriculum in Hong Kong.

The next few years represent the most critical moment for the development and institutionalization of general education in both public and higher education in Hong Kong and the greater China region. The 3+3+4 mandate represents government commitment with additional, though limited, resources. There are also supports available from other initiatives, such as the Fulbright General Education program, funded privately. The Hong Kong General Education Project (HKGEP) is another example. Mr. Po Chung, a prominent philanthropist in Hong Kong and founder of DHL in Asia, has donated over US$1 million to Hong Kong universities to support American Fulbright general education scholars to come to Hong Kong. The Hong Kong government has matched the fund with another US$1 million. So far, Hong Kong universities have hosted 20 Fulbright general education scholars each year between 2008 and 2012. While the Hong Kong American Center has served as the administrative platform for this project, administrations from different campuses have fully participated in the selection progress. In the meantime, the new four-year program has also meant a substantial expansion of academic staff by 10–20 percent and additions to the existing expertise on different campuses.[5]

Despite these unique circumstances and opportunities for expansion and further development, universities from all three areas share similar challenges in developing a vibrant and effective GE program. General education is a complex operation and carries a myriad of challenges, which could be grouped into three broad categories, namely, program design, delivery and administration.

Design

Program design is the very first step for any effective general education program. With reference to specific models, there are a plethora of approaches available. As reported by Lin Mei-chin in Chapter 6, a recent survey was conducted on the organization of GE programs among 292 American four-year colleges and universities between 1975 and 2000. Four popular models were identified over this 25-year period, namely, "core distribution areas," "traditional liberal arts," "culture and ethics" and "civic/utilitarian." In the meantime, there are other well-known GE models that have been discussed among general education scholars and practitioners, including the "Great Books" program (Chicago), the Honors College (Colorado), service-learning (NYU), first-year experience or freshman seminar (UCLA), capstone experience/synthesis (Columbia) and study abroad experience (Brown).

Locally, there are two specific challenges in GE program design. First and foremost, any GE program has to align itself with each institution's history, culture, vision and mission. Since each individual university has its unique strengths and traditions, the matrix of their graduates may also be different. For example, at HKBU, the Center for Holistic Teaching and Learning organized a six-part seminar series of teaching and learning experience sharing (TALES), providing strategies and tips for alignment of general education to Baptist University's Christian heritage of whole-person education. TALES 1 specifically discusses the intended learning outcomes (ILOs) for general education and how they support HKBU six graduate attributes of the whole person – spiritual/individual, intellectual/rational, social/cultural, physical/material, humane/community and vocational/professional. Similarly, as discussed by Lin Mei-chin in Chapter 6, Fu Jen University, a Catholic institution in Taiwan, also takes whole-person education as its core institutional mission. To align its GE program goals with this core mission, Fu Jen developed the so-called four Cs framework in its curricular design, which covers culture, curriculum, co-curriculum and community. After several years of experimentation, the Center of Holistic Education was placed in charge of general education, and whole-person education became officially known as general education in 1990.

In addition, an effective GE program structure should be coherent and not a "smorgasbord" (in Harry Lewis' words). The demands on context are fewer but the demands on principled undertaking may be greater. In other words, there is always the challenge of balancing the depth and breadth of the general curriculum. A case in point: GE scholars commonly agree that the "distribution model" tends to compartmentalize knowledge and approaches. As discussed by several authors in the collection, including Hu Xianzhang and Cao Li (Chapter 5), Li Manli and Shi Jinghuan (Chapter 7) and Hedley Freake (Chapter 8), Chinese universities have struggled with this balance in their program design for years. For example, Li Manli and Shi Jinghuan describe the typical undergraduate program for mainland Chinese universities that has to incorporate two kinds of Ministry of Education mandated courses, including compulsory courses on political theory, military training, English language, sports and the so-called *wenhua suzhi jiaoyu* (Culture Quality Education) courses together with any discipline-based and institutionally mandated courses. As they write: "the general education curriculum lacks organic links and cannot be integrated into the total undergraduate program. Neither professors nor students consider general education courses as fundamental academic training but rather as an opportunity to expand knowledge and to learn a bit about everything." This statement has highlighted a common problem in GE program design among Chinese universities.

Delivery

As showcased by the different case studies in this collection, three elements must be in place for the implementation of any successful GE programs.

First, a workable staffing model for general education should be developed with strong support from all the stakeholders, including faculty and students as well as senior management. As testified by the contributors to this book, faculty buy-in is critical to the successful delivery of any GE program. Often teaching GE is regarded as less important to the academic majors, and does not help research, publications and thus faculty promotions. Accordingly, a number of questions have been raised about their workable staffing models by Chinese universities. How will regular faculty be enticed to take on GE courses and given due recognition at the unit level? Will there be a new type of academic staff specializing in teaching and advising students? Some Hong Kong universities have increasingly recruited a new grade of academic staff who are designated as "teaching fellows" with no research obligations. Is this trend the same as or similar to the lower-paid, less prestigious and fast-growing "adjunct faculty" rank seen in the United States? The relevant concern here is that a two-tiered staffing system could lead to disparities and resentment among academic staff.

In response, a number of recommendations have been made on sustaining a core group of faculty engaged in general education, such as establishing professional development opportunities, e.g. summer faculty seminars, creating special incentives, for instance faculty stipends, course release and public recognition, and developing a strong network of support on campus, as along the lines of NYU's GE electronic blackboard, consisting of faculty space, media matrix and virtual commons. In the meantime, a few institutions have allocated additional resources for the establishment of endowed chairs in general education. As part of its centennial anniversary hires, HKU, for example, has recruited a few new chair professors, whose explicit responsibilities would be to serve a leadership role in general education and the transition to the four-year degree program. In short, a core group of faculty dedicated to teaching GE is needed to run GE programs effectively.

Second, academic departments are often confronted with the challenge of training or retooling some of their faculty to teach GE courses. Indeed, teaching a GE subject is different from teaching a regular disciplinary class. Although the subject matter could be the same, students in GE classes often have a broader range of academic background, more divergent motivation and varying engagement levels. In this sense, GE courses may demand pedagogical adjustments for instructors.

Third, an effective GE program should build in a regular and vigorous assessment system. Some GE scholars have called for a fully developed quality assurance scheme.[6] Indeed, this assessment challenge needs to be addressed at all levels, from individual academic units to faculty, institutions and the entire higher education system. Instruments have been developed on different campuses for quality assurance. To create a useful platform for dialogue, the last three chapters in the current volume are specifically designed to address learning outcome assessment, making sure that GE programs are achieving their intended outcomes.

Administration

As a university-wide program, taught by a multidisciplinary faculty, general education also has an administrative dimension or infrastructure that may require our special attention. Between 2004 and 2006, for example, the University of California system organized a system-wide "Commission on General Education in the 21st Century." The Commission has since made eight specific recommendations about an appointed and dedicated leadership, committed resource allocations and regular professional training opportunities.[7] At the top of the list is the office and leadership role of a chief undergraduate education officer/director. To institutionalize general education, the report recommends an Office of General Education or Academic Programs, placed at the university level in the Office of Academic Affairs. The designated GE officer/director should be charged with coordinating the curriculum, liaison between the advisory committee and the teaching units (colleges and departments.), conducting GE faculty training and organizing GE seminars, workshops and even weekly or monthly luncheons.

Indeed, as showcased by several authors in the present volume, a successful incumbent must be a strong advocate for GE, an effective bridge-builder and liaison for GE and a scholar and competent teacher in GE. He or she should be responsible for promoting good pedagogical approaches and hosting programming activities, such as GE workshops, symposia and summer institutes; he or she should also take the leadership in assessing and improving student learning to achieve the intended learning outcomes for GE and other courses. Since GE is a university-wide program, outreach and networking with all the stakeholders should be a priority for anyone who occupies that office. As part of the transition to the new four-year undergraduate program, all the eight UGC-funded universities in Hong Kong are in the process of setting up, if they have not already done so, a centrally located GE office. CUHK, for example, has a decade-old GE unit, administered by a dean for the staffing, administration and evaluation of the GE program. Two years ago, HKU established a pro-Vice-Chancellor position for Teaching and Learning Initiatives, overseeing general education. Recently, PolyU has also launched a general university requirement (GUR) office.

How do we teach general education?

This volume should be taken as a springboard for dialogue on this practical topic among noted GE scholars and teachers from Hong Kong, Taiwan and mainland China. As the contents page shows, the book is organized around four major themes of general education, namely (1) concepts and objectives of general education; (2) curricular development for general education; (3) pedagogical approaches to general education; and, (4) strategies for general education assessment. We will use the remainder of this introduction to provide a few highlights from each chapter for our readers.

Goals and objectives

In the now classic 1945 publication, *General Education in a Free Society: Report of the Harvard Committee*, the authors outlined the primary goal of general education as providing a broad, yet focused survey of courses that will promote critical thinking and increase students' awareness of the world around them. In 2000, AAC&U sponsored a two-year national initiative on twenty-first-century general education, revisiting the goals and objectives of general education. The concept of general education seems to be culturally neutral, but it is not. As the three chapters in Part I demonstrate in detail, general education may mean very different things for different educational systems from different societies. What is more, because of their different natures – public versus private, Christian versus secular, for instance – even universities in the same area may have different understandings of general education.

Huang Chun-chieh's opening chapter provides readers with an overview on the tensions between what he calls "the new tide of post-Cold War capitalist globalization" and Chinese cultural traditions and indigenous knowledge in the twenty-first century. After highlighting some of the major phenomena of today's "academic capitalism," he recommends some "coping strategies" which will help universities on both sides of the Taiwan Strait "plant deep culture roots so that students may avoid becoming rootless orchids in the great tide of globalization and lose themselves and their cultural identity." Song Shanggui in Chapter 3 discusses the intended objectives of general education from the perspective of university culture. Using the "learning to care" program as a specific example, proposed by the 1989 "Education for the 21st Century" international symposium in Beijing, sponsored by UNESCO, Song argues that the existing Chinese university culture, which is characterized by an emphasis on "engineering over science" and "science over liberal arts," must be transformed for the sake of general education reform. Calling it "the hidden curriculum of general education," the author has illustrated his point by drawing our attention to the various dimensions of the university culture, ranging from the teaching process, faculty development, campus environment to university administration. For example, Song proposes one of the core objectives of general education is to "nourish students the qualities of 'being kind to others' and 'caring for society'." Thus, universities should first take the concept of humanistic care as their top administrative priority, and only after "a student-centered and service-oriented concept is developed and fused into all administrative activities can the university create a good humanistic environment."

The third chapter in Part I, by Leung Mei Yee, wraps up this engaging discussion on the goals and objectives of general education by tracing the formation and development of general education from the tradition of liberal education. Despite the fact that some scholars view liberal education and general education as interchangeable concepts, Leung distinguishes the two by describing the classical concept of liberal education as both a "universal education ideal" and a "concrete curriculum," while the modern concept of general education represents only a concrete curricular paradigm. Thus, "placing liberal education on the level of an education philosophy and regarding general education as a curriculum element in realizing the ideal of a liberal education," she concludes, "not only help in clarifying the relationship between the two, but are also extremely important to the future development of general education curricula."

To a varying extent, all three authors in Part I have emphasized the three key objectives of general education for Chinese universities, namely, (a) how curricular programs, and for that matter our university culture, help students receive a broadly based education and foster their critical thinking and learning skills; (b) how they help students maintain their cultural identity, under the onslaught of globalization, and acquire cross-cultural literacy and competency; and (c) how general education contributes to the public good by training more "citizens," rather than "netizens," who enter society not only with their technical expertise but also a strong sense of civic and global responsibility.

Curricular development

The four chapters in Part II offer a rare comparative perspective on GE curricular development among over a dozen institutions of higher education from Hong Kong, Taiwan and mainland China. Drawing upon the recent research data collected by the Center for Liberal Education at Tsinghua University and based on their own rich and lengthy experience as GE administrators, Hu Xianzhang and Cao Li, the authors of Chapter 5, showcase three GE models operated by three of China's most prestigious universities, including the Beida model of general elective courses plus major discipline platforms, the Fudan model of undergraduate college plus the core curriculum and the Tsinghua model of core curriculum plus pilot projects. After outlining the basic framework of general education that has been firmly established by Chinese universities over the last two decades, the authors highlight some existing problems in curricular development in the mainland, including continued marginalization of GE courses as simple adds-on, the popularity of "wet courses," which water down course content for entertainment purposes and lack of a strong faculty buy-in on Chinese university campuses. In comparison to the mainland, Christian institutions of higher education in Taiwan and Hong Kong often integrate the concept of whole-person education into their course designs. For example, in Chapter 6, Lin Mei-chin from Fu Jen University discusses in detail the four Cs framework of culture, curriculum, co-curriculum and community adopted by Fu Jen in its GE curricular design.

Taking examples from Peking, Zhejiang, Tsinghua, Huazhong, Fudan and Zhongshan universities, Li Manli and Shi Jinghuan, authors of Chapter 7, discuss the tension between the philosophy of liberal arts education and market economy in contemporary Chinese society and its impact on undergraduate program development. Through a detailed analysis of course offerings, extra-curricular activities and administrative structures at those leading mainland universities, the authors have provided some very useful case studies for GE scholars and practitioners. The last piece in Part II, by Hedley Freake, a residential Fulbright Scholar at Hong Kong Polytechnic University for the 2009/10 academic year, provides both a summary of the GE programs developed by the eight UGC-funded universities in Hong Kong and compares them with one another and with those operating in the United States. Further, Freake has used Hong Kong Polytechnic University as a useful case study to illustrate the complex and often painstaking efforts of curricular changes in Hong Kong. Comprehensive in data and insightful in perspective, the chapter is a must-read for anyone who is interested in understanding the details of GE program design in the Hong Kong context.

In short, all the four chapters in Part II address, to varying degrees, two types of curricular questions: models and structures. In terms of curricular models, the conversation has focused on the benefits and problems of the "common core" and the "distribution requirement," both of which were borrowed from Harvard, or a combination of the two. In the meantime, specific questions have been asked by the authors as to how Chinese universities structure their GE courses in the local context. For example, should they be knowledge-based, discipline-based, skills-based or inter/multidisciplinary theme-based? And, for some campuses, there is also an ongoing dialogue about the necessity of a local or regional program focus, such as the requirement for China studies. Finally, two of the authors have discussed the idea and practice of residential education as part of the GE movement, such as Fudan College in Shanghai and Yuan Pei College in Beijing.

Pedagogical approaches

The success of any GE program depends not only on a well-designed curriculum, but also a successful and effective delivery system. Part III attempts to address the issue of teaching strategies adopted by Chinese GE teachers and practitioners. While the first three chapters approach critical pedagogy from a specific disciplinary perspective, namely general science, medicine and mathematics, the last chapter aptly devotes itself to faculty training, a fundamentally important dimension in the delivery of general education.

John Babson, a trained physicist who has been teaching general education over several decades in Honolulu, Korea, Japan and Hong Kong, starts Chapter 9 with a scathing critique of C. P. Snow's famous concept of the "Two Cultures," claiming that "science is not to be viewed as separate or in contrast to the humanities but instead fundamentally a product and driver of the humanistic tradition." He then gives a nuanced analysis of the scientific method, which represents nothing less than a good exercise in humanistic thinking. Finally, Babson provides readers with a "tool box" for the practical pedagogy of teaching general science in the Hong Kong classroom. Taking a similar stand on the relationship between humanities and science, Fan Ka-wai, in Chapter 10, approaches the subject from the perspective of Chinese medicine. The author argues passionately that the wide gaps between two sets of cultures, the cultures of sciences and humanities and the cultures of China and the West, should be and can be narrowed through general education. "In my opinion," Fan writes, "teaching Chinese medicine as a general education course can achieve both goals, bridging science and humanities as well as China and the West." Specifically, the author discusses the Problem-Based Learning (PBL) approach, a dialogue-focused pedagogy in teaching a course on Chinese medicine he has proposed at the City University of Hong Kong. Chapter 11 by Wang Lixia, a long-time math professor and published scholar in math education, shares her expertise and experience in teaching GE math courses in Beijing. To her, an ideal math education should be by its nature general education and demands "an organic, holistic and progressive" approach. Accordingly, teaching math is more than just teaching numeracy, but should integrate three equally important components, namely, mathematical theory, literacy and application. Readers should find it helpful in what she has called the "context-driven" approach, where she divides students into three separate groups, namely math majors (M students), science and engineering majors (SE) and non-SEM students. To meet their specific needs, she has developed a number of electives, including "History of mathematics" and "Mathematical culture."

Chapter 12, the last piece in Part III, co-authored by Liang Jia-chi and Wang Lin-wen, wraps up the discussion of pedagogy by addressing the key issue of faculty development in general education. Drawing upon their own involvement in faculty training at Yuan Ze University in Taiwan, the authors introduce the concept of pedagogical content knowledge (PCK), where they detail the five key elements in PCK for faculty development, including the spirit, discipline, students' understanding, approaches and assessment in general education. Perhaps what readers may find most helpful in the chapter is their discussion of the quasi-in-service system (CLIPPER) they have designed for their junior colleagues on campus. The CLIPPER system's seven dimensions are explained in detail, which include community, literature, inspiration, paradigm, practice, engagement and resources.

In summary, all the four chapters in Part III address some key pedagogical questions and explore useful strategies in teaching GE courses. Some of the questions raised may include: how do faculty members generate student interest in GE classes which might not be directly related to their own academic programs? Unlike teaching academic majors, how do instructors deal with GE students' diverse academic backgrounds and different levels of academic preparation? And how do GE instructors make sure that they can accommodate students' different learning styles in and outside the typical classroom?

Outcome assessment

Nowadays, there is a broadly shared consensus among educators and university administrators that a successful GE program should build in a regular and vigorous assessment system, assessing and improving student learning to achieve the intended learning outcomes for general education.

The three chapters in Part IV examine assessment work in education through three divergent perspectives. Huang Chun-chieh starts off the discussion with a powerful critique of the broadly shared problems in evaluation and assessment in the fields of social sciences and humanities in Chinese higher education. Going beyond teaching and general education, Huang challenges the general academic standards adopted by Chinese universities in both teaching and scholarship. He argues that the use of indices in assessing research outcomes stifles innovation and leads to an exclusive focus on "quantitative" standards, overemphasis on natural science and technology and stress on research over teaching. To correct the problem, he proposes three new standards for evaluation, which include innovation in knowledge, student enlightenment and contribution to society. In comparison, Chapter 14, by Lai Kwok Hung and Xu Hui Xuan, has a very narrow but carefully placed focus on learning outcome assessment of GE courses, particularly those with a service-learning component. Based on their research (content analysis of journals, data generated from questionnaires, participant observation and focus interviews) on three pilot credit-bearing service-learning courses offered in the academic year 2008/9 at the Hong Kong Institute of Education, the authors have presented a carefully prepared case study from the perspectives of course lecturers, student affairs practitioners as field instructors, service agency supervisors of community groups as well as student participants. The discussion of their research methodology and its limitations at the end of the chapter should also serve as important reference point for readers.

In Chapter 15, the last chapter of the volume, Feng Huimin brings to a close the assessment discussion by carefully documenting some specific difficulties and problems in GE assessment, including the haphazard nature of assessment work, ambiguity in GE objectives, lack of benchmarking, monolithic methodology, inadequate consideration of faculty and student input and lack of institutional support and resources. Feng points out that the bottom line is that inconsistencies in classifying GE learning outcomes have made its assessment an impossible task to accomplish. In response, she recommends applying Benjamin Bloom's taxonomy to GE assessment and group GE indices into three broad categories in the domain of knowledge, the domain of skills and the domain of emotions. "Corresponding to the three domain of learning outcomes," Feng writes, "the teaching objectives of general education can also be divided into objectives of knowledge, abilities and emotions."

In a nutshell, the discussion in Part IV boils down to three organizing questions. The first is about benchmarking, e.g. what kind of standards do we use in outcome assessment? Second, consideration must be given to methodologies, namely what kind of methods do we employ in evaluating GE classes? And, finally, what kind of assessment tools have been developed for GE assessment? In other words, are we using the same kind of methodologies we are familiar with in learning outcome assessment, such as (a) student portfolios, (b) exit interviews, (c) alumni surveys, (d) faculty focus groups and (e) employer questionnaires?

We want to conclude our introduction by highlighting the book's unique features, which include: (1) it is multi-disciplinary (written by noted GE scholars from fields ranging from science to philosophy); (2) it is comparative in nature (identifying both local and regional similarities and differences in general education, given the tremendous diversity both within and among Chinese societies); and (3) it is comprehensive (covering every dimension of general education from curricular design to learning outcome assessment). We hope you will find that these features make the book enjoyable and useful reading.

Notes

1 William F. Pinar, *What is Curriculum Theory?*, 2nd edn. (New York and London: Routledge, 2012), p. xvii.
2 Quoted from "'Not Me but You': Profile of a Service-Learning Program in India." In Howard A. Berry and Linda A. Chisholm, *Service-Learning in Higher Education around the World: An Initial Look* (New York: International Partnership for Service Learning and Leadership, 1999), Appendix V, pp. 121–29.
3 D. Bourn, A. McKenzie and C. Shiel, *The Global University: The Role of the Curriculum* (London: Development Education Association, 2006).
4 Task Force on Higher Education and Society, *Higher Education in Developing Countries: Peril and Promise* (New York: World Bank, 2000), pp. 117–18.
5 For details, see the progress report, "The Progress of Hong Kong's Universities in Implementing the 3–3–4 Reforms: A Status Report on Preparations and Prospects," prepared by Martin J. Finkelstein, Fulbright Senior Specialist, Hong Kong University and Elaine M. Walker, Visiting Scholar, Hong Kong University, July 5, 2008.
6 In 2007, Hong Kong Polytechnic University sponsored an assessment conference, papers from which appeared in Steve Frankland, ed., *Enhancing Teaching and Learning through Assessment* (Dordrecht: Springer, 2007).
7 For details, see "General Education in the 21st Century: Report of the University of California Commission on General Education in the 21st Century." Center for Higher Education Studies, University of California, Berkeley, April 2007. Online. Available HTTP: <http://cshe.berkeley.edu/publications/publications.php?id=254>.

Part I

Concepts and objectives of general education

2 Globalization and higher education in Greater China

Trends and challenges

Huang Chun-chieh

Introduction

During the last decades of the twentieth century, the world witnessed a rapid turn of the page of history. The former Soviet Union disintegrated, the European Union was formed, NAFTA (North American Free Trade Area) was established, ASEAN (Association of South East Asian Nations) appeared and China emerged; each of these events influenced the others and shook up the old geopolitical, economic and cultural orders. In academia, rapid developments in biochemical sciences and technologies, nanotechnology, telecommunication technology, cognitive science, etc., spurred the knowledge-based economy and strengthened the trend toward globalization – through which the rich and powerful countries increasingly control and exploit the poor and weak ones.

The impact of these new trends on institutions of higher education around the world is unprecedented in force and magnitude. In this rising tide of globalization, each country faces a higher level of competition, in turn intensifying the conflict between "globalization" and "nationalization" within each institution of higher education. These trends also upset the balance between equality of opportunity and pursuit of excellence in higher education, triggering conflicts between preserving local culture and anticipating future change, between diversification and unification of the functions of higher education, between cultivation of personal interest and contribution to society, with the result that they are ever more difficult to negotiate and balance.[1] In response to the serious new challenges faced by institutions of higher education in the twenty-first century, UNESCO issued, in 1998, the "World Declaration on Higher Education in the Twenty-First Century: Vision and Action."[2] Also, Beijing University's centennial celebration (May 2–4, 1998) included a seminar on higher education; university presidents from many countries came to discuss problems facing college education in the twenty-first century.[3] And on November 13, 2005, National Taiwan University held a forum of world university presidents to discuss trends and issues of higher education in the twenty-first century, focusing on the tension between globalization and localization, the impact of the knowledge-based economy on higher education and university management of the competing demands between democracy and efficiency. Among the many problems faced by institutions of higher education, forum participants stressed that universities should make sure that universities keep close tabs on the changes in organization and instruction that are brought about by technological innovation and economic production.[4]

As the universities in Greater China enter the new era of globalization in the twenty-first century, on the one hand, each university faces many problems that are common to other universities around the world, such as changes in financial management and administration, establishment of new evaluation systems, reform of curriculum and content,[5] and innovative technology research; on the other hand, in facing all of these phenomena, universities on both sides of the Taiwan Strait feel great pressure and have made serious errors in their evaluations since the purpose and standards of these evaluations have not been well defined. Evaluation is a problem also faced by universities overseas; for example, the rising tendency to emphasize the "quantity" over "quality" of research results[6] and for political power to intrude and command academic work.[7] In the new age of globalization, while each of the universities in Greater China has its own special problems, many of the challenges they face are peculiar to Greater China, including:

- how to maintain the balance between transmitting national cultural traditions and inculcating the new globalization outlook;
- how to re-establish and maintain the subjectivity and autonomy of higher education in this era of rapid technological development in the twenty-first century;
- how to strike the balance between creating personal interest and enhancing social welfare in Greater China, where there is a huge gulf between rich and poor.

Although these problems are universal in the twenty-first century, they are especially acute for universities in Greater China and warrant particular attention.

Traditional values and dialogue among civilizations in the age of globalization

The first challenge to higher education in Greater China in the twenty-first century is how, in the midst of the rising tide of globalization, to "baptize" the college students into the spirit of traditional Chinese culture, so that they can participate creatively in the new age of dialogue among civilizations. The great rupture between tradition and modernity that occurred in Chinese culture during the past several centuries accounts for why this issue poses such a major challenge for higher education in Chinese society.

During the twentieth century, while Asia went through a stormy historical process, it could be said that the Chinese people had written China's contemporary history with their own tears and blood. It was against this historical backdrop of Western powers' encroaching on the about-to-collapse China that China's modern institutions of higher education were set up. Hence, universities in twentieth-century China had the mission of driving China onto the path of being rich and powerful. In 1895, Peiyang University (Beiyang daxue, 北洋大學) was established with the mission of teaching science and technology. In 1898, Peking University (Jingshi daxuetang, 京師大學堂) was established with the mission of cultivating a modern bureaucracy. By the turn of the twentieth century, institutions of higher education all over China had the goal of helping China to catch up with the Western powers in science and technology so as to be free from colonization and exploitation.

In that age of pragmatism, higher education in China was tactically developed for the purposes of increasing national wealth and power. It was these presumed practical effects of education that were valued. The original purpose of education was forgotten and did not receive serious attention. Coming to the present day, technology is still a key focus in higher education in the effort to build a prosperous country. In addition to developments in mainland China, the Japanese colonial government in Taiwan established the first modern university in 1928, Taihoku (Taipei) Imperial University, 台北帝國大學 (present-day National Taiwan University, 國立台灣大學). The purpose of establishing this university was to support imperial Japan's strategy of encroaching on South East Asia. The Japanese were also interested in strengthening their knowledge of tropical medicine and developing South East Asian cultural resources. The first president of Taihoku Imperial University, Shidehara Tadao, 幣原坦 (1870–1953), advocated that Taiwan was a base for Japan's entry into the South East Asian region. The humanities and natural sciences received about equal regard in that mission. He further emphasized that this imperial university was established expressly for the sake of completing these political objectives.[8]

During the past several centuries, institutions of higher education were established in Greater China as a strategy of survival under the pressure of the Western powers. At the same time, the phantom of capitalism loomed over Greater China, stealing the souls of the Chinese people and subordinating the traditional sphere of education to non-educational spheres, thus leading to a serious commodification of education. With this historical distortion of several centuries, institutions of higher education in Greater China increasingly neglected traditional culture and values. Consequently, young Chinese intellectuals who received their college education in China felt estranged from their traditional culture – often to the extent of despising it.

The serious split between "tradition" and "modernity" bequeathed from twentieth-century higher education in China makes it difficult for Chinese intellectuals to face the challenges of the twenty-first century. In contrast with the way in which political, economic and cultural forces interacted in the geopolitical context of the twentieth century, the twenty-first century has witnessed the rapid development of the telecommunications industry and more and more "citizens" of each country are becoming "netizens" of the world. What is replacing the geopolitical territory of the twentieth century is a post-Cold War cultural identity, so the possibility of a clash of civilizations has accordingly been heightened.[9] In 2001, the World Trade Center in Manhattan became "ground zero" of the 9/11 terrorist attack, signaling the vital need for real dialogue among diverse civilizations in the twenty-first century.

In this age of dialogue among civilizations, China's rapid economic development during the past 30 years has received widespread attention.[10] By exploiting Chinese labor and abundant natural resources, together with Taiwan's high-tech industry and economic development, and supported by Hong Kong's international experience and resources, the new "China Circle" will possibly rise up on the heels of North America and Europe to become the new economic center of the twenty-first century.

However, viewed from the century-long development of higher education in China, the sort of training received by young Chinese intellectuals at institutions of higher education has increasingly cut them off from their own cultural traditions, values and ideals. As a result of the serious split between "tradition" and "modernity" in education, even today they are still unable to enter deeply into the treasures of their own cultural legacy, and thus unable to play an active role in the age of dialogue among civilizations.

The tide of "globalization"

Besides the traumatic history of the past centuries, after the Second World War, the tide of globalization exacerbated the tension between "tradition" and "modernity," bringing frustration and suffering to the Chinese people. The tide of globalization, in many guises, turns out, in effect, to be a matter of the economically rich countries extending their power to suppress the development of other parts of the world. These economically powerful countries are, for the most part, also politically and militarily powerful; they are the countries that consume the most energy resources. These influential powers also control the international banking and financial organizations, such as the World Bank and the International Monetary Fund (IMF). They have the power to direct the international capital markets, for example through the World Trade Organization (WTO). They possess state-of-the-art developments in the high-tech industries, such as information technology, aeronautics, space technology, biomedical technology, as well as controlling the latest developments in the arms industry. They always form alliances in order to obstruct and encroach upon other countries' advances. Therefore, the tide of globalization always works to strengthen the long-term advantage of the most powerful countries in political and military affairs.[11]

The basic reason why "globalization" has developed into a weapon for the strong, rich countries to wield over the weak, poor countries is that, under the domination of the strong, rich countries, "globalization" becomes a compelling general necessity that goes deeper and wider than the special conditions of each country and its international activities. The "globalization" tide is a relentless, unstoppable geopolitical-economic control force. In recent decades, it has been presented as a rationale for destroying cultures and ways of life. It is not far-fetched to say that globalization provides "a rationale for killing people" (*Yi li sha ren*, 以理殺人). In this way, the poor countries of Asia and Africa are caught up in the web of globalization, sucked in by an irresistible force. They are compelled to draw loans from the IMF in order to join the WTO. They cannot resist being sucked into the vortex of the global system of capitalism centered on the USA. In other words, "globalization" is the rising tide of economic power that is rolling over each of the weak, poor countries; it does not offer the tools that they might use to become really prosperous. Consequently, the rewards of "globalization" easily become the "exclusive domain" of the strong, rich countries just as, within the context of a single country, the "nation" becomes the exclusive internal affairs club managed by the capitalist class.

The tide of "globalization" has meant that higher education in Greater China has started to face the problem of rapidly losing its cultural tradition and values. This problem manifests itself mainly in the following ways:

- Traditional Chinese cultural education is increasingly being neglected in higher education in Greater China. In the general education courses designed to cultivate the students' basic abilities, the position of traditional Chinese culture, such as the humanities and arts, is weakening. Not only are such courses being increasingly squeezed out of the curriculum by technology-related courses, but the research trend enforced on the faculty detracts from the professors' ability to incorporate edifying educational content in their courses on Chinese literature, history and philosophy.
- Under the slogans of "globalization" and "internationalization," some universities in Greater China now offer most of their courses in English as an index of their degree of internationalization. We should keep in mind that languages are not merely tools of communication; at the same time, each language is the rich repository of cultural values. Under the objective condition that English has become the *lingua franca* of international education and scholarship, it is important for universities in Greater China to emphasize English instruction. But, to exaggerate the use of English as their working language under the pressure of "globalization" makes scholars from non-English-speaking countries face "relentless fierce competition from scholars in the same field from other countries under conditions most unfavorable to themselves."[12] Naturally, it is beneficial for one's research results to reach the international community of scholars through established international channels; but if we continued to over-exaggerate English instruction, the university's function of maintaining and developing ethnic cultural traditions will be killed off under the insidious manifold forces of globalization.

Intimate linkage of "tradition"

Facing the high tide of globalization, how can universities in Greater China promote effectively the traditional culture and its values? This is certainly a major challenge.

Facing the challenges of the tension between "tradition" and "modernity" and the hegemony of Western cultures over Eastern cultures, universities and colleges in Greater China can select from among various coping strategies. The most direct and effective one, naturally, would be to strengthen instruction and research in East Asian literature, history and philosophy, especially to delve into the classics and values of East Asian cultures to improve college students' familiarity with their "tradition."

The so-called "classics", in fact, are the records of profound spiritual dialogues. But, there is a key difference between the classics of China and those of the West. The "Other" addressed in the spiritual dialogues of the Western classics is God, while the "Other" addressed in the spiritual dialogues of the Chinese classics is "Man," or perhaps the "Sage" or "Wise Man". Regarding the "bible" of East Asia, the *Analects* of Confucius, the Japanese Tokugawa (1600–68) Confucian scholar Itō Jinsai 伊藤仁齋 (1627–1705) proclaimed it was "the ultimate book in the universe (*saijō jikyoku uchudaiichisho*, 最上至極宇宙第一書)."[13] The reason why Itō Jinsai praised the *Analects* so highly was that this book presented the eternal true principles governing human life "in everyday upright human relationships." The twentieth-century Japanese sinologist Yoshikawa Kōjiro 吉川幸次郎 (1904–80) also expressed endless praise for the philosophy of life of the Chinese classics.[14]

In fact, the reason why the Chinese classics are worthy of continued study and reflection, even in the age of globalization, is that the Chinese classics embody the unfathomable mysteries of spiritual transformation in the context of everyday upright human relationships, so people can concretely realize the abstract, general values in the stream of life. In the new age of dialogue among civilizations, we should offer ample instruction in the Chinese classics so that college students have the opportunity to hold the hands of the ancients, walk with the ancients and read through the classics in order to communicate with them. By deepening college students' interest and roots in local cultural resources, they will become well-grounded young intellectuals who can, in the age of globalization, engage in dialogues with youth from other cultures so as to share their values and achieve a higher degree of mutual understanding.

New technological developments and the subjectivity of higher education in the twenty-first century

The second major challenge facing higher education in Greater China lies in the rapid development of new technology: How can the university preserve and develop the subjectivity of college education? The reason why this challenge is so crucial for universities in Greater China is identical with the one identified by C. P. Snow (1905–80) in England: the great divide between the cultures of "science and technology" and "the humanities."[15] During the past century, this division has become especially serious and pronounced at institutions of higher learning in Greater China.

The impact of technological development on college education

Since the Second World War, technological development has advanced at a furious pace. For example, in 1945, the United States successfully tested the first atomic bomb. In 1946, the first electronic calculator appeared. In 1953, human DNA was decoded. In 1957, the Soviet Union launched the first satellite, Sputnik I. In 1959, the integrated circuit was invented. In 1960, the laser was invented. In 1961, the Soviet Union launched the first manned spaceship. In 1969, the American astronaut Neil Armstrong (1930–2012) walked on the moon. In 1969, the US Defense Department completed the Arpanet computer network that was subsequently developed into the Internet in the 1980s and the World Wide Web (www) in the 1990s, which has changed the pattern of human life incalculably. In 1978, the first test-tube baby was born. In 1982, the first artificial human heart was implanted into a person. In 1990, a research project on the human genome was launched in Europe and the United States;[16] by 2001, ahead of schedule, the human genome sequencing project was completed, thanks to the joint efforts of scientists around the world. During the past 20 years, developments in telecommunication technology, nanotechnology, genetic medicine, life science and cognitive technology have stirred great changes in academic attitudes in the university community, leading to the appearance of the following two noteworthy phenomena:

1   An increased degree of commercialization of knowledge at universities and colleges. The rapid development of new technology has greatly changed the age-old production methods, creating new business opportunities in which the new knowledge serves as the key to rapidly increasing wealth. Additionally, since the modern university community is developing in a capitalist production network, the degree of commodification of new knowledge created at the university is increasing. In recent years, major universities have set up centers for innovation and incubation to serve as a bridge between industry and the academic world. This is precisely a manifestation of the commodifying trend of knowledge.

Because technological development is leading the commercialization of knowledge, on the one hand, the university community is warping into a sort of weird "academic capitalism".[17] As this trend incubates and develops, it leads to the overturning of the original mission of the university as the pursuit of truth. On the other hand, great business opportunities created by technical research at the university strengthen the trend for government to get actively involved in guiding research. Moreover, as the mutual dependence of science and technology grows stronger, the resulting technological production becomes the ground of the legitimacy of universities and colleges in the eyes of the sponsoring government and tax-payers, which makes the relations between university administrators and political power-holders grow ever more intimate.

This trend tends to kill off the critical function of the university as the conscience of society, turning the university into a sort of think tank of the capitalist production system. The university becomes a training ground for personnel who benefit the vested-interest classes of capitalist society.[18]

2   University students and teachers easily fall into the trap of quantitative thinking. The rapid development of technology influences the worldview and the academic views of the college students and teachers in Greater

China such that they take on a sort of "quantitative mode of thinking." This quantitative mode of thinking defines the intellectual sphere of the modern university as the realm of modern technology, and thus they always tend to adopt a "quantitative" position and rarely a "qualitative" one when considering questions and issues in research and education. For example, in Taiwan, emphasis is placed on number of Science Citation Index (SCI)-listed articles, number of patents awarded from research projects, amount of profit earned from cooperation between academia and industry, and so forth. However, less emphasis is placed on the inspiration the teachers give to the students, the benefit the teachers give to the students in maturing and enriching their lives, the criticism the teachers voice over unfairness and injustice in society and the question whether the university is contributing to the development of the human spirit. In recent years, at universities on both sides of the Taiwan Strait, faculty promotion assessments and course evaluations have been conducted on a quantitative basis. For example, Shanghai Jiaotong University (上海交通大學) announced that the evaluation criteria for the "2004 Global University Academic Ranking" are "Number of Nobel laureates," "Number of frequently cited papers," and "Number of publications in top journals," such as *Nature* and *Science*. At about the same time, the *Times Higher Education Supplement* in London published a list of "The Top 200 Universities in the World" (2004). This list was compiled from scores given by 1,300 scholars from 88 countries based on the following five standards: "International recognition" (50%)," "Average frequency of citation of faculty writings" (20%), "Teacher–student ratio" (20%), "Number of international faculty," and "Number of international students" (5% each). Among these standards, the first is certainly subjective, and it tends to favor the older universities with long histories in major countries. On October 9, 2005, the ROC Ministry of Education issued a press release entitled, "'Project Aspiring for Top Universities': Assessment Results and Explanation." The fourth point under the first item of this press release affirmed that, in future, universities would receive funding based on the MOE assessments according to the present-day international standards. For the project to be effective, the following standards were recommended:

- cultivation of talents: increase the quality and number of high-tech and special area personnel training and related industrial production personnel;
- increase the number of articles published in SCI- or SSCI-listed journals;
- increase in the number of internationally outstanding teachers and researchers;
- increase in the number of concrete cooperations between domestic and foreign universities and research institutions;
- growth of the average annual rate of guiding cooperative research plans between academia and industry.

These university evaluation standards all, in various ways, exhibit "the trap of quantitative thinking." This kind of "quantitative thinking" deeply injures the idea of the university, overturns the character of the university and distracts from the real function of college education. In fact, as a result of such "quantitative thinking," the university is turning away from its original position as a temple of the pursuit of truth and the academy that raises the maturing spirits of its students, and becoming a profit-making SCI-papers-vending machine, gradually killing off the precious subjectivity of the university and encouraging intellectual creativity to be used for non-academic purposes, e.g. as tactics in the search for wealth and power. In effect, this makes the university faculty become mere SCI paper workers and college students become digits of quantification. This is an unfortunate development of college education.

Rejuvenating college students' subjectivity

Looking into this future, how should the universities in Greater China respond to these challenges?

The universities in Greater China can respond to these challenges in a variety of ways. However, the most important strategy of response should lie in the renewal of the autonomy of the university. This should take two main forms. In the first place, as to the universities' falling into the "toolification" trend, we should strongly uphold and preserve the original purpose of college education. If we intend to lead the university back to its original purpose as an academic institution, the university must strengthen the reform of university-level common and general instruction. In particular, it should offer curricula for the research and study of Chinese and Western classics in order to acquaint college students with the greatest insights of China and the West, to engage them in intimate dialogues. Second, as to the universities' tendency to overemphasize formalism in operation and evaluation, we should stress the original purpose of college education as being to enlighten the student about life and to enrich human life generally.

Economic development, gap between rich and poor and social responsibility

The third challenge to college education in Greater China is this: under the new situation of an ever-increasing gap between rich and poor in tandem with economic development, how can the university work toward the formation of a fair, just society in which each sector is prosperous and in which each person will have a fair and equal chance to be educated and create his life?

This challenge has become particularly important in recent years because the gulf between rich and poor has become wider on both sides of the Taiwan Strait. Since the start of the twenty-first century, the poverty gap in Taiwan society has become very wide indeed. According to the ROC Executive Yuan statistics on annual household income for 2004, the average income for the top 20% was NT$1,792,000 while that for the bottom 20% was NT$297,000. The average income for the top 20% was 6.03 times that for the lowest 20%. Although the difference was greater in 2003, 6.07 times, that the income gap between rich and poor remains great is an indisputable fact.[19] Among students at National Taiwan University, those from Taipei City and County account for 57.6% while those from rural counties, such as Miaoli, Jiayi, Hualian, Xinju, Taidong, etc., account for less than 1%, respectively.[20] The statistics for mainland China are equally telling. For the years 1998, 1999, 2000 and 2001, disparity between the richest and poorest household incomes was 4.4 times, 4.5 times, 5 times and 5.3 times, respectively.[21] Comparative statistics between 1985 and 2002 reveal that, while the income disparity between rich and poor in 1985 was 3.74 times, the gross amount of difference in renminbi was 901 in 1985, but grew to 17,680 in 2002, or 19.6 times greater.[22] According to the Beijing City Bureau of Statistics, the ratio of income disparity between rich and poor households in Beijing rose from 4.7:1 to 5.8:1 from 2003 to 2004. In Jiangsu, the disparity in income between rich and poor households grew from 5.39 times in 2000 to 9.91 in 2003 and reached 10.71 in 2004. According to national statistics for cities of over 50,000 households throughout China, the income disparity between the richest 10% and poorest 10% households was 9.5 times during the first six months of 2004.[23] In general, the income disparity situation between rich and poor households in Taiwan has been improving gradually in recent years.[24] In mainland China, nevertheless, under the high tide of reform and starting in recent years, not only has the gap between affluent and destitute households widened, but the gap between the highest and lowest personal incomes has increased greatly. Moreover, the relative difference in incomes between the prosperous cities along the coast, like Shanghai, and the poor provinces in the northwest is growing ever more extreme and unsustainable.

Under these new socio-economic conditions on both sides of the Taiwan Strait, college education stands at a historic crossroads. The knowledge transmitted in modern college education can support each student's competitiveness in the job market after graduation, so college students graduate with a relatively advantageous position in the capitalist division of labor system, thus creating personal economic benefits for the students. As the market value of the graduates increasingly becomes a criterion in considering the value of college education, the curriculum itself increasingly is geared toward job competitiveness. This benefit increasingly determines what the students and their parents consider to be a hot program, a hot curriculum.

Taking a deeper look, we find that university production consists in the activity of transmitting knowledge. But, in the grip of the capitalist socio-cultural-economic system, it receives the severe constraints of the logic of the capitalist market economy. The university campus nowadays is filled with consumerism, and the way the university functions increasingly embodies and reproduces the characteristics of corporate culture.[25] Universities on both sides of the Taiwan Strait are developing rapidly in this direction. Moreover, carried along by the globalization tide that is the mainstream of the twenty-first century, students receive the sort of education that will land them in the best positions in the employment market. But the operation of the world economy is becoming less free: when a person enters the world job market and is placed in the world employment system, he or she can only float along as a single element in the cut-throat capitalist system, pouring all of him- or herself into capitalist production.

The new tide of post-Cold War capitalist globalization has had a huge impact on higher education. Higher education is increasingly market-oriented, and the knowledge transmitted in the university is increasingly commodified.[26] As university research and instruction evolve gradually into something increasingly opposed to the original goal of the university, the resultant self-estrangement of the university becomes an inevitable tragedy. This sort of production context affects many universities on both sides of the Taiwan Strait. As early as 1949, National Taiwan University President Fu Sinian 傅斯年 (1896–1950) pointed out: "The university was established for scholarship, for youth, for Chinese and world cultures."[27] Sadly, students nowadays have put aside Fu Sinian's ideal. They are happy to be trained to fit into capitalist society and study hard to reap the economic and class benefits.

Even more chilling are the constant efforts of economic liberals to apply the principles of the marketplace to education. When these economists issue a call for students to have ever more freedom and choices,[28] they completely forget that, by making college education tantamount to a market economy, they are expanding the benefits of the economically affluent class and creating a class-restricted sense of freedom such that the farmer and laborer classes continue to toil with less freedom just because they cannot receive the best education.

Consequently, the question arises of where does the social responsibility of the university lies: in entering into "collaborations" with the capitalist system, or in creating benefits to all sectors of society? This is the third serious issue facing college education on both sides of the Taiwan Strait in the twenty-first century.

Conclusion

With the development of globalization and the knowledge-based economy, higher education on both sides of the Taiwan Strait faces major challenges in the twenty-first century. The present chapter focuses these challenges in terms of several issues: (a) the transmission and development of traditional culture, (b) the impact of rapid technological development on the university and (c) the social responsibilities of the university. By analyzing and tracing the development of these three issues, we can begin to work out positive strategies for responding to them.

We advocate that higher education in Greater China in the twenty-first century should plant deep cultural roots so that students may avoid becoming rootless orchids in the great tide of globalization and lose themselves and their cultural identity. We also advocate that the university should shed its excessive pragmatism and formalistic habit of thinking, and return to the original goal of education. The university should also review the challenge to take up its social responsibilities, supporting the idea that the university plays the role of conscience in society, thus creating great benefits for all of the people in society, not just the advanced capitalists.

These strategies for responding to three issues all remain mindful of the original spirit of college education. In this age of separation between science/technology and the humanities, between East and West, we must work to renew the idea of the university and make the university into the temple of exploring and upholding truth, so it can be the field of conscience in society. By renewing the spirit of college education, universities on both sides of the Taiwan Strait will be able to take a leading role in the twenty-first century so that in the new age of dialogue among civilizations we can bring the most positive elements into play.

Notes

1 Clark Kerr, in association with Marian L. Gade and Maureen Kawaoka, *Higher Education Cannot Escape History: Issues for the Twenty-First Century* (Albany, NY: SUNY Press, 1994).
2 UNESCO, "World Declaration on Higher Education in the Twenty-First Century: Vision and Action," October 9, 1998. Online. Available HTTP: <http://unescdoc.unesco.org/0011/001138/113878eb.pdf>
3 Wei Xiu and Ma Wanhua, *The University of the 21st Century: Proceedings of the Forum of Higher Education in Conjunction with the Centennial of Peking University*, May 2–4, 1998 (Beijing: Peking University Press, 1998).
4 See James J. Duderstadt, *A University for the 21st Century* (Ann Arbor: University of Michigan Press, 2000, 2002).
5 See Tamil Salmi, "Facing the Challenges of the Twenty-First Century." *Perspectives: Policy and Practice in Higher Education*, 6(1) (February 2002): 8–12.
6 See Lee Harvey, "The Power of Accreditation: Views of Academics." *Journal of Higher Education Policy and Management*, 26 (July 2004): 207–33.
7 See Kauko Hämäläinen, "Common Standards for Program Evaluations and Accreditation?" *European Journal of Higher Education and Management*, 26 (July 2004): 291–300.
8 Shidehara Tadao, "Taiwan no qakujitsu teki kachi" 台湾の学術價值. *Taiwan Jiho* 台湾時報 (December 1923): 25–34.
9 Samuel P. Huntington, *The Clash of Civilizations and Remaking of the World Order* (New York: Simon & Schuster, 1996).
10 See Barry Naughton, ed., *The China Circle: Economics and Technology in the PRC, Taiwan and Hong Kong* (Washington, DC: Brookings Institution, 1997).
11 Huang Chun-chieh, *Quanqiuhua shidai daxue tongshi jiaoyu de xintiaozhan* 全球化時代大學通識教育的新挑戰 [*New Challenges for University General Education in the Age of Globalization*] (Kaohsiung: Tongshi jiaoyu xuehui, 2004). See especially chapter 1, p. 8.
12 Ding Xueliang 丁學良, *Sheme shi shijie yiliu daxue?* 什麼是世界一流大學? [*What is a World-Class University?*] (Beijing: Beijing daxue chubanshe, 2004), p. 104.
13 Itō Jinsai 伊藤仁齋, Rongo Kogi 論語古義 [*Ancient Meaning of Confucius' Analects*]. In Seki Giichirō 關儀一郎 ed., *Nihon Meika Shisho-Chūshaku* 日本名家四書詮釋全書 [*Complete Works of Commentaries of Famous Scholars in Japan*] (Tokyo: Ōtori Shuppan, 1973), vol. 3, p. 4. Itō Jinsai, Dōshi Mon 童子問 [*Inquiries of a Child*]. In Ienaga Saburō 家永三郎 et al., eds., *Kinsei Shisoka Bunshu* 近世思想家文集 [*Collected Works of Modern Thinkers*] (Tokyo Iwanami Shoten, 1966, 1981), vol. 1, p. 204.
14 Yoshikawa Kōjiro 吉川幸次郎, *Shinajin no Koden to sono seikatsu* 支那人の古典とその生活 [*The Classics and Lives of the Chinese*] (Tokyo: Iwanami Shoden, 1943).
15 C. P. Snow first pointed out this problem in a lecture he gave at the University

of Cambridge on May 7, 1959. See C. P. Snow, *The Two Cultures* (Cambridge: Cambridge University Press, 1998).

16 *The New Age of Discovery* (*Time* magazine, special issue) (January 1998).

17 Sheila Slaughter and Larry Leslie, *Academic Capitalism: Politics, Policies and the Entrepreneurial University* (Baltimore and London: Johns Hopkins University Press, 1997).

18 The mission of the university is the pursuit of the truth, thus it should not be at the service of powerful corporations or political authorities to conduct research for their practical benefit. See José Ortega y Gasset, ed., *Mission of the University*, trans. Howard Lee Nostrand (New Brunswick and London: Transaction Publishers, 1991, 1992), esp. pp. 47–56. This sort of university ideal is being seriously challenged at university campuses on both sides of the Taiwan Strait.

19 See <http://www.stat.gov.tw/public/Attachment/59911302371.doc>

20 Kuo I-ling, 郭奕玲 "Yige Taiwan, liangge shijie" 個台灣, 兩個世界 [*One Taiwan, Two Worlds*]. See <http://magazines.sina.com.tw/businessweekly/contents/800/800-001_1.html>

21 *Tianxia zazhi* 天下雜誌 [*Commonwealth*], no. 272 (April 1, 2003): 89.

22 Zhongguo laogong tongxun 中國勞工通訊 [*China Labor Information*]. Online. Available HTTP: <http://big5.clb.org.hk/public/contents/article/revision_id=65105&item_id=65104>

23 Data from New China website 新華網 [Xin Hua net], "Zhongguo pinfu chaju youmeiyou bei kuada?" 中國貧富差距有沒有被誇大 [*Has the Gap between Rich and Poor in China been Exaggerated?*] See <http://big5.xinhuanet.com/gate/big5/news.xinhuanet.com/comments/2005-03/ 11/content_2682008.htm>

24 See <http://www.dgbas.gov.tw/public/data/dgbas03/bs7/yearbook/ch8-13&14.xls#a28>; <http://www.dgbas.gov.tw/public/attachment/581814552071.doc.>

25 See Eric Gould, *The University in a Corporate Culture* (New Haven: Yale University Press, 2003).

26 See Derek Bok, *University in the Marketplace: The Commercialization of Higher Education* (Princeton: Princeton University Press, 2003).

27 Fu Sinian 傅斯年, "Guoli Taiwan daxue disici xiaoqing yanshoci" 國立台灣大學第4次校慶演說詞 [*Observance of the Fourth Anniversary of National Taiwan University*], presented on November 17, 1949. See *Fu Sinian xuanji* 傅斯年選集 [*Collected Works of Fu Sinian*] (Taipei: Wenxing shudian 文星書店, 1967), chapter 9, pp. 1573–74.

28 See, for example, Milton Friedman, "The Role of Government in Education." In *Capitalism and Freedom* (Chicago: University of Chicago Press, 1982), chapter 4. See also Milton and Rose Friedman, *Free to Choose: A Personal Statement* (New York: Harcourt Brace Jovanovich, 1980).

3 The significance of university culture building for general education

Song Shanggui

Introduction

Since the 1990s, China has been implementing cultural quality education in higher education. Initially general education was introduced as a major form of cultural quality education from the developed countries, Hong Kong and Taiwan. Since then a wave of general education has swept over universities in the mainland, general education research has received critical attention and a large body of research on both theory and application has been pub lished. However, in this large body of literature, most of the studies approach general education from the perspectives of curricular design and delivery, and researchers are mostly concerned about how to achieve the intended objectives of general education in helping students gain comprehensive knowledge and develop a sound mind and healthy character through curricular activities. Little attention seems to be given to university culture and its impact on general education. I believe that university culture is one of the core elements for the university, which will have both a direct and indirect impact on student growth in various forms and through different channels. This chapter attempts to explore the interdependent relationship between university culture and general education and ways of improving general education from the perspective of the establishment of a university culture.

The meaning and characteristics of university culture

University culture was born at the same time as the university. The broad concept of culture is very rich in meaning and wide in extension. It includes all the knowledge, values, life attitudes and styles that have emerged in the process of human development, covering all the civilizations formed throughout human history with their respective understanding and transformation of nature and their self-development. Any discussion of university culture must first start with interpretation of the context of culture. As Tony Becher pointed out: "An inquiry that starts by reviewing higher education, or some component of it, as a cultural system must, at the very least, seek to single out the underlying pattern of concepts, values, and activities that give it a coherent identity."[1] In this chapter, I take the narrow definition of culture as a social phenomenon that is distinct from sociopolitical and economic activities. University culture refers to the cultural carrier of the society that exists in the university, i.e. the commonly accepted values, the structure of the university's educational system, behavior protocols for the university as an institution and for individual faculty and students, the code system developed in the process of university adminis-tration and education, and other cultural phenomena able to help define the characteristics of the university.

First, university culture is a set of unique university values, which are widely accepted by the faculty and students and institutionalized in the university's physical features and management activities. It has both an enduring nature in historical inheritance and has been constantly developing and changing under internal and external influences. For example, knowledge exploration and cultural inheritance can be viewed both as the basic function of the university and the defining characteristics of university culture. In the process of inherit-ance, integration and knowledge innovation, the university shapes a distinctive culture with an emphasis on respecting science and facts, not blindly following authority or book knowledge, as well as the value and educational view which are characterized by the search for truth.

Second, university culture is a systemic structure. The modern university has developed a complete system for its education, curriculum, administration and operation, which has institutionalized educational concepts and laws formed and preserved in its historical development, and which also highlights the individual features of different universities. Universities from different countries in different historical periods have gradually formulated their distinctive educational systems and administrative styles over time, which have become important elements of the university culture. Unique features in their educational system have deter-mined significant differences in their curricular system, content and process. We could well take these differences as disparities or characteristics in university culture. For example, American universities were established after the model of British and German universities, but they did not copy their rigid European-style curricular management system. Instead, they have created a management system of their own which is more flexible and free. Today we can easily identify differences between the two university management systems from the perspec-tive of university culture.

Third, university culture is a code of conduct. As we all know, the formation of university culture cannot happen overnight, but involves a long process of historical accumulation and sublimation. In this process, each university will develop specific behavioral guidelines, which not only regulate the behavior of the university as a whole (how to define its mission, conduct educational activi-ties and fulfill and complete its social responsibilities, etc.), but also regulate indi-vidual (faculty, students and administrative staff) behavior (teaching, learning, research, management and service activities, etc.). In a broader sense, those distinctive codes of conduct on each campus are formulated from the general educational objectives of creating and transmitting knowledge and promoting progress in human civilizations. All university people, in completing their work and learning tasks, intentionally or unintentionally follow those codes of conduct which have existed for several decades or centuries. Universities conduct their activities under these invisible but powerful codes of conduct, in order to realize their educational ideals. At the same time, the codes reflect the characteristics of universities and their unique institutional cultures.

Fourth, university culture is the organizational structure and symbolic system formulated during the growing process of a university. University organizational structure includes characteristics of all internal components within the university, relationships between the components (such as working relations, power relations, emotional relations and relations of interest, etc.), institutional establishments, bureaucratic type and management system, etc. The symbolic system of a university represents a sign system that indicates specific meanings generally accepted by all members of the university. It includes names of internal units, titles and terms of reference for different members, and symbolic meanings of ceremonies, logos, insignia, designs, mottoes and slogans.

University culture is a special organizational culture, and the university's mission and its inherent characteristics make university culture different from ordinary organizational culture. First, university culture is a culture in pursuit of academic achievements. Academic activities are the foundation and core of the university. University culture is also a culture in pursuit of truth. University activities are organized around explorations and discussions among faculty and students about the universe, nature, society and human nature. Teaching and learning are essentially a scholarly process of rigorous exploration and truth seeking. Therefore, university culture despises shallowness, vanity, falsehood, short-sighted vision and drifting with the tide; instead, it advocates rigor, logic, experiment, experience, practice and step-by-step persistence and hard work. In addition, university culture is a culture of strong critical spirit. The nature of science is to boldly question and sort out knowledge, carry on traditions by discarding the dross and selecting the essence which manifests the needs of critical differentiation and eliminating falsehood and retaining the truth; scholarly and cultural exchange need the process of criticism and counter-criticism; the creation of knowledge and the pursuit of truth require that we surpass and criticize others and ourselves; the progress of human civilization needs the critical spirit to surpass reality and achieve desired goals. In the process of constant criticism, a university develops its unique value judgments and rational demands and, therefore, university spirit. Once formed, the university spirit will transform itself into a powerful vitality, enabling the university to play a special role in guiding social values, gathering knowledge and talents and inheriting and developing culture in a complex social life.

Finally, university culture is a culture that has developed over time and preserved its uniqueness and independent nature. The university is the strongest social institution. The university has a long history, a history that is even longer in the process of creating its brand in comparison to other social organizations, thus possessing a stronger sense of history in its formed values, institutional framework, code of conduct and other unique cultural symbols. The university is also more independent and self-governing than other social organizations, and it can still operate independently under the influence of mainstream trends, values and culture. The university is able to examine society as an outsider and play the role of a social critic at all times. This sense and quality of independence makes the university not only the creator of knowledge and ideas, but a leader in advanced culture.

In short, university cultures have their commonalities, but they demonstrate even more unique qualities in the dimensions discussed above. Whether the university has a long or brief history, it must bear some distinctive features of its own. In general, the longer a university has existed, the more distinctive its cultural features are. Reading the history of their development among well-known Chinese and foreign universities, it is easily apparent that significant differences exist in "culture" between well-established institutions and relatively new ones. While the centuries-old well-known universities are trying to reform their cultures and contemplate a "paradigm" shift to "modernize" their traditions in the face of the new trends of "globalization," "the knowledge-based economy" and "post-modernism," many new Chinese universities with a 50- or even a 20-year history are still locked in the debates over the unique features of university culture. They barely have time to figure out the ways to build their own university cultures before another wave of new socio-economic, political and cultural reforms are pushed upon them.

The interdependent relationship between general education and university culture

The development of university culture gave birth to general education

The evolution of university culture has significantly influenced activities in higher education. Tendencies of university culture in a certain period often determine the orientation and models of education at the time. Though the relationship between university culture, university educational activities and social factors is very complex and we cannot simply describe their causal relationship in a linear way, we can still distinguish the major impact of university culture on educational activities from a historical perspective. A preliminary examination of the outlines of European university culture development and a comparison with the prominent features of contemporary educational activities show some valuable connections between the two.

Long before the industrial revolution, the concept of humanistic education had been a dominant force for European universities. Aristotle's concept of liberal education and Newman's idea of free education and the famous "Yale Report" in nineteenth-century America, all reflect the importance of humanistic education. In Europe, even before the Renaissance, humanistic education had developed into a complete system, and a strong humanistic tradition and heritage had already emerged among universities. With help from the great progressive forces of the Renaissance, the West began the first scientific revolution in the seventeenth century, and scientific ideologies emerged. Over the next century, modern science had already made great progress by the time a number of Western capitalist countries launched the first industrial revolution in the mid-eighteenth century, and science and technology began to show their huge role in pushing for social development. Accordingly, scientific knowledge had increasingly become an important content area in education, and the idea of science education had become an important educational philosophy. Advocates for science education strongly promoted the role of science and technology in society, and cast aside those elements of traditional humanistic education that were out touch with reality. But at this time science education did not have sufficient influence or power.

Science and technology developed rapidly throughout the nineteenth century, and increasingly affected all aspects of human social life. British universities first began large-scale reforms in traditional university educational ideas and curriculum. The role of science and technology was increasingly gaining acceptance, and scientific knowledge began to replace humanistic knowledge as the major content area for university education. In response to the fact that science education was gaining increasing importance, advocates of humanistic education, such as Robert Maynard Hutchins and Matthew Arnold, began to challenge the advocates of scientific education, including Herbert Spencer and Thomas H. Huxley. Hutchins believed that "education leads to understanding; it has no more 'practical' aim. It is interested in the development of human beings through the development of their minds. Its aim is not manpower, but manhood."[2] But the humanistic scholars' challenge to science education did not shake its dominant position in higher education. At the outset of the twentieth century, science and technology continued to develop rapidly; disseminating and developing modern science and technology had become the most important social function and task for higher education institutions. As a result, those science advocates went increasingly to the extreme, even opposing any speculative activities, promoting technological determinism and believing that science and technology could completely transform nature and solve all social problems. Accordingly, the task of higher education was to equip professionals with modern scientific and technical knowledge and skills. In the meantime, the importance of science and technology in society made the younger generation believe science and technological knowledge and skills were a precondition for make a living. Driven by those dual forces, university programs and curricula became more and more specialized and career-oriented, and the proportion of science and engineering majors and courses was increasing at the expense of the humanities and social sciences curriculum. This mentality of science supremacy was dominant for the majority of the twentieth century. Guided by these educational philosophies, university education placed undue emphasis on specialty skills and professional training, and overlooked cultural and humanities education. Universities became good only at training the so-called "technocrats" and "machinists," who only knew how to operate machines and create wealth.

Since the mid-twentieth century, while scientific and technological development has brought great wealth to mankind, it has also increasingly revealed its negative impacts on human life: environmental degradation, ecological imbalance, resource depletion, physical and mental illness caused by the increasingly rapid pace of life, morally degrading and decadent values driven by material interests, more brutal wars and the growing disparities between the rich and poor. These problems, alongside the development of science and technology, forced people to rethink the impact of education on human nature, and the role of general education in higher education with a humanistic focus has regained people's attention. With the publication of *General Education in a Free Society* (a.k.a. the "Red Book") and the general education reform movement represented by Harvard University, a movement to revive general education was first started by universities in the developed countries of the West. In 1984, the National Endowment for the Humanities (NEH) published *To Reclaim a Legacy: A Report on the Humanities in Higher Education*, which provided a detailed analysis of student knowledge in the humanities, and called for the revival of general education in response to the serious deficiencies it uncovered. Driven by this report, American institutions of higher education launched a curricular reform movement to strengthen general education. The release of this report was also seen as a milestone in the "return" of liberal arts education in Western developed countries.

In April of 1987, the UK government published a white paper titled *Higher Education: Meeting the New Challenge*, which proposed to make enhancing humanities scholarship one of the goals for higher education, and encouraged high-level scholarly achievements in the humanities and social sciences. In 1988 the UK government enacted the Education Reform Act, which made it a clear goal for education to strengthen moral education, and teach students to be honest, self-reliant, responsible and respectful of other people's values. In 1989, UNESCO (the United Nations Education, Scientific and Cultural Organization) hosted "Education for the Twenty-First Century," an international symposium in Beijing, which once again called people's attention to humanistic education, and proposed the "learning to care" program (care about our health, care about our families, friends and colleagues, care about others, about society and our national economic and ecological welfare, care about human rights, care about other species, care about the state of the planet and care about truth, knowledge and learning). Once again the importance of humanities education became the issue for educational policymakers and scholars. From various perspectives, people have stressed the importance of humanities education in contemporary society with its highly developed science and technology. As George Papadopoulos, the former deputy director of the Education Directorate of the Organisation for Economic Co-operation and Development (OECD), said:

> The need for such a role is particularly essential to safeguard against the unintended consequences of technology-based, competition driven and media-dominated societies which, if left unfettered, might result in the "dehumanisation" of values and culture. This is not a question of rejecting scientific and technical progress. It is rather one of ensuring that such progress is healthily woven into the social and cultural fabric and fundamental human values.[3]

This so-called "new humanism" has taken hold in Western countries. Over the past 10 years, many top universities in Europe and North America have implemented various general education reforms, such as the "integrated curriculum project," the "core curriculum," the "interdisciplinary curriculum," the "basic curriculum," the "humanities research curriculum" and so on. These general education advocates oppose early specialization and over-specialization, and, instead, emphasize curricula in the humanities, arts, social sciences and philosophy. The initial goals of these reforms are to strengthen the integration of humanities education and science education, especially increasing the proportion of humanities education in the curriculum. We can clearly see the trend of "return" for general education in higher education philosophies of Western countries.

The constraints on general education by the development of Chinese university culture

In China, although humanistic education was highly recommended by educators in ancient times, general education did not get the attention it deserved following the introduction of higher education into China. In the 1930s, although pioneers in Chinese higher education, such as Cai Yuanpei, Mei Yiqi and Zhu Kezhen, had already realized the important role general education played in personnel training, and tried to enhance humanities education among universities, people's understanding of general education was shallow and its acceptance was limited at that time; in addition, the idea of "National Salvation through Science" was very popular among intellectuals, so science and technology became the core content of education for the limited number of Chinese universities. From the same period, the tendency of "engineering over humanities" had taken hold among Chinese universities in their educational philosophies and specific educational management activities (such as academic major design, curriculum development, academic resources management, etc.); this tendency has not changed substantially with the passage of time.

Since 1949, Chinese higher education has copied wholesale the Soviet model of higher education. After the 1953 restructuring of Chinese colleges and departments, many comprehensive universities were broken up into professional colleges. The academic major design and curriculum development had become increasingly specialized; priority was placed on the development of disciplines and programs in science and technology, and the humanities became of secondary importance. The "anti-rightist" political movement of 1957 and the subsequent "10 chaotic years" brought disaster to the humanities and general education in Chinese higher education. Ever since the reform movement and opening up to the outside world, Chinese higher education was brought back to life by the policies of restoring order and market-oriented economic reform. However, Chinese universities did not shake off the shackles of emphasizing "engineering over science" and "science over liberal arts." For most institutions, especially those science and engineering colleges, humanities education was still being neglected and students were given deficient humanistic training (human spirit, human knowledge and practice, etc.)

It has been 15 years now since Chinese universities launched the cultural quality education movement. Some prestigious universities, such as Huazhong University of Science and Technology, Peking University and Tsinghua University, have carried out a series of educational reform experiments around the theme of promoting the integration of humanities education and science education, which has set good examples for other Chinese universities. Many universities also introduced a variety of experiments in general education reforms, trying to enhance the general education curriculum by modifying and improving GE teacher training programs. National educational authorities have set up dozens of cultural quality education stations, lending administrative support to the reforms. In the meantime, the cultural quality education reforms have aroused strong interest among mainland Chinese universities in studying general education theory and experience from Western countries as well as from Hong Kong and Taiwan, which in turn have promoted general education research on the mainland. Today, the concept of general education has been accepted by most university administrators and educators. People believe that general education plays an irreplaceable role in developing "well-rounded" students with respect and self-esteem, a sense of democracy and law, freedom and equality, and fairness and justice. Among China's mainland universities, general education has begun to return to its rightful place. The studying and acceptance of the concept of general education has played a crucial role in the development of Chinese universities. This can be seen as clear evidence for the positive impact on educational practices of university culture.

University culture exerts a powerful influence and directly impacts the following generations of educators and administrators in terms of educational philosophies and activities. The specific university cultural environment in which university educators and administrators received their own higher education will affect their understanding of general education directly or indirectly. This early understanding of general education will become an important factor impacting their educational or administrative activities when they become university educators or administrators themselves. For example, the traditional cultural environments of "engineering over science" and "science over arts" in mainland China universities still seriously confine the thinking and behaviors of many educators today. Therefore, transforming existing university culture is probably the most important task for Chinese higher education and general education reform.

The positive impact of university culture on general education

The goal of general education is to develop well-rounded graduates. As the pioneers of general education had already realized, achieving this goal demands more than just a series of courses:

> But while we admit that general instruction is not enough for our purpose, we also call attention to the fact that the school as it stands is equipped to exercise an influence over its pupils through media other than formal

teaching. The school is an organization in which a certain way of life is practiced. The pupil acquires a habit by the process of unconscious absorption.[4]

As this quote indicates, university organization, a specific way of life and other
factors that may have potential influence over students can all be regarded as the
cultural tradition and quality a university has formed in its long-term development. University culture influences general education primarily at two different
levels: first its direct impact on general education activities, including direct
impact on teaching activities, especially on the general education curriculum,
and the impact on faculty members; and second the indirect impact of university
culture on students through other means, which may create a similar or the
same educational effect as general education, and which can be taken as general
education in the broadest sense (the hidden curriculum), including the impact
of university cultural environment on students' development, and the impact
of university cultural factors on teaching and administrative activities and on
general education.

University culture's direct impact on general education

Cultural factors in the teaching process

The university teaching process is both the key step in the implementation of
general education and also a major means of achieving the goals of general
education. It is important to explore the role of cultural factors in the teaching
process as a key factor in enhancing the effect of general education. Specifically,
we should start the process as follows. First, university teaching as a way to
pursue truth and the culture of rigorous scholarship in university teaching
activities play an irreplaceable role in developing students' scientific spirit and
academic ethics.

Second, there are multiple objectives for the humanities, social sciences and
natural sciences curricula. Teaching should not be confined to the mere transfer
of knowledge but take into consideration pedagogical values. There is no direct
and natural relationship between the transfer of natural science knowledge
and its cultural implications, but it is undeniable that teaching knowledge of
the humanities is still an important form of general education for most college
students in terms of values, ideas, cognitive methods and the forms and habits
of external behavior, which all depend on competency in and understanding
of the humanities. However, the cultural factors in teaching activities are far
more influential than the knowledge itself. In fact, the cultural influence faculty
members may have exercised in their professional and other personal interactions
with students may be more telling than the knowledge they have imparted. In
this sense, faculty should not only achieve the goals of humanities education and
science education through subject instruction, but also enrich student minds
through teaching and learning activities, their interactions with students and
other campus activities, nurturing student cultural competency, ethics, good
habits, scientific literacy and the scientific spirit.

Third, humanities and social sciences disciplines and departments should play a full role. In the 1990s, many polytechnic universities established colleges and schools of humanities as a major measure to enhance humanities education and achieve the goal of developing well-rounded students. Over the years, this practice has shown positive outcomes. Many specialist science and engineering institutions have launched new majors in humanities and social sciences and set up relevant departments. This addition has not only complemented their existing disciplines, but also plays a positive role in enhancing students' humanities background through curriculum design, faculty development, campus activities and interdisciplinary initiatives. Years of practice show that offering humanities majors and setting up humanities colleges have institutionalized humanities education at polytechnic universities. Curricular activities offered by humanities departments and schools play an irreplaceable role in fostering the humanistic atmosphere in higher education and contributing to student training in the humanities.

Fourth, we need to understand clearly the implications of integrating humanities education with science education. Integration should not simply be a matter of add-ons, but enhancing internal relations and mutual penetration between the two fields, providing a new "integrated" approach to general education. By adjusting academic majors and subjects, we aim to create a better program structure, update program teaching plans and bring into a more prominent role the design of those majors and subjects that seamlessly integrate humanities education and science education. Curriculum design should focus more on basic knowledge and skills education for academic majors, increasing the proportion of comprehensive courses, and rectify the tendency to over-specialization.

Fifth, we should handle the relationship between knowledge education, values education and emotional education properly. Currently all course instructors are faced with the challenge of balancing the teaching of the mind and the heart. The best answers to the challenge include the following: instructors must have an in-depth understanding of course content and formulate their own views and ideas; they should select teaching content in a scientific way; they should adopt a flexible pedagogy that encourages student class participation; they should develop a clear outline of scientific development though teaching that organically integrates scientific ideas, critical thinking and knowledge instruction; and they should consciously promote scientific values in curricular and extra-curricular activities and help students experience healthy and positive social sensitivities through experiential learning.

In addition to classroom teaching, experiential learning activities also serve as an important way to achieve general education goals. Developing student competency in humanities and science is never a mere process of knowledge acquisition, but a gradual formation and development process of character and temperament building through knowledge-based social practices that combine knowledge acquisition and emotional experiential learning, proactive thinking and critical judgment. Therefore, for the improvement of student literacy in the humanities and sciences, it is important to re-design and re-organize experiential learning based on the pedagogical concept of integrating humanities and science education. The teaching objectives of the traditional practicum are to introduce students to the practical use of theoretical knowledge and acquire the ability to solve real-world production and social problems using theoretical knowledge and skills. This outcome design certainly makes sense, but it may have neglected humanities and science education. Practical courses should and can reflect the requirements of humanities and science education. The curricular design of experiential learning should take full account of the requirements of humanities and science education, and take full advantage of the rich case studies from social practices and social phenomena and guide students to experience and comprehend the human spirit and scientific spirit.

Faculty development and teacher–student interaction

Influenced by an over-emphasis on institutional, professional and curricular specialization, a tendency towards mutual isolation between arts and sciences also reveals itself. For most faculty members, their knowledge base and ability are confined to a narrow disciplinary area. They fail to understand the implications of humanities and science education, and their knowledge base and perspective do not allow them to meet the requirements of an integrated humanities and science education. For most humanities faculty, science and technology, especially of the high-tech kind, seems unfathomable, so it would be hard to expect them to integrate knowledge of modern science and technology into the instructional process and help to promote student competence in science. Similarly, it is also very difficult for teachers of science and engineering to have the concepts and knowledge of the humanities embedded in their teaching. The lack of cultural competency among faculty members will directly impact a university's cultural quality and development potential. An ideal university should be a holy place in which intellectual giants gather, but our universities in the real world have a long way to go to reach that ideal.

Science and engineering faculty as well humanities and social sciences faculty are confronted with the task of improving their literacy in the humanities and science. Although acquiring humanities and science knowledge can help improve humanities and scientific literacy, there is no causal relationship between pure knowledge learning and literacy improvement. In fact, our education system has precisely the shortcoming of over-emphasizing knowledge acquisition at the expense of self-improvement. Therefore, discipline-trained faculty should not only be proficient in their own specialized area, but also have some basic knowledge of history, philosophy, literature, art and modern science and technology, and work on their self-improvement in ethics and behavior patterns, value systems, emotions and character, critical thinking skills and interpersonal relationships, professionalism and sense of responsibility, as well as the scientific mode of thinking, scientific attitude and rigor and the pragmatic spirit. Humanistic and scientific literacy and spirit achieved by faculty self-improvement will help create a campus environment with a strong humanities and science orientation for students. Universities should appropriately arrange professional development opportunities for faculty in multi-disciplinary or interdisciplinary training for the overall improvement of faculty quality.

University culture's indirect impact on general education

University culture not only helps to achieve general education goals through curricular activities, but also, to a greater extent, through the subtle but indirect influence over students by the cultural factors embedded in the overall campus environment. Environmental factors of education include the university's ecological and physical environment, organizational and administrative environment, cultural and social environment and interpersonal environment. The ecological and physical environment refers to the university's geographical location in the country and region, its climate and material conditions, such as dorms, equipment and facilities. Organizational and administrative environment refers to the university's status, type of organization, management system, presidency, faculty composition, classes and associations. Cultural and social environment refers to the university's ethos, traditions, customs, values in the social environment, beliefs, rules and patterns of thinking, folkways, religion, general mood of society and so on. Interpersonal environment refers to interpersonal communications and mutual influence among faculty, administrators and other support staff and between them and the students. Improving the educational environment should start with educational philosophy, administration and resource investment and distribution as well as specific aspects of management measures. The ultimate goal is to have a comprehensive organizational and management plan, trying to build a sound university environment with a strong atmosphere in both humanities and science. Based on the stability of those environmental factors, we can broadly classify the indirect impact of university cultural environment on general education into the impact of the static cultural environments and the impact of the dynamic cultural environments.

Impact of static cultural environments on general education

Factors of static cultural environments include the stable historical and cultural traditions formed in a university's long-term development, the unique university value system (such as dominant educational philosophy, pedagogy, activities, judgment standards for educational activities and other social values), time-honored university rules and regulations, educational and other social activities, codes of conduct accepted and acted on by staff and students and long-established interpersonal environments. These factors did not come overnight, nor could they be easily changed overnight. These factors are not reflected in the curricular process directly, but, embedded in the campus environments, they exercise their influence over faculty and students in an implicit, indirect and diffused way, thus impacting student morality, ideas, behaviors and even their daily attitudes and habits. In a broader sense, we can categorize them as part of the hidden curriculum of general education.

Static cultural factors should be not only internalized in everyone's mind and behavior (in terms of thoughts, ideas, traditions, customs, systems and rituals), but also institutionalized in specific cultural facilities and carriers. Universities should take developing campus cultural facilities seriously and highlight their functions in humanities education, making full use of various historical, cultural and science education factors, such as university history archives, museums, science halls and libraries. In the meantime, universities should pay attention to the collecting and display of information on historical figures and events related to the university and achievements by famous alumni. Universities should establish and promote a system for their logos and insignia, set up special university holidays, design and customize the rituals, procedures and content of major university ceremonies (such as university day and commencement), organize various cultural activities regularly, create an active, open and rich campus cultural environment for the formation and development of a healthy character and positive values.

Dynamic cultural environment factors include extra-curricular activities in sports, arts, entertainment and other social practice activities. University-sponsored extra-curricular activities offer another important way for humanities and science education. Universities can promote humanities and science education and improve student overall quality indirectly by offering lecture series, symposia on humanities and science education, knowledge contests, technological invention and innovation exhibits, exceptional talent shows, sports competitions and other extra-curricular activities. For example, public lectures not only provide an important forum for researchers to exchange ideas and present their unique views and scholarship, but also an effective way for students to receive humanities and science education. Scholars' unique views and innovative scholarship in their specialty often have significant implications for the students' thinking and values. Multidisciplinary lectures and specialized seminar activities can compensate for over-specialization, broaden students' thinking, develop wide-ranging interests and enable students to understand methodologies and ideas from different academic research disciplines, all of which contribute to students' humanities and science education. In addition, various seminars, contests, technological invention and innovation activities and other extra-curricular activities on campus help increase interactions between faculty and students, among students themselves and between students and the university, which enables students to pick up new ideas, methods and concepts from others for a better understanding of the community, other people and themselves. In the meantime, all those rich and varied activities will help cultivate student minds, develop students' interests in learning, train their scientific thinking skills and allow them to fully comprehend the meaning and values of life.

Impact of dynamic cultural environments on general education

In comparison to factors of static cultural environments, dynamic factors can be adjusted and changed in a short time. We can create more favorable cultural environments for student development by improving university administration and adjusting educational activities. For example, we often see banning orders posted on campus by the university (e.g. "No Spitting," "No Loud Noises," etc). Behind these orders are cultural factors that reflect educators' lack of respect and trust for students (or faculty members). If a student lives in such an environment for four years, how can he be expected to learn to respect and trust others? From the viewpoint of invitational education put forward by William W. Purkey and Betty L. Siegel, "The students are able, valuable and responsible, and should be treated accordingly."[5] Everything in the university, from the physical campus to everyone's mind and behavior, and every single factor and activity are all infused with the power of education. If we can line up these factors scientifically, work on them and bring into play their cultural influence, then everyone in the university will be a general education teacher and the whole university will become a general education classroom.

Among dynamic cultural factors, educational administration has important implications for general education. Administrative activities are important factors that directly impact educational effectiveness. To achieve the goal of integrating humanities and science education, universities must attach great importance to the cultural components in the administrative process and its impact on student growth. They should bring into full play the positive impact of administrative activities, develop a student-centered philosophy and fully reflect the humanistic care concept of education and service in their system design and specific administrative practices.

The concept of humanistic care in educational administration

One of the core objectives for general education is to equip students with the qualities of "being kind to others" and "caring for society." Universities should first take the concept of humanistic care as their top priority in educational administration. In reality, many universities still promote the concept of "teach by control." Administrators assume the roles of leaders and judges, and students are taken as objects to be educated and controlled, who must obey orders submissively. Administrative activities often operate under the premise of command and control, and lack the most basic concepts of service and humanistic care. Therefore, the top priority for university administrators is to change their management philosophy and style. Only after a student-centered and service-oriented concept is developed and infused into all administrative activities can the university create a good humanistic environment and let the students enjoy humanistic care, value and dignity, whereby they become the young generation who know how to respect others and have a caring attitude to society. University administrators at all levels, including staff in administration, teaching and logistics, should adjust their roles accordingly, making it their primary responsibility to provide students with humanistic service, to respect and trust every single student and exercise their administrative responsibilities in an interpersonal environment of equality, understanding and harmony.

Significance of education management system reform for general education

The internal management system and operational mechanism within the university, while regulating campus academic activities, also serve the function of educating students. University administrators should be fully aware of the educational functions of their administrative activities, and create more space for students' development through the continuous improvement of the management system.

Administration of the curriculum is the core of administrative activities, and the key to educational effectiveness. Reforming the curricular management system is an important task in achieving the integration of humanities and science education. In its system design, curricular management should ensure that students have sufficient learning choices (including self-selection of majors, courses and independent study time), provide students with abundant educational resources and organize academic and social practice activities that promote individual development and innovation for student participation. For example, the academic credit system reform launched by Chinese universities in the 1980s has provided more space, to a certain extent, for students in self-selecting courses and developing personal academic interests. This institutional reform has also provided systematic support for the further development of general education. Implementation of the credit system helps to integrate majors and disciplines, avoid one-sided development for students due to over-specialization and provide more choices for students' free development. Establishing the credit system thus reflects our greatest respect for students' interests, and exemplifies the concept of humanistic care. Together with credit system reform, many universities have also set up the advisor system, with the goal of helping students select their courses and solve academic problems in the learning process. They appoint top faculty members as student advisors, offering various consulting services for students in course selection and other learning activities, providing stronger scientific guidance for student growth, helping students choose their development directions and resolving their confusions and problems. Both domestic and foreign case studies have shown that the advisor system plays an irreplaceable role in reflecting the humanistic care for students and promoting comprehensive student character development.

Requirements for education administrators

In addition to the system guarantee, we must improve the personal qualities of the administrative staff if we want to reflect a student-centered philosophy in administrative activities and make every student gain a sense of equality, respect, understanding and trust in his or her communications with educators and administrators. For historical reasons, the professional and moral qualities of Chinese university administrators are uneven. Additionally, under the influence of the long-existing tradition of administrative bureaucracy at Chinese universities, it is common among institutions to manage university affairs in a bureaucratic way.

Without an awareness of the need for respect and service for students, administrators and students lack a sense of mutual equity and respect. Therefore, we must do more to enhance administrative staff training and raise their personal and professional proficiency, which are the preconditions to creating a good management and cultural environment.

After more than ten years of educational reform and theoretical deliberations, there is an established body of research literature on such issues as understanding the significance of the establishment of university culture and its functions. However, our understanding of the relationship between university culture and general education and the role of university culture in the process of achieving general education goals remains very superficial, and a large number of theoretical issues remain to be studied more deeply. With the spread of general education reform, people will look at general education and its contributing factors from an even broader perspective, present the relationships between general education, university culture and other important factors in higher education in a more comprehensive way, bring into full play the guiding role of theories in general education reform and ensure the continuous and healthy development of general education.

Notes

1 Burton R. Clark, ed., *Perspectives on Higher Education: Eight Disciplinary and Comparative Views* (Berkeley and Los Angeles: University of California Press, 1984), p. 168.
2 Robert Maynard Hutchins, *The Learning Society* (New York: F. A. Praeger, 1968), p. vii.
3 George Papadopoulos, "Learning for the Twenty-First Century: Issues." In Jacques Delors, ed., *Education for the Twenty-First Century: Issues and Prospects* (Paris: UNESCO, 1998), p. 46.
4 Harvard University Committee on the Objectives of a General Education in a Free Society, *General Education in a Free Society: Report of the Harvard Committee* (Cambridge, MA: Harvard University Press, 1945), p. 171.
5 William W. Purkey and Betty L. Siegel, *Becoming an Invitational Leader: A New Approach to Professional and Personal Success* (Atlanta, GA: Humanics Publishing Group, 2003), p. 7).

4 From liberal education to general education

Change and continuity in the philosophy of university education

Leung Mei Yee

Introduction

General education as a curriculum concept appeared with the campaign to reform the higher education curriculum in the United States at the beginning of the twentieth century. Advocated by a small number of scholars, it was first tried in various forms in different colleges. The lack of consistency in the philosophies that supported the various experiments and the differences in the processes of implementation and outcomes resulted in much criticism and debate. After World War II, with the increasing number of students entering university and with the shock of the devastating war, general education was given a second look by universities. Notwithstanding, on more than one occasion in the 1970s it was described as the "disaster area" of the undergraduate curriculum (Lucas, 1994, p. 268), which led to serious reviews and reforms of general education. Since the 1980s, numerous universities have been busy reviewing and redefining their general education curricula. Following the ups and downs in the general education movement, not only has general education become a basic component of the undergraduate curriculum of most American universities (Johnson, 2002, p. 10),[1] but the importance attached to it by universities has only increased (Johnson, Ratcliff and Gaff, 2004, p. 10).[2] Additionally, general education has progressively received greater attention in places outside the United States. In 2000, the Task Force on Higher Education and Society convened by the World Bank and UNESCO published a research report on the prospects of higher education in developing countries in the twenty-first century. The report devotes a whole chapter to explaining the importance of general education and encourages the relevant countries to ensure that, while they are developing higher education, at least some of their universities provide a broad-based general education (Task Force on Higher Education and Society, 2000, pp. 117–18).[3]

However, despite these seemingly favorable prospects, academia has never achieved a consensus on the meaning of the term general education, and there has never been a unanimous answer to the question, "What is an ideal general education curriculum?" Furthermore, those universities that have implemented various types of general education programs have encountered all manner of problems in their planning, triggering open opposition or passive resistance within the schools, and unending review and reform of existing courses. It can be said that, in the last century, the development of general education has given rise to a singular phenomenon: as a curriculum, its emergence and broad acceptance demonstrate the practicality of its existence, however, the experience of planning general education curricula also shows that achieving the ideal to which it aspires is not an easy task, despite the variety of methods and approaches that different schools have adopted. In spite of this, the "failures" in the actual implementation of general education have not resulted in its disappearance from the university curriculum, but have, on the contrary, sparked more discussions and driven its further development. Why is a curriculum that is universally recognized as of great importance in higher education circles suffering such vagueness in its philosophy and practice? Why is the creation of a curriculum so difficult? Why have all of these difficulties not led to the disappearance of general education from university education, but have instead seen it go from strength to strength? The reasons that have given rise to these phenomena are myriad and complex and are intimately connected with the entire developmental history of general education. This author does not intend, nor does she have the ability, to clarify them one by one here. The aim of this chapter is solely to attempt, by looking at the relationship between general education and another concept with which it is often used interchangeably – liberal education – to show that there is an inextricable relationship between the process of development of general education and changes in the objectives of higher education. It will briefly show that in the course of the transformation of the university from being a place for nurturing the elite to being one for educating the masses and from being a place for training the human intellect to being one for researching profound knowledge and serving society, the philosophy and curriculum format of liberal education have, to different degrees, moved in the direction of general education. Furthermore, general education, as a program that seeks to realize the university ideal and respond to the demands of the real world, finds itself wedged between philosophical continuity and real-world change, regularly facing strong tensions and even difficult predicaments.

Liberal education or general education?

In the debates on general education during the 1970s and 1980s, numerous scholars felt that conceptual confusion hampered its effective implementation, accordingly, university teachers and administrators needed to reach a consensus – which would serve as the guideline for curriculum design and teaching – and communicate with students, parents and society (Boyer and Levine, 1981, pp. 2–3). What particularly caught the attention in the midst of this conceptual confusion was the regular use of general education and liberal education as interchangeable concepts. Some scholars felt that the concepts of general education and liberal education were essentially equivalent (Li, 1999, pp. 13–15). However, according to the research carried out by the American scholar G. E. Miller (1985, pp. 234–35), general education and liberal education were fundamentally different curricular concepts, which in terms of both their basic assumptions and objectives constituted fundamentally different paradigms. Liberal education, founded on rational assumptions, oriented toward essentialism and based in the methods of logic, was concerned with ideas in the abstract, with the conservation of universal truths handed down through the years and with the development of the student's intellect. General education, founded on instrumentalist assumptions, emphasizing skills and abilities, oriented toward the existential condition of the student and based in the methods of educational psychology, was concerned with experimentation and problem-solving for individual and social action, with the present and the future and with the development of the individual. Miller (1985, pp. 4 and 244) felt that general education was a specific curricular concept, more specifically, that it was a self-consciously developed, comprehensive program that developed in students the attitude of inquiry, the skills of problem-solving, the individual and community values associated with a democratic society and the knowledge needed to apply these attitudes, skills and values so that they could fully develop their abilities and function as full participants in a society that was continuously changing through democratic processes. Some participants in the debate felt that the distinctions that Miller drew between the two concepts were, to a certain extent, helpful in analyzing curricula; however, these distinctions were, in fact, never widely adopted nor were they ever successful in forging a consensus on what constitutes general education (Smith, 1993, p. 245).

We think that Miller's analysis of general education as a curriculum conceptual paradigm is useful in helping us to reflect more profoundly on the particular qualities of a general education curriculum. However, his attempt to draw absolute distinctions between liberal education and general education was not very successful, mainly because he treated liberal education merely as a form of curriculum, placing it on the same conceptual level as general education. However, a more in-depth analysis of papers that discuss liberal education and general education shows that liberal education can simultaneously appear at two different levels, that of a "universal education ideal" and that of "concrete curriculum." As to the concept of general education, it seeks to break away from liberal education to serve as a concrete curriculum paradigm while at the same time retaining certain ideals of liberal education. Consequently, it is inevitable that the two concepts are at times used interchangeably, but they are not entirely equivalent.

Liberal education: the core of Western educational thought

"Liberal education" was first conceptualized by the Greek philosopher Aristotle. Its core concept, "liber", is liberty, i.e. the liberation of the intellect. Liberal education was also the education of the "freeman".

Aristotle's educational theory was an extension of his political philosophy and ethics (Howie, 1968, p. 20). Ethics, based on the realization of man's value and emphasizing man's being free, affirmed that man himself was the objective and was not the tool of another. In contrast to the education of the "non-freeman", which achieved a utilitarian objective through the study of a certain skill, liberal education sought to foster in man the development of his qualities and the perfection of his rationality and moral character. The student was required to affirm the value of knowledge itself and incessantly pursue happiness in life, not use knowledge as an instrument to please others or seek gain.[4] The person cultivated through liberal education would not be deceived by the ignorant, distracted by immediate special interests or make rash judgments or decisions out of a sudden impulse. Moreover, there was a necessary connection between educational objectives and social ideals (Howie, 1968, p. 25). An education that fully developed a person's rationality and moral integrity was not a private or individual education. As the member of a city-state, the happiness of the individual first required the happiness of the entire city-state. Consequently, from a political perspective, the educational undertaking was public, and the citizens of a city-state should receive an education that could help in realizing the objectives of the city-state.[5] Understood in this way, liberal education was closely connected with the realization of the individual's potential, the nurturing of his moral character and how he met his responsibilities within the community. However, it must be noted that the right to receive a liberal education was restricted solely to freemen in the city-state, and the slaves engaged in labor for others were not its target.

Liberal educational thought has consistently had an important influence in the history of the development of Western education and although there have been differences in the specific educational systems and the contents taught due to different social and historical settings, the ideal of "nurturing the full development of the intellect, and making it rational and responsible" has been essentially retained. As the full development of the rationality of each educated person was demanded, thought could not be narrowly oriented, so breadth of educational content was favored. Christian schools of the Middle Ages developed the seven liberal arts of grammar, rhetoric, logic, geometry, arithmetic, music and astronomy, and the Renaissance had "classical humanities" that covered such studies as oratory, history, philosophy, mathematics, astronomy, natural science, and so forth. In both cases, their subjects were wide ranging, covering both what today are known as the arts and sciences, hence the alternative Chinese translation of liberal education, "*boya jiaoyu*," literally "broad and refined education." Even today, there are a fairly large number of small liberal arts colleges in the United States that offer curricula based on the so-called modern liberal arts of the humanities, social sciences and natural sciences, that effect their teaching through small seminar-type classes, allowing close interaction between teacher and students, and that emphasize the comprehensive development of the student's potential. As to the average large universities, although their school philosophies and curriculum formats are quite different from those of liberal arts colleges, they commonly call the education that they offer a "liberal education." It was not until the nineteenth century that the term "general education" formally appeared in American higher education (Huang, 2006), so it can be said to be a quite modern educational concept.

From liberal education to general education

During colonial times, higher education in the United States mainly nurtured talent through a Christianized liberal arts education aimed at serving church and state. In addition to inculcating Christian principles, educational objectives included nurturing in students a good moral character and enhancing their skills in thinking, writing and reasoning so as to build up a broad knowledge base (Lucas, 1994, pp. 105–6). Their curricula were mainly based on the liberal arts studies that had developed since the Renaissance. Concisely put, they included mathematics to train logical thinking, Greek and Latin classics to nurture taste, oratory to enhance speaking skills and Christian ethics to establish a model for living.[6] It could be said that there was a certain consistency between the conscious educational objectives of the school founders of the time and the actual curricula: the objective was a liberal education and the curriculum was liberal arts, hence the name liberal education. However, by the nineteenth century, traditional liberal education had fallen into a quandary, challenged as it was by the times.

The rise of the industrial revolution had caused a change in the social demands placed on higher education. A demand gradually arose in society, requiring that university-trained talent be congruent with social development and drive the economy. Starting in the nineteenth century, some schools of higher learning in the United States began to incorporate new disciplines or practical disciplines, e.g. law, medicine, modern languages and engineering, into their university curricula, and started to try systems of electives which allowed students to select courses based on their own interests, abilities and career orientations. The traditional classic humanistic curriculum that stressed equal competence in the arts and sciences was clearly out of step with the times. In the face of this challenge, Yale College, one of the leading American liberal arts colleges of the time, published a *Report on the Course of Instruction in Yale College* in 1828, re-emphasizing that the college's educational objective was to lay the foundation for a higher and comprehensive education. This foundation-laying work had to be broad, deep and sound, and had to take account of two great points, namely the *discipline* and the *furniture* of the mind, expanding its powers, and storing it with knowledge (Yale Report, 1993, p. 28). Discipline of the mind was to nurture good thinking habits through vigorous, steady and systematic effort, and the knowledge stored in the mind was to be comprehensive and balanced. Accordingly, "it has been an object to maintain such a proportion between the different branches of literature and science, as to form in the student a proper balance of character" (Yale Report, 1993, p. 28). As to specific curriculum content, the report stressed that the Greek and Roman classics were an indispensable part of a liberal education as they were "the most effectual discipline of the mental faculties" (Yale Report, 1993, p. 36). In other words, the objectives and spirit of a liberal education were seen as intimately connected with and inseparable from traditional liberal arts education curricula and content.[7] Even in the last half of the nineteenth century, the perspective that equated liberal education with an education in the Greek and Latin classical liberal arts caused those educators active in curriculum reform to view liberal education as an obstacle to university progress. At the end of the 1870s, the president of Columbia University lamented the "idea that our undergraduate college with its commitment to liberal education stood in the way of the right development of the institution as a whole" (Cross, 1995, p. 7).

The establishment of the Universität zu Berlin in 1810 marks the appearance of the modern university idea that sees research as its primary task. American students who were studying in Germany at this time brought back with them this idea and methodology, which rapidly took root in American universities. The electives system and professional training became the choice of an ever-growing number of universities and students. In 1869, the new president of Harvard University, C. W. Eliot, implemented the electives system, scoring a significant success. Eliot felt that as students' intellects and interests differed, their potential could only be developed through a curriculum that respected their individual differences, and that a university education had to satisfy society's demands for talent (Li, 1999, p. 58). At the turn of the twentieth century, Columbia University shortened its four-year liberal education program and gave qualified students the option to begin work in the university's professional schools after two years of study (Cross, 1995, p. 9). Looked at from the perspective of developing the individual's potential and concern for the happiness of the community, the electives system and professionalization do not necessarily run contrary to the spirit of a liberal education. However, the educational system reforms contained a major flaw: too early knowledge specialization produced students who lacked a comprehensive development and had an outlook that tended toward the narrow and superficial. Additionally, curricula lacked comprehensiveness, students from the same university, in the absence of basic and common courses, did not know one another let alone communicate or understand one another. As a remedy for the flaws of the electives system and professionalization, curriculum reform under the name of "general education" began to be tried in different guises in different American universities. Each university also had its own definition of "general education," but, generally speaking, the general education that developed at this time attempted to restore a semblance of comprehensiveness and completeness to the curriculum. Broadly speaking, it could be divided into two categories: the first was an approach that attempted to remedy the unorganized and fragmented nature of an absolutely free electives system by developing a major system, while additionally requiring the student to take courses in disciplines outside his or her major but within defined limits, so as to ensure that he or she had exposure to knowledge in disciplines other than his or her major, the most famous of these being Harvard University's distribution requirement (Li, 1999, p. 61); the other was an approach that considered the objectives of a university education head-on, which was based on the common concerns and experiences of mankind and set certain general knowledge courses as mandatory courses for all students, so as to give students a common study experience and the opportunity to jointly explore questions that ought to be of concern to and understood by them; Columbia University's introduction to contemporary civilization established in 1919 is a typical example (Cross, 1995, pp. 12–14).

It can be said that by the 1920s and 1930s, the new curricula had superseded traditional liberal arts education. However, as, at the level of university philosophy, school authorities still believed in the importance of a holistic education, a task that could not be fulfilled by a major or a professional discipline, general education became the realm in which the ideal of a holistic education was to be realized. Therefore, during the 1920s and 1930s, the two terms liberal education and general education could be used interchangeably, even synonymously (Lucas, 1994, p. 252).

Liberal education in general education

However, commencing in the 1940s and 1950s, there were already educators who were attempting to draw a clear distinction between the two. Of particular note was the conscious use in 1945 by the president of Harvard University, J. B. Conant, in *General Education in a Free Society* (1945) of the term "general education" rather than "liberal education" to describe a curriculum that was in close keeping with social requirements.

In the Introduction to the report, Conant clearly explained that his appointment of a committee to research the issue of general education, not liberal education, in a free society mainly arose from two considerations: (1) he had requested that the committee's study consider both high school education and college education, because the most important educational issue at the time addressed "the great majority of each generation" not just the comparatively small minority who attended four-year colleges (Conant, 1945, pp. viii–ix); and (2) if it were called "liberal education" many specialists would have "testified eloquently to the fact that their specialty if properly taught was in and by itself a liberal education"; in contrast, no department could claim that its courses could cover all of general education (Conant, 1945, p. ix). Put otherwise, the main distinctions between liberal education and general education were that: (1) the former was an elitist education for the minority, and the latter was education for the mass of students under universal education; and (2) liberal education was closely associated and connected with a certain type of traditional disciplines, thereby burdening it with limitations. Calling it general education served to cast off the limitations that liberal education had accumulated through the course of its historical development and give the new curriculum greater inclusivity and more development space.

However, in Conant's report, general education and liberal education are not two completely unrelated educational concepts, and general education does not simply supersede liberal education. World War II had brought higher education circles face to face with serious educational questions: why did Germany, with its relatively advanced educational system and leading scientific knowledge, become the seedbed of Nazism? Was rapid technological development sufficient to destroy all of human civilization? Consequently, Conant felt that "[t]he heart of the problem of a general education is the continuance of the liberal and humane tradition. Neither the mere acquisition of information nor the development of special skills and talents can give the broad basis of understanding which is essential if our civilization is to be preserved." Just the knowledge of a discipline and the ability to read and write several foreign languages did not provide a sufficient educational background for citizens of a free nation, for such a program lacked contact with both a man's emotional experience as an individual and his practical experience as a gregarious animal (Conant, 1945, p. viii). Conant believed that universal education had to be established on the basis of a common Western cultural tradition as it upheld the dignity and mutual obligation of man (Conant, 1945, pp. 46, 51). Clearly, in Conant's mind, general education was in fact the successor to the ideals of a liberal education, namely the pursuit of both individual and community values. History, the arts, literature and philosophy were the most important concrete tools in the process of making these ideals a reality, as students were required to come into contact with these disciplines related to value judgment at different stages of maturity. They had to be able to distinguish "right" from "wrong," both in the ethical and mathematical senses, if they were to become persons with inner strength who did not have a narrow outlook (Conant, 1945, p. ix). Consequently, the general education that Conant advocated was not only the transmission of broad knowledge, but also the nurturing of the soul and the capacity to make judgments; additionally, the perfection of the individual's abilities also required a broad, mainly humanities-based education. This can truly be said to be a liberal education shorn of the traditional Greek and Roman classics.

General Education in a Free Society squarely proposes the establishment of a general education that takes the spirit of liberal education as its guiding principle and emphasizes that the curriculum needs to transmit common cultural traditional values. This orientation was not identical to that of Harvard University's general education at the time and was much more akin to the general education at Columbia University. The report's recommendations reverberated strongly through American universities, where many revamped their general education under its influence. However, the report received less than enthusiastic support from Harvard's faculties, and the curriculum proposals were not genuinely implemented. That the report received such a welcome at Harvard is not at all surprising as, at the time that Conant was again advocating a liberal education philosophy, Harvard was already moving toward an even newer university model.

The "multiversity" and general education

In 1963, the president of the University of California, C. Kerr, put forward the idea that the real modern university was a "multiversity." This was a true characterization of both the University of California and of Harvard University. Kerr (2001, pp. 14–15) pointed out that, in contrast to the university ideal advocated by Cardinal Newman in the nineteenth century, namely that the university was a community consisting of masters and students whose mission was the transmission and study of liberal knowledge, the modern comprehensive research university is an inconsistent institution. It is not one community but several – the community of the undergraduate and the community of the graduate; the community of the humanist, the community of the social scientist, and the community of the scientist; the communities of the professional schools; the community of all the nonacademic personnel; the community of the administrators. Its edges are fuzzy – it reaches out to alumni, legislators, farmers, businessmen … A community … should have common interests; in the multiversity, they are quite varied, even conflicting … many parts can be added or subtracted … with little notice taken.

The multiversity is comparable to a modern metropolis, with its infinite variety that can easily cause some to get lost, while others manage to make it to the top; students are more vocationally oriented and find themselves in an intensely competitive atmosphere; they identify less with the total community and more with the subcultures of smaller communities (Kerr, 2001, p. 31). In addition to the teacher and researcher, the faculty also had the consultant and administrator. For an increasing number of members, teaching was no longer the central concern. The specialties and interests of colleagues were becoming increasingly diverse, resulting in fewer common topics of conversation (Kerr, 2001, pp. 32–33). Under such conditions, building of a consensus and establishment of a general education curriculum in which all members participate and which includes common standards and shared values becomes a mirage that is likely out of reach, because the members of the different communities in the university have nothing in common beyond the name of the university.[8] Such a university is extremely adaptable and very competitive, able to develop knowledge and cutting-edge technology at a dizzying pace, but has given rise to a major problem with respect to the teaching of students.

In 2006, H. R. Lewis, former president of Harvard University, in his book *Excellence without a Soul* echoed the same sentiments elaborated by Kerr almost half a century earlier. He clearly states that there is a tense relationship between the excellence pursued by the modern comprehensive research university and the ideal education objectives: professors are ever more oriented toward their cutting-edge research, teaching performance has become secondary and assisting students in becoming adults is of even less importance (Lewis, 2006, p. 8). Teaching consists only of transmitting knowledge, and when the university student experiences an existential dilemma brought on by the transformation in study method, he can only find assistance from the ever more specialized support staff, as the teachers simply do not care (Lewis, 2006, p. 13). The university gives students a great deal of freedom in choosing their courses; however, elite students who have expended great efforts to enter a top school do not necessarily have the skills to lay the foundations for their futures and are consequently not necessarily equipped to handle the freedom that the university offers (Lewis, 2006, p. 12). During the curriculum reforms of 2002, the reformers emphasized, on the one hand, that undergraduate students should have a common foundation, while, on the other, they emphasized that students had to have the freedom to choose their own courses. When breadth and choice become curriculum objectives, a so-called common foundation becomes nothing more than empty talk and students are left to wonder what they can learn (Lewis, 2006, pp. 23–25).

Generally speaking, the current realities of comprehensive research universities, including their faculty systems, curriculum structures and resource allocation, are all moving in the direction of specialization. Educating students can hardly be the first priority. However, if a university, as an educational institution, does not relinquish its ideal of educating people, then liberal education remains a task incumbent on every university and, consequently, general education, as the repository of the spirit of a liberal education, cannot but be seen as important. But the reality is, general education forms only a part of a university curriculum, notably a part that is generally not deemed important by teachers and students. Tasking it with the mission of thoroughly shaping students' abilities, attitudes and sense of social responsibility is daunting. With the achievement of such a lofty ideal as its goal, but without genuine discussion, reflection, real commitment and support in the university community, general education will inevitably become the "major disaster area" in a university curriculum.

Liberal education and general education in the twenty-first century

In 2000, the Association of American Colleges and Universities, which has more than 1,150 member institutions, launched a two-year nationwide discussion to review the quality that higher education in the twenty-first century should have. Since its establishment in 1915, the association has taken the promotion of a liberal education as its mission, and in the 2000–1 discussions, liberal education not only became one of the focal points but was determined to be the quality education that all students should receive (Association of American Colleges and Universities, 2002, p. 24). The national panel's report clarified the relationship between the concepts of liberal education and general education. It defined liberal education as "a philosophy of education that empowers individuals, liberates the mind from ignorance and cultivates social responsibility ... 'General education' and an expectation of in-depth study in at least one field normally comprise liberal education" (Association of American Colleges and Universities, 2002, p. 25). General education is "[t]he part of a liberal education curriculum shared by all students. It provides broad exposure to multiple disciplines and forms the basis for developing important intellectual and civic capacities" (Association of American Colleges and Universities, 2002, p. 25). In other words, general education is not identical to liberal education but is a specific program for realizing the philosophical ideals of liberal education, is indispensable and is the only segment that students at institutes of higher learning can experience in common. Placing liberal education on the level of an educational philosophy and regarding general education as a curriculum element in realizing the ideal of a liberal education not only help in clarifying the relationship between the two, but are also extremely important to the future development of general education curricula. That is because it is only through the clear definition of the objectives of university education and the tasks that general education is to assume under these objectives, that we can have an idea of the degree of difficulty of such tasks, and resources can be allocated accordingly. General education must be reviewed and assessed with reference to the tasks as clarified and the resources actually available for the curriculum so that an apt judgment can be rendered and the direction of reform and development can be determined.

At present, each university has different objectives in creating its general education curriculum, ranging from remedying the deficiencies in overly specialized curricula, broadening students' horizons, enhancing students' basic abilities and assisting students in realizing themselves to educating responsible citizens, making students aware of common cultural traditions, developing in them a concern for the issues of common concern to mankind, and so forth. All of these objectives are, in fact, to a greater or lesser degree related to liberal education as an educational ideal, but generally lack clear exposition. Broadening horizons can be said to be the most basic requirement of general education, and is relatively easy to accomplish. Creating a common student experience and developing in them a sense of concern are relatively straightforward responses to the question of the objectives of general education, but are relatively difficult to accomplish. Some scholars have proposed that general education is a dynamic program that needs to adjust and respond to the changing needs and interests of students, society and the expanding realms of knowledge (Johnson, Ratcliff and Gaff, 2004, p. 26). This of course is undeniable. However, if change occurs only in response to changes in external conditions, a program is likely to be unclear in orientation, incoherent and fragmented. If we agree that one of the major themes in the development of general education curricula is the creation of coherence (Johnson and Ratcliff, 2004, pp. 85–95), then taking a closer look at the contemporary significance of the idea of an "educated person" in liberal education, considering and discussing anew such questions as what kind of student the modern university should produce, what kind of social responsibility university students are expected to assume, and so forth may be not only of some help in creating coherence in general education curricula, but also relevant to establishing coherence in the entire undergraduate study experience of university students through the combination, from a more macro perspective, of the general education curriculum with other parts of undergraduate education. Accordingly, getting university communities to jointly think about such issues as the overarching university philosophy, educational ideals, and so on should be the first important step in promoting the development of general education.

Notes

1 In 1990, 86 percent of American colleges and universities had formal general education courses that were compulsory for all students.
2 In a survey conducted on its member institutions by the Association of American Colleges and Universities in 2000, 99.6 percent of the responding institutions said that their institution placed a higher priority on general education in 2000 than it did ten years earlier (Johnson, Ratcliff and Gaff, 2004, p. 10).

3   The whole of chapter 6 of the report is devoted to a discussion of general education.

4   "And any occupation, art or science, which makes the body or soul or mind of the freeman less fit for the practice or exercise of virtue, is vulgar; wherefore we call those arts vulgar which tend to deform the body, and likewise all paid employments, for they absorb and degrade the mind. There are also some liberal arts quite proper for a freeman to acquire, but only in a certain degree, and if he attends to them too closely, in order to attain perfection in them, the same evil effects will follow. The object also which a man sets before him makes a great difference; if he does or learns anything for his own sake or for the sake of his friends, or with a view to excellence the action will not appear illiberal; but if done for the sake of others, the very same action will be thought menial and servile." Aristotle, *Politics*, cited in Zhang, 1994, p. 294.

5   The original reads as follows, "education should be one and the same for all, and that it should be public ... the training in things which are of common interest should be the same for all" (Zhang, 1994, p. 293).

6   As an example, the curriculum at Harvard University in 1642 included 12 courses, logic, rhetoric, history, ethics and politics, catechism, Greek, Hebrew, Arabic, Syriac, botany, mathematics and astronomy (Huang, 2006, p. 4).

7   In his *General Education in American Universities*, Huang Kunjin (2006, p. 7) states that, "The Yale Report, 1828, has been deemed the beginning of the general education movement, however, in reality, its objective was the defense of classic liberal arts courses. It is more appropriate to say that it was liberal education in the narrow sense, rather than general education."

8   In particular, Kerr (2001, p. 15) points out that a university's name is important because it "stands for a certain standard of performance, a certain degree of respect, a certain historical legacy, a characteristic quality of spirit. This is of the utmost importance to the faculty and to students, to the government agencies and the industries with which the institution deals." Unfortunately, Kerr did not elaborate on what the specific contents of "historical legacy" and "quality of spirit" were.

References

Association of American Colleges and Universities (2002). *Greater Expectations: A New Vision for Learning as a Nation Goes to College* (Washington, DC: Association of American Colleges and Universities).

Boyer, E. L. and Levine, A. (1981). *A Quest for Common Learning* (Lawrenceville, NJ: Princeton University Press).

Committee on the Objectives of a General Education in a Free Society, Harvard University (1945). *General Education in a Free Society* (Cambridge, MA: Harvard University Press).

Conant, J. B. (1945). "Introduction." In Committee on the Objectives of a General Education in a Free Society, Harvard University, pp. v–x.

Cross, T. P. (1995). *An Oasis of Order: The Core Curriculum at Columbia College* (New York: Office of the Dean, Columbia College).

Howie, G. (1968). *Aristotle on Education* (London: Collier-Macmillan).

Huang, K. (2006). 美國大學的通識教育. 美國心靈的攀登 [General Education in American Universities – The Rise of the American Spirit] (Beijing: Beijing University Press).

Johnson, D. K. (2002). "General Education 2000 – A National Survey: How General Education Changed Between 1989 and 2000." Unpublished doctoral dissertation, Pennsylvania State University.

Johnson, D. K. and Ratcliff, J. L. (2004). "Creating Coherence: The Unfinished Agenda." In J. L. Ratcliff, D. K. Johnson and J. G. Gaff (eds.), *Changing General Education Curriculum* (San Francisco: Jossey-Bass), pp. 85–96.

Johnson, D. K., Ratcliff, J. L. and Gaff, J. G. (2004). "A Decade of Change in General Education." In J. L. Ratcliff, D. K. Johnson and J. G. Gaff (eds.), *Changing General Education Curriculum* (San Francisco: Jossey-Bass), pp. 9–28.

Kerr, C. (2001). *The Uses of the University*, 5th edn. (Cambridge, MA: Harvard University Press).

Lewis, H. R. (2006). *Excellence without a Soul: How a Great University Forgot Education* (New York: Public Affairs).

Li, M. (1999). 通識教育——一種大學教育觀 [General Education – A View on University Education] (Beijing: Tsinghua University Press).

Lucas, C. J. (1994). *American Higher Education: A History* (New York: St. Martin's Press).

Miller, G. E. (1985). "The Meaning of General Education: The Development of the General Education Paradigm and Practices." Unpublished doctoral dissertation, Pennsylvania State University.

Smith, V. (1993). "New Dimension for General Education." In A. Levine (ed.), *Higher Learning in America 1980–2000* (Baltimore and London: Johns Hopkins University Press), pp. 243–58.

Task Force on Higher Education and Society (2000). *Higher Education in Developing Countries: Peril and Promise* (Washington, DC: World Bank).

The Yale Report, 1828 (1993). In G. Willis, W. H. Schubert, R. V. Bullough, Jr., G. Kridel and J. T. Holton (eds.), *The American Curriculum: A Documentary History* (Westport, CT: Greenwood Press), pp. 25–38.

Zhang, F. (ed.) (1994). 古希臘教育論著選 [Selection of Works on Education in Ancient Greece] (Beijing: People's Education Press).

Part II
Curricular designs for general education

5 Meaning and methods

Some thoughts on the role of general education and curriculum design

Hu Xianzhang and Cao Li

In recent years, a number of China's prestigious universities, driven by the goal of achieving "first-rate" university status in a globalized world, have been engaging in various curriculum reviews and educational reforms. A good number of universities have initiated reforms in curriculum design, administrative structure and modes of learning and teaching. In the process of change and renovation, there has emerged a wide variety and range of research interests and practice in general education (GE). Over the last few years investigation of general education and curriculum design across China and in a number of Asian and American research universities has been carried out by the Center for Liberal Education of Tsinghua University. Basing the discussion on these surveys and research, this chapter starts with a survey of the origin and development of general education in the West and in China, and then proceeds to showcase the rise of general education in China in recent years. It then discusses the position of general education in higher education and how such a position should orient and affect curriculum design. The recently developed core courses and general education programs of Harvard and Columbia universities in America and Fudan, Beida and Tsinghua in China are illustrated and discussed as typical modules indicative of both achievements and problems. The chapter concludes by suggesting possible approaches to dealing with the problems.

The origin and development of general education

Many believe that GE originated from the concept of "liberal education" proposed by Aristotle. In his *Politica*, Aristotle advocated that freemen receive education in order to develop their rational mind and seek truth. This presupposes that education is not for making a living but for the ideal of free and pure philosophical "meditation." University liberal education of the Middle Ages was based on the "seven arts," grammar, rhetoric, logic, arithmetic, geometry, music and astronomy, which together formed the content resource and discipline base of university liberal arts education. In terms of content, liberal education focused on providing basic knowledge in humanities and sciences; as for methods and objectives, it aimed to foster students' rational thinking and raise their intellectual level. It is different from specialized vocational education and technical education, but it is also related to both. *The Yale Report of 1828*, published by

Yale University, was the first modern university report on "liberal education." It mainly discussed the relationship between "Liberal Education and Collegiate Life" and "Liberal Education and the Classical Curriculum," proposing that the essence of university education is "liberal education" or "liberal arts education," with classics and the humanities as its core. In the mid-nineteenth century, British educator John Henry Newman inherited and developed the tradition of rationalism and classical humanities education. In 1852 Newman published his masterpiece on education, *The Idea of a University*, which suggested that the ideal of a university was not to pass on practical knowledge and skills, but to teach an arts-and-science-based "liberal education," emphasizing the nourishment of rational thinking and the pursuit of truth. It is fair to say that the concept of "liberal education" advocated in *The Idea of a University* was the synthesis of modern liberal education ideas, which became the cornerstone for GE in future years. The ideal of "liberal education" which Newman advocated, centered on classical liberal arts education, rational thinking and self-education, has had a broad and profound impact on the development of higher education around the world, both in his own time and subsequently. However, the term "general education" itself should be credited to Professor A. S. Packard of Bowdoin College. A year after the Yale Report was released, in 1829, Professor Packard used the GE concept for the first time in an article for the *North American Review*, defining it as "a classical, literary, scientific and comprehensive education that provides comprehensive and complete knowledge base for professional training."[1] Since then, general education has been a goal, gradually promoted among some prestigious American universities while allowing change over time.

Charles William Eliot, president of Harvard University for 40 years (1869–1909), first brought up the issue of cultural roots in university education: "The American university has not yet grown out of the soil. It must grow from seed. It cannot be transplanted from England, France or Germany ... The American university will be the outgrowth of American social and political habits."[2] It was on this understanding that during the rest of the nineteenth century certain premier universities tried to strengthen general education in order to help universities take root in American cultural soil. Two representative figures were President R. M. Hutchins of the University of Chicago and President James B. Conant of Harvard University, both of whom made significant contributions to the concept of general education. They shared an emphasis on building a common cultural foundation among students. Accordingly, while providing a comprehensive and complete curriculum basis for professional education, general education contributed the unique feature of having students transformed by culture, with much focus on reading Western classics in the process of education.

Thus, since early in the twentieth century, top American universities, such as Columbia, Chicago, Yale and Harvard, have implemented general education courses under the respective titles of "Western civilization," "contemporary civilization" and "great books guided reading" as the basis and core of undergraduate education. In 1945 Harvard University published *General Education in a Free Society*, also known as the "Red Book," on general education. The book is a historic document that offers a comprehensive documentation and analysis of the status and role of general education in higher education, and had wide influence on American universities after World War II.[3] The central aim of the "Red Book" was to adjust the curricular design and training objectives of higher education in an increasingly stratified and diverse society, in order to build a future American cultural entity that would lead society and influence the world. Ever since, American general education has emphasized the roots and heritage of culture and civilization on university campuses. The "Red Book" also pointed out that general education was intended to develop responsible citizens with integrity and that they should possess four basic skills, including the ability "to think effectively, to communicate thought, to make relevant judgment and to discriminate among values." This objective, emphasizing rational thinking, responsibilities and cultural roots, later became the basic requirement of general education in higher education.

In 2005, in response to *Excellence without a Soul*,[4] which depicted the embarrassing situation in American higher education under the pressure of a commercialized economy and globalization, AAC&U (the Association of American Colleges and Universities) launched a ten-year discussion on "What is General Education?" in order to promote the ideal of the university and the value of general education. AAC&U defines liberal education and general education as follows respectively:

Liberal education is a learning methodology that enables individual learners to deal with complexity, diversity, and change. It provides students with broad background knowledge (e.g. science, culture, and society) as well as in-depth specialized knowledge. Liberal education teaches students a sense of social responsibility and helps them gain strong and transferable intellectual and practical skills such as communication, analytical and problem-solving skills, and a demonstrated capacity to apply knowledge and skills to the real world.

General education is a part of liberal education shared by all students. It exposes students to diverse disciplines, laying the foundation for developing important intellectual, practical and civic capacities. Therefore, general education could also be called "core curriculum" or "liberal arts education."[5]

The above definition describes in general terms the basic meanings of liberal education and general education and their relationship: liberal education is a concept and methodology while general education serves as the important conduit and means to practice liberal education. And its core contains mainly subjects of the sciences and humanities. Due to general education's central role in liberal education and the impact of American universities, people tend to use "general education" in place of "liberal education." In other words, general education originates from liberal education. As a concept and methodology, liberal education is not only concerned with general knowledge, but also specialized education and training, thus covering the whole education process. General education is regarded as the most important way to liberal education as it aims to provide a liberal arts foundation through a multi-disciplinary approach and serves as the key to specialized training and even lifelong learning.

Since the beginning of the twenty-first century, universities worldwide face many common challenges and problems. Accordingly, to keep up with the times, general education has shouldered more historical missions and contemporary responsibilities. Nowadays, on the one hand, many universities emphasize the return of general education to its classic traditions, while, on the other hand, they advocate that general education must face reality, the future and mankind's common problems. The interdisciplinary and cross-cultural nature of GE's orientation and objectives has, therefore, received unprecedented attention.

General education in China

In the first half of the twentieth century, Chinese higher education was influenced by the United States and accepted the GE concept to varying degrees. Mei Yiqi, president of Tsinghua University from 1931 to 1948 was known for the statement that "general knowledge is primary and specialized knowledge is secondary." He mandated general education for the freshman year, asking students to understand and prepare themselves for the natural sciences, humanities, social sciences and other fields. In the 1950s, to meet the need for professional talent in the planned economy and industrial development, Chinese higher education followed the Soviet model and did an extensive overhaul of its colleges and departments. As a result, specialized education was emphasized more than ever before, and general education faded out of the university curriculum. Since China's reform and opening up, especially since the 1990s, with the rapid development of modernization, the national policy of rejuvenating the country through science and education and the vision of building a moderately prosperous society poses in a more prominent way the task of improving the cultural and scientific quality of the overall population. In September 1995, to address the over-emphasis on specialized education at the expense of liberal arts education and the development of well-rounded students, the Ministry of Education hosted the "First Working Conference on Improving the Cultural Quality Education of College Students among Piloting Universities" at Huazhong Polytechnic University (since renamed Huazhong University of Science and Technology). The concept of "cultural quality education" was first introduced officially at the conference, marking the beginning of the cultural quality education. Fifty-two universities were selected as trial bases for the implementing cultural quality education piloting project. In March 1998, the First National Working Conference for University Teaching passed the resolution "Some Recommendations on Improving the Culture Quality Education," which in the same year was publicly announced as "Higher Education [1998] Document #2." The document stated that "the basic quality of college students includes moral quality, cultural quality, professional quality and physical and psychological quality, among which cultural quality is the foundation. The cultural quality education we are reinforcing refers to humanistic quality education."

In 1999 the Ministry of Education formally approved the establishment of 32 cultural quality education bases (including those shared by several universities) operated by 53 universities. In 2005, the Department of Higher Education and the Cultural Quality Education Steering Committee of the Ministry of Education jointly hosted a conference "In Commemoration of the 10th

Anniversary of Cultural Quality Education and the 4th Working Conference of Cultural Quality Education in Higher Education" at Tsinghua University. Zhou Ji, Minister of Education, attended the conference and conveyed President Hu Jintao's concern for quality education. President Hu encouraged educators to find solutions and ideas by way of systematic research. Minister Zhou stressed the special significance of cultural quality education in developing a modern educational system with Chinese characteristics. According to him, cultural quality education should be taken as the starting and breakthrough point for a complete reform of education, for the implementation of state education policy in training all-round talents and advancing quality education and it should be continually promoted step by step.[6] Following the conference in June 2006, the Ministry of Education approved a second round of 61 cultural quality education bases operated by 104 universities. In this process, a considerable number of mainland universities have trialed and explored various forms of cultural quality education with unique characteristics that fit their own situation. The content and platforms of cultural quality education have gradually shifted from the preliminary stage of extra-curricular activities and general electives to the implementation of a substantial undergraduate general education curricular system. A seminar on the development of a national cultural quality education system and its core curriculum was held at Tsinghua University in 2004, which garnered widespread attention for GE curriculum set-up and its quality control. In 2006, Tsinghua University took the lead in establishing its cultural quality education core curriculum. Other universities such as Southeast University, Nankai University and Harbin Engineering University set up similar cores as a result. The establishment of a cultural quality education core curriculum provided a landmark for the beginning of the second stage of cultural quality education development.

With the development of cultural quality education and the rise of undergraduate education reform and experiments, the adoption and implementation of general education gradually became the focus of undergraduate education reform at many universities. Around 2000, a number of key universities, including Peking University, Tsinghua University, Fudan University and Nanking University, began to pay attention to and promote general education. Those institutions define undergraduate education as "broad ranging specialized education based on general education," and take the corresponding measures of organization and implementation: specialty-free recruitment and training, set-up of core courses, specialty-free platform courses or general education core courses. Some universities have even established undergraduate colleges. Fudan University, for example, set up Fudan College in 2005, with a vision to develop it into a College of Arts and Sciences. With Fudan College in place, all 3,000 Fudan University incoming freshmen enter Fudan College for general education. In 2006, Nanjing University established Kuang Yaming College, where students are trained to become "all-round talents" in the broad categories of arts or science. In 2007, Peking University officially opened Yuan Pei College, the first specialty-free undergraduate college, in order to implement liberal arts education. Zhejiang University, in 2008, established Qiushi College, offering general education to first-year students before they decide on their majors. In

2009, Sun Yat-sen University opened its Liberal Arts College, trying to return to liberal education and classical humanities to meet and tackle the challenges and problems of the new age. In the same year, Tsinghua University launched the Tsinghua School Program, where the Qian Xuesen mechanics class, a course named after the late famed Chinese nuclear scientist, was among the first to explore new ways of combining undergraduate education with graduate studies and research, stressing the importance of education in liberal arts for science and engineering students. The establishment of several undergraduate colleges in China has obviously helped to institutionalize general education in the baccalaureate programs at Chinese Universities, and GE is considered as the "chosen path" towards reform in Chinese higher education.[7] Presently, both "general education" and "quality education" are used in many Chinese universities with a belief that college education needs to be strengthened along the lines of quality education with a strong emphasis on laying a common foundation of knowledge and culture for all students regardless of their diverse majors or specialisms.

The orientation and design of the general education curriculum

Guided by the GE concept, the general education curriculum constitutes the common core courses required to be taken by all undergraduate students. Due to different historical and cultural circumstances and the various institutions of different types and levels, the GE curriculum varies from campus to campus. Our task is to explore the common requirements and basic goals they all should meet.

The American educator R. W. Tyler, "the father of modern curriculum theory," believed that four fundamental questions must be answered in developing any curriculum. They are:

1   What educational purposes should the school seek to attain?
2   How can learning experiences be selected which are likely to be useful in attaining these objectives?
3   How are learning experiences organized for effective instruction?
4   How can the effectiveness of learning experiences be evaluated?[8]

Some scholars believe that even today the four issues raised by Tyler still "occupy the center of curriculum areas."[9] We believe that these four issues also have reference value for building a general education curriculum. Inspired by Tyler's questions, we will discuss general education curriculum design from the perspectives of objectives, content, methods and assessment below.

Defining objectives for the general education curriculum

In establishing a general education curriculum, we must first determine the educational objectives. This means we need to answer the following questions first: what type of knowledge, what set of skills, what cultural outlook and values do we expect our students to have? Specifically, the focus of today's general education is to help students develop:

- Holistic and integrated knowledge structure. The primary implication of general education resides in the word "general." General education courses provide not only a proper knowledge base in humanities and science to follow up specialized studies, but also an appropriate key for lifelong learning, community service and sustainable personal development. Therefore, general education courses must be characterized by both their foundational and versatile nature, a unique feature that helps college students, in face of a blending culture of science and humanities and under the influence of a rich world cultural heritage, develop competency in humanities and science, and inspect and treat the general and specialized knowledge they have acquired from an integrated, progressive, multi-faceted, multi-angle, and cross-disciplinary perspective, understand their development process and their relation with other fields so as to raise student awareness and ability in making cross references, especially in the areas of innovation and creativity.
- Independent learning, critical thinking, communication and aesthetic skills. GE is not only the teaching and learning of a multi-disciplinary general knowledge, but also an education in methodology. The pursuit of truth and continuous innovation is the essence of a scientific spirit and independent learning, and critical thinking skills are the basic elements of creative talents and also the defining characteristics of a self-defined individual, since interdisciplinary competency and cross-cultural communication skills serve as both the source and motivation for creativity. Therefore, developing students' independent learning, critical thinking and communication skills should be the starting point in the GE curriculum and remain important focuses.

   Aesthetic education is of great significance for training a well-round person. As Schiller, the German classical aesthetician and philosopher, stated: "[T]ransition from a passive state of feeling to an active state of thinking and willing cannot, then, take place except via a middle state of aesthetic freedom … There is no other way of making sensuous man rational except by first making him aesthetic."[10] He emphasized that aesthetic education was "to establish a sense and sensibility to turn human beings into a harmonious 'whole person'." Many famous Chinese and foreign scientists such as Albert Einstein, Qian Xuesen, Chen Ning Yang and Tsung-Dao Lee, all have a profound understanding of integrated science, humanities and arts. They all thought this understanding played a crucial role in nurturing creative thinking and the well-balanced growth of human beings. Thus, aesthetic education should be incorporated into the general education curriculum.
- Character building and sense of responsibility. General education is education about world outlook and values. Its ultimate goal is to foster well-rounded, balanced and holistically developed men and women, advocating for the unified development of one's intellect, ability and moral character,. Therefore, curricular design should reflect the goal of "value education."

A common core that is truly important to our students – as persons and citizens – should be established and carefully developed so that students' intellectual capacity and moral ideals, their sense of citizenship and social responsibility, are cultivated.

Content and structure of the general education curriculum

The GE curriculum may differ at Chinese and foreign universities in terms of structure and format. However, we can still find certain commonalities and development logics in general education curricular and pedagogical models due to their similarities in terms of aims.

American general education curriculum development

Generally speaking, general education in the United States has witnessed three major stages of development since the twentieth century. Stage one began when Columbia University started teaching the "Contemporary Civilization" course; stage two was marked by the "Great Books" curricular plan launched by the University of Chicago in the 1930s and 1940s; stage three refers to the practice of general education modeled after the "Red Book" at Harvard University between the 1940s and 1970s. The "Contemporary Civilization" course was started against the background of World War I; its content covers various contemporary problems and situations facing mankind, including natural and geographic resources, human nature, Western historical outlines and other contemporary issues. The "Great Books" course originated from the "General Honors Course" at Columbia University. Each week students read one book from among the 50 or 60 recommended classics, and discuss it in class. With strong support from President Hutchins of the University of Chicago, the "Great Books" project was later implemented in the undergraduate college of general education. The project involved readings and discussions of a set of classic titles that covered the relationship between human beings and society as well as among human beings themselves, including works that touched upon the philosophical basis of American democracy, and major social and cultural issues, the value of freedom and the issue of its control, Aristotelian doctrine and issues related to physical science and biological science. The "Great Books" project was later taken to St. John's College by Hutchins and has been maintained till today as a model for most American liberal arts colleges. Below we introduce the general education models adopted by Harvard University and Columbia University, two representative US research universities.

THE HARVARD MODEL: FROM CORE CURRICULUM TO THE NEW GENERAL
EDUCATION PROGRAM

Under the guidance of President Conant, Harvard University published the "Red Book" in 1945. It emphasized that general education should help American students develop a common cultural foundation and highlighted the importance of understanding Western history and cultures. It required students to take at least six general education courses, at least one for each in the humanities, social sciences and natural sciences. Arts-related courses were added in the *Report of the Committee on the Visual Arts at Harvard University* released in 1956. Later during the introspection caused by the Soviets' successful launching of Sputnik ahead of the USA it was believed that the USA was lagging behind largely because of its lack of art education.[11] Guided by "Project Zero" at Harvard University, many institutions of higher education have included art education in their general education curricula in order to develop student concepts of aesthetics and the artistic imagination, an important quality that is related to creativity. In the 1960s and 1970s, the general education movement in the USA was in decline as a result of the larger academic environment where research took priority over teaching and specialization took priority over general education. Most general education programs adopted the distribution model with discipline-based courses. In 1973, to push for a new round of general education reform, Derek Bok, president of Harvard University, appointed Henry Rosovsky dean of the Faculty of Arts and Sciences. Rosovsky emphasized that universities should not only provide students with career training, but also make them cultured through general education so that they are able to think and write clearly and effectively; judge and evaluate nature, society and themselves; understand other cultures with a broad vision; understand and analyze ethical and moral issues, and make the right judgments and choices; while also specializing in certain fields of study.

Accordingly, in 1979 Harvard University published the *Harvard University Report on the Core Curriculum*, and, after some pilots, began to fully implement the core curriculum plan in 1982. At the beginning, the core curriculum included five areas, including literature and art, science, historical research, social analysis and foreign cultures, and moral reasoning was added in 1985. On average, there were ten courses for the students to choose in each area. Later, in response to the students' poor writing skills, a writing course as a compulsory requirement was added. In 2007, Harvard University proposed the "New General Education Program," and, starting in 2009, the new program gradually replaced the requirements of the existing, 30-year-old core curriculum. The new general education plan covers eight broad categories: (1) aesthetic and interpretive understanding; (2) culture and belief; (3) empirical and mathematical reasoning; (4) ethical reasoning; (5) science of living systems; (6) science of the physical universe; (7) societies of the world; (8) the United States in the world. The new program has basically adopted the distributive compulsory model, where students are required to take one course in each of eight broad categories during any of the four years. Harvard University General Education Committee declared that while the core curriculum emphasized the "ways of knowing," the new plan focused on "connecting what students learn in the classroom to the life they will lead after college." The new program encourages innovative pedagogies, including non-traditional, non-standard teaching methods and assignments.[12] The new Harvard University program has received mixed reviews in the USA. Supporters believe the new program is more inclusive and open;

its emphasis on the sciences, international vision and diversity addresses real issues in American society. The detractors argue that the new program provides nothing but a big open-shelf GE supermarket for students to pick and choose their distributed electives over four years. The all-inclusive content and format, they argue, have actually weakened GE's recognized core values and rigorous style. In view of this situation, it seems obvious the merits and drawbacks of the new program still need to be tested in practice.

THE COLUMBIA UNIVERSITY MODEL: THE CORE CURRICULUM

Columbia University is yet another American institution of higher education that is noted for its general education program. Currently, it operates its GE program under the framework of the core curriculum. The core curriculum is divided into ten subject groups: contemporary civilization, literature humanities, art humanities, music humanities, frontiers of science, science requirement, global core requirement, university writing, foreign language requirement, and physical education requirement.

Among them, contemporary civilization is the longest-running course that is noted for its top-notch faculty and unique pedagogy at Columbia University. By exploring a whole range of political, social, ethical and religious issues, the course introduces students to the structures and core value systems of different societies and prepares them to become active and informed citizens. It is a year-long course with a small class size of 22 students. It emphasizes the study and discussion of different classics. Classic texts are chosen based on their historical influence, their enduring significance and their potential to provoke productive discussion. "Literature humanities" aims to enhance students' understanding of the main lines of literary and philosophical development that have shaped Western thought for nearly three millennia; "Art humanities" teaches students how to look at, think about and engage in critical discussion of the visual arts. The course focuses on the formal structure of works of architecture, paintings and other media, as well as the historical context in which these works were made and understood. "Music humanities" has awakened in students an appreciation of music in the Western world, it has helped them respond intelligently to a variety of musical idioms and it has engaged them in the debates about the character and purposes of music that have occupied composers and musical thinkers since ancient times. The science requirement is intended specifically to provide students with the opportunity to learn what kinds of questions are asked about nature, how hypotheses are tested against experimental or observational evidence, how results of tests are evaluated and what knowledge has been accumulated about the workings of the natural world. Three courses in the science requirement (at least ten credits) must be completed to meet this portion of the core curriculum. Frontiers of science integrates modern science into the core curriculum to change the way students think about questions of science and about the world around them. Global core courses focus on a specific culture or civilization, tracing its appearance and/or existence across a significant span of time and sometimes across more than one present-day country or region, or address several world settings or cultures comparatively. The foreign language requirement is a four-semester subject, and departmental placement examination is permitted to demonstrate equivalent competence. Passing physical education is a requirement for the degree. All students are also required to pass a PE exam, including a swimming test. Because of its small class size, core curriculum focus and integration of classics of civilization and frontiers of science, Columbia University has gained wide recognition and even become a role model for many other American universities.

The United States is a nation of immigrants with diverse cultures and ethnicities. Its problems as well as its vitality come from this feature of diversity. In addition to the research universities, the USA has many state universities, liberal arts colleges and community colleges. In recent years, almost all these kinds of institutions have been actively promoting general education. AAC&U even passed the high-profile "Liberal Education and America's Promise (LEAP)" resolution, pushing American general education to a new level. It is noted that in many American universities, general education programs, whether following the distribution model or the core curriculum model, have curricular designs with distinctive interdisciplinary, cross-cultural and border-crossing characteristics. While honoring tradition and the classics, such an approach calls for critical attention to practical issues and new academic frontiers.

The general education curriculum in mainland China

In mainland China, the general education curriculum system generally includes required courses in political theory, general elective courses (also known as cultural quality education courses), PE and required military training, foreign language courses and computer literacy courses, among others. Since math and physics are considered foundation courses for science and engineering majors, they are often included in the general education curriculum by some polytechnic universities. Here we mainly discuss the general elective courses and cultural quality education courses through models operated by Beida, Fudan and Tsinghua universities.

THE BEIDA MODEL: GENERAL ELECTIVE COURSES AND MAJOR DISCIPLINES PLATFORM

In September 2000, Peking University offered 150 quality education general elective courses. Now there are 202, which are divided into six areas: mathematics and natural sciences (36 courses); social sciences (50 courses); philosophy and psychology (20 courses); history (38 courses); language, literature, arts and aesthetics (48 courses); sustainable development in society (10 courses). According to the document issued by Peking University Office of Educational Administration in December 2010, all students should have completed at least 12 elective credits. Science and engineering majors are required to complete at least two credits in the areas of mathematics and natural sciences and sustainable development in society, and four credits in linguistics, literature, art and aesthetics, of which at least one credit must be in arts and aesthetics and at least two credits in the rest of the other three areas. Arts majors are required to complete at least four credits in the two areas of mathematics and natural sciences and sustainable development in society, and two credits in linguistics, literature, art and aesthetics, of which at least one credit which must be in arts and aesthetics. All undergraduates are required to complete at least two credits in the other three areas. In 2009, on the basis of quality education general elective courses, Beida started major discipline platforms built and shared by related colleges and departments, further strengthening the general education curriculum. Major platform courses are divided into two categories: the basic platform courses and open platform courses. Each college or department is required to offer two basic platform courses according to the needs of other colleges and departments, and a certain number of open platform courses.

The major discipline platform courses include: engineering and science platform courses (offered by the following ten departments and colleges: School of Mathematical Science, School of Physics, College of Chemistry, School of Biological Sciences, School of Electronics Engineering and Computer Science, College of Urban and Environmental Sciences, School of Earth and Space Sciences, Department of Psychology, College of Engineering); the humanities platform courses (offered by the following six departments and colleges: Department of Chinese Language and Literature, Department of History, Department of Philosophy, School of Archaeology and Musicology, School of Foreign Languages, and School of Arts); social sciences platform courses (offered by the following six departments and colleges: School of Government, School of International Studies, Law School, Department of Sociology, Department of Information Management, School of Journalism and Communication); economics and management platform courses (offered by School of Economics, Guanghua School of Management and the Center for Sociological Research and Development Studies of China). The establishment of major discipline platforms further expanded and consolidated the general education curriculum at Peking University, laying the foundation for establishing an undergraduate college for the future. In addition to establishing and developing a university-wide general education system, in 2007 Beida established Yuanpei College, a non-specialized undergraduate college, on the basis of the original "Yuanpei Plan," which is a great step forward in undergraduate education reform and general education development.

THE FUDAN MODEL: UNDERGRADUATE COLLEGE AND CORE CURRICULUM

Fudan University is the first mainland research university to have established an undergraduate college, and also the first mainland institution that clearly proposed general education. The establishment of Fudan College in 2005 provided important institutional and operational support for promoting and implementing general education at the college level. Along with the establishment of Fudan College, all freshmen are required to take a year-long general education program within Fudan College, and continue to receive general education after they declare their majors in the second year. There are six modules that constitute the core in the general education program, with the guiding principle: "Break through the single 'professional horizon' and 'knowledge horizon', offer the students the courses that can help them cultivate basic humanistic quality, intellectual vision and spiritual insight for training new Chinese citizens in the new era." The six core modules are: historical classics and cultural heritage, philosophical wisdom and critical thinking, dialogues among civilizations and world vision, technological advancement and the spirit of science, ecological environment and life care, creative arts and aesthetic experience. A total of 12 credits are required for each student with 2 credits from each module (one course). It is recommended that students take one course per semester and complete the requirement in six semesters. Fudan University emphasizes reading the classics, cutting-edge knowledge and small-class discussion. Among mainland universities, Fudan is a university that clearly places general education at the center of undergraduate education reform. Therefore, it is ahead of other mainland institutions in setting up a college system, policy formulation, faculty development and outcome achievement. It is said that Fudan University is currently planning the establishment of a larger college of arts and sciences so as to provide a more sustainable and open institutional framework for a more deliberate and solid integration between general education and specialized education.

THE TSINGHUA MODEL: CORE CURRICULUM AND PILOT PROJECTS

In 2001, Tsinghua University proposed the idea of "broad ranging specialized education based on general education" for undergraduate studies, and instituted a 13-credit cultural quality course requirement. Since 2006, Tsinghua has started to implement the "core curriculum" plan, and initiated higher and more rigorous benchmarks for the curricular system, faculty resources, teaching content and delivery in order to address the existing problems of tailoring course offerings to random availability. The core curriculum emphasizes the common foundations in humanities and science, cultural connotations, methodological significance, interdisciplinary perspective and global awareness. It promotes the study of Eastern and Western classics and achievements of civilization. It honors and carries on Tsinghua's tradition of "integration of China and the West, amalgamation of tradition and modernity, and integration of liberal arts and science." It tries to break through disciplinary barriers and limitations and broadens intellectual horizons, focusing on cultivation of character and development of critical thinking and the spirit of exploration and innovation.

In April 2009, Tsinghua University revised the *Guide for Culture Quality Education Electives* and issued *Measures for the Management of Tsinghua University Culture Quality Education Core Curriculum*. As a result of several years of hard work, core curriculum courses have increased from an initial 20 to nearly 100. In the meantime, the university has adjusted and updated the names and structure of the core curriculum courses. From the Fall semester of 2011, the cultural quality education curriculum will consist of four categories: culture quality education core courses, freshman seminars, cultural quality education lectures (also known as "new humanities lectures") and other cultural quality education electives. A total of 13 credits are required, at least 8 of which are required to be from the core. The eight broad categories of the core curriculum have been revised as follows: philosophy and ethics; history and culture; language and literature; art and aesthetics; environment, technology and society; contemporary China and the world; personal life and development; and mathematics and natural sciences.

Over the last few years, in addition to continuously adjusting and reforming the general education curriculum, Tsinghua University has encouraged individual schools and faculties which are willing and ready to initiate pilot projects on undergraduate education reform. In 2010, the School of Economics and Management initiated pilot projects on undergraduate education reform, making substantial adjustments in the undergraduate program, which emphasized general education and individual development. The new program proposes that the objectives of general education are not just the laying of foundations for specialized education, supplementing learning or simply for students' immediate career prospects, but for the lifelong benefit of the students. In this sense general education stands on its own in terms of purpose and value. In the new undergraduate program, general education courses account for 50 percent of the total. It focuses on six core courses: Chinese civilization; world civilizations; critical thinking and moral reasoning; art and aesthetics; China and the world; and introduction to life science. It also highlights three basic skills, Chinese, English and mathematics, which are mandatory subjects for all students. It tries to achieve the "trinity" by developing value concepts (values, character and ideals), building capacities (curiosity, imagination and critical thinking), and imparting knowledge (core accomplishments of human civilization). In terms of development of the individual, the School also launched new initiatives. For example, out of the 140 required credits, it leaves 20 open for students to choose as "free electives," providing more opportunities for a second degree or a minor. In the meantime, it also provides different enhancement programs for special talents among juniors and seniors.

In 2009, Tsinghua University launched the "Tsinghua School Program." Qian Xuesen Mechanics Class has the largest number of students so far in the program. For three years now, this class has adhered to the idea and practice of liberal education by requiring students to take a set of recommended courses in humanities and art including great minds and the university; contemporary art; modern Chinese history; Western civilization, etc., all conducted by prestigious professors in small-class and seminar format. In order to have students fully absorb the knowledge passed to them in the lecture room, a 1:1 ratio of hours for in-class and out-of-class work and activities was introduced and enforced. Students are therefore "forced" to read, write and discuss outside class in addition to in-class lectures. The course objective is to focus on developing students' habits and skills in critical thinking and innovative learning. Students are led to develop "problem awareness" and "experiential learning methods," while exploring the formation and development of the cognitive process and creative thinking. The adoption of these measures and methods aims to break away from the random and superficial nature of survey courses and general knowledge courses, overcome the so-called "dim sum" or fast-food" teaching style, and encourage in-depth learning and debates.

In view of GE designs both inside China and overseas we believe that an emphasis on arts and science, knowledge acquisition and the development of individual talents is equally important for the balanced enrichment and cultivation of students' minds. At the same time, since general education serves the purpose of teaching values and cultures, it is necessary to place the best of Chinese and world civilizations at the core and provide cognitively challenging and culturally rooted courses according to local realities and historical demands, so as to achieve the goals of education in the areas of culture, values and methodology.

The implementation and assessment of the general education curriculum

The way the general education curriculum is implemented will have a large impact on teaching effectiveness. For a long time, from primary education to higher education, "making a tool" instead of "making a person" often served as the educational objective, and it is a popular practice to take the amount of knowledge acquired and the ability to draw upon that knowledge as the standard for testing. In educational philosophy and methods, the instructor-centered teaching process of passing on and "spoon-feeding" constrains students' initiative and enthusiasm and restricts their creativity. German philosopher and educationalist Karl Jaspers said: "The concerns of educational activities are how to achieve the realization of bringing human potentials and capacity into play at the utmost, and how to fulfill a complete growth of human inner intelligence. That is to say, education is to educate the human soul, but not an accumulation of rational knowledge and cognition."[13] General education, which plays a fundamental role in university education, should be committed to helping students with critical thinking, pursuit of truth and self-improvement, improving their own spiritual life and cognitive skills. Therefore, the general education curriculum needs a paradigm shift from knowledge-planting and spoon-feeding introductory courses to cognitively challenging and culturally rooted research and seminar courses. Under these circumstances, small-group discussions with TA-guided tutorials are among the important elements in the teaching process.

In the meantime, an effective education and teaching process needs the safeguard of a scientific assessment system. Mainland Chinese universities like Tsinghua University have adopted the combined approach of end-of-term student evaluations, peer reviews and inspections by senior administrators, which have been successful to a certain degree. The two areas in GE assessment in need of improvement are: (1) setting up clearly defined assessment goals; (2) giving instructors a more positive role to play in assessment. In this regard, so-called course-embedded assessment (CEA) may be a good model to follow. This method was initiated by the University of Northern Colorado at the beginning of the century. In response to past problems with standardization of tests, survey questionnaires and teaching material evaluations, the university set up a general education assessment committee, which is charged with designing teaching objectives and evaluation criteria and organizing training seminars for teachers where they discuss course syllabi and assessment principles and methods. Then according to the above principles and classroom dynamics, instructors conduct assessment as the course advances and submit an assessment report by the end of the course, which covers student learning outcome targets, student test results, grading criteria and reflections on and recommendations for improving teaching effectiveness. There are real cases that have proved the method's effectiveness. The key point is the effective integration of the general education curricular objectives, teaching process and evaluation indexes. It mobilizes teachers' enthusiasm in curriculum development as well.

General education in Chinese higher education should continue to improve its assessment system while learning from and modeling it after good examples from other countries. With the integration of the CEA method with the existing assessment tools and the introduction into the assessment system of alumni recollections and evaluations of the teaching process, new breakthroughs are expected to improve the assessment system.

Existing problems and solutions in the general education curriculum

Although consensus is gradually emerging, and the basic framework is established, there are still at least three major difficulties and problems facing mainland Chinese universities in the implementation of a high-quality general education program and the set-up and delivery of the core curriculum.

Structural problems for the undergraduate curriculum

Unlike American Ivy League universities, for Chinese universities general education serves as a project to reform the established practice of emphasizing specialized education at the cost of general education. General education often ends up as a simple add-on to the original curriculum. Thus, the implementation of general education has a lot to do with smoothly restructuring the undergraduate curriculum. For example, Tsinghua University has various general electives in its undergraduate program. However, there is little connection and integration among them. So, based on the interconnected nature of quality education, it is necessary to establish a general education system with a design scheme that would integrate the various constituents of general education courses including political theory, foreign languages, physical education and the cultural quality core. This scheme would enable a better-constructed platform for general education on which the overall framework and the specific curriculum can be more strategically structured, with the elements of general education and specialized education more organically integrated, both with a clearer focus, supported by a wider consensus and stronger institutional management. It is also necessary to adjust the undergraduate curriculum design according to disciplinary training objectives and requirements, in order to address the public perception of the structural conflict between specialized education and general education.

Therefore, general education curriculum design must be placed within the context of the university's entire curricular and educational reform. For instance, one of the major impediments to assuring the quality of the general education curriculum in mainland universities is the overcrowding of undergraduate courses. The students are so overloaded in their major studies that it is difficult for them to do any in-depth learning in general education. In comparison to premier universities overseas, most Chinese undergraduates take too many courses each semester in the first three years. Some students enroll in up to ten courses per semester. At Harvard and other top-ranking world universities, students normally enroll in four or at most five or six courses per semester, and special approval is needed to take more. It is impossible for students to invest enough time to study general education courses in an intense way if the total number of undergraduate courses is not reduced. Drawing upon the experience of major foreign universities, it is necessary, as part of adjusting the overall undergraduate curriculum, to set a limit on the total number of courses a student can take, in order to guarantee learning quality and improve the real learning outcome. Some people believe students cannot become well qualified in a certain field if the hours of specialized learning are not guaranteed. The key to understanding the issue lies in the overall orientation of undergraduate education. Different types and levels of higher education institutions take a divergent view on the issues because of the different orientations of their undergraduate programs. For research universities, it is reasonable to expect them to break free from the shackles of "specialization" and "instrumentality" in undergraduate education for a better liberal arts foundation. Once a high-quality general education is in place, college graduates are more likely to be equipped with the potential to become outstanding talents and leaders in various special fields with a richly equipped mind, profound knowledge, broad vision, innovative spirit and creative ability. To address the conflict in student credit hours, in addition to reducing the number of specialty-based courses, it is also important to promote the concept and method of liberal and quality education in the curriculum and the teaching of specialized training.

Course content and pedagogy

The term wet course (the opposite of a dry, solid course) is popular among students, and captures the disappointment caused by some general education courses in terms of both the teaching process and outcome. A considerable number of GE courses go overboard to make everything fun and entertaining. While students are diverted in a light-hearted and delightful manner in terms of both course content and requirement, such courses fail to pose challenges to their cognitive ability, imagination and reasoning power. Though it is important to make classes interesting and attractive, academic courses cannot always cater to the interests of knowledge consumers, just as the university cannot always cater to the demand of the market. Very often, it happens that the instructor provides an overview with a single textbook with no reading, writing or discussion requirement; students pay little attention in class and invest no time after class; all they do is "listen leisurely" for a couple of hours per week, finish an end-of-term report and earn academic credits without any significant effort. It needs great determination and effort to improve this.

To enhance the overall quality of the core curriculum and to raise the benchmark for teaching and learning, general education needs a paradigm shift from introductory and general knowledge courses to cognitively challenging and culturally rooted in-depth courses. It becomes imperative to promote and implement the reading, writing, discussion and tutorial elements in the teaching of the core so as to help guarantee some necessary time investment outside class. A better shared vision among instructors and students and greater joint efforts are called for to make real progress in the areas outlined above. General education courses should not simply be a matter of sorting out and summarizing general knowledge from various fields. They are there to encourage and help students to explore the cognitive process and the formation of knowledge and to relate one subject to another. It is especially important to mandate reading and writing requirements, and create opportunities for students' voluntary participation. These should be taken as directions for various general education courses. Better-informed decisions need to be made to achieve the balance and integration between entertainment and cognitive challenge, the general and the specialized, the standardized and individualized mode of liberal education.

Another important aspect of general education is the in-depth study and analysis of major intellectual achievements, both Chinese and foreign, ancient and modern. Thus, reading of the great books and texts themselves (as opposed to general introductory materials) and seminar discussions are important elements of general education, especially when we come to the question of courses in the humanities. In the digital era, where the culture of reading and reading habits (also, to some degree, the habit of thinking) are seriously challenged and eroded by the visual culture and virtual cultures, it is particularly important to guide and require college students to acquire and maintain good reading and thinking habits, and expose them to the great classics of the world in an intimate way, because those great classics have attempted to raise and answer the most profound and enduring questions in human life, the intensive reading and research of which can help students learn and understand their own culture and foreign cultures, their traditions and development as well as interactions with others in the long process of human civilization, while helping them grow into qualified citizens with historical awareness, contemporary concern, sound reasoning power, good judgment and a capacity for lifelong learning and reflection.

Faculty development and sustainability

Former Tsinghua President Mei Yiqi's saying, "a university is so named because of its master professors," is the word of wisdom for general education. Currently, general education often lacks faculty participation, especially senior faculty involvement. As for the reasons, first, it is due to the concept that specialized education is the priority; second, general education is not yet properly placed in a truly fundamental central position. The problem needs to be addressed by changing concepts and policies, where university presidents' awareness and strong leadership play a key role. Also, various incentives need to be in place to mobilize faculty members' enthusiasm in teaching general education courses, for example, to set up chair professorships, offer position bonuses and encourage new initiatives and involvement with awards and grants, while the most important thing is to prioritize undergraduate GE teaching in both policy-making and practical management.

Another key element related to faculty development is the development and training of well-qualified teaching assistants. Because Chinese universities have had a late start in setting up the teaching assistant system, especially for the humanities, the task of teaching assistants is normally limited to preparing teaching materials for the lecturing professors, grading term papers and answering questions online. They have little opportunity to sit in on the class and interact with students. So, those who are good at organizing small-class discussions and offering tutorials are few and rare. Strengthening the teaching assistant system is a key step forward, including having a practicum requirement for those PhD students engaged in the core curriculum. Teaching assistants have to attend class regularly, get to know lecture notes well, know readings by heart and form their own questions and ideas for organizing tutorials and discussions. Breakthroughs and progress need to be made in this regard together with innovation in curriculum design, improvement in course organization and faculty development.

Today, Chinese higher education shoulders the historic mission of helping China in its transition to becoming a nation of innovation and bringing about its great rejuvenation. The *National Mid- and Long-Term Educational Reform and Development Plan* reaffirms that "While adhering to the people-oriented policy, the full implementation of quality education is of strategic significance for educational reform." We believe that promoting university general education is an important measure and a fundamental step forward for implementing quality education as it relates to the long-term effects of talent training and potential of future specialists. It will have a significant impact on the future of the nation and the prospects of the country. Therefore, a strategic perspective is very important in the course of promoting general education as a cultural course and one of the effective means to upgrade the quality of Chinese higher education to bring it to the forefront of higher learning in the world.

Notes

1   S. Packard, "Review of *The Substance of Two Reports of the Faculty of Amherst College to the Board of Trustees, with the Doings of the Board Thereon.*" *North American Review*, 28, 1829, p. 300.
2   Richard Norton Smith, *The Harvard Century: The Making of a University* (Cambridge, MA: Harvard University Press, 1998), p. 27.
3   Committee on the Objectives of a General Education in a Free Society, Harvard University, *General Education in a Free Society* (Cambridge, MA: Harvard University Press, 1945).

4 A term used by Harry R. Lewis in *Excellence without a Soul: How a Great University Forgot Education* (New York: Public Affairs, 2006).
5 AAC&U, "What is Liberal Education?" Online. Available HTTP: <http://www.aacu.org/leap/what is liberal education.cfm>, accessed March 22, 2010.
6 Hu Xianzhang, ed., *Ten Years of Exploration and Development: On the Tenth Anniversary of Cultural Education Movement* (Beijing: Higher Education Press, 2006), pp. 8–12.
7 See Gang Yang, "The Way of University and Cultural Consciousness." In Hu Xianzhang and Cao Li, eds., *The Idea of a University and the Spirit of Humanities* (Beijing: Tsinghua University Press, 2006), pp. 215–34; Wu Ming, "General Education Took Off in China." *21st Century Economic Report*, December 25, 2006, p. 20.
8 Ralph W. Tyler, *Basic Principles of Curriculum and Instruction* (Chicago: University of Chicago Press, 1996), p. 1.
9 Daniel Tanner and Laurel Tanner, *Curriculum Development: Theory into Practice*, 2nd edn. (Upper Saddle River, NJ: Prentice Hall: 1995), p. 84.
10 J. C. F. Schiller, *Letters on Aesthetic Education*, trans. Xu Hengchun (Beijing: China Federation of Literary and Art Circles Press, 1984), pp. 116 and 108.
11 Harvard University, *Report of the Committee on the Visual Arts at Harvard University* (Cambridge, MA: Harvard University Press, 1956), p. 100.
12 Harvard College Program in General Education. Online. Available HTTP: <http://generaleducation.fas.harvard.edu/ibc/ibc.do>, accessed April 2, 2011.
13 Karl Jaspers, *What is Education?*, trans. Zou Jin (Hong Kong: SDX Joint Publishing Company, 1991), p. 4.

6 The relationships in curriculum designs of general education and whole-person education in higher education

Lin Mei-chin

Introduction

What is the ultimate goal or the main purpose of institutions of higher education? Is it to educate students to become fully developed whole persons, to discover new facts or theories, or to train students to be specialists in a certain field? While generating new knowledge and training students to become masters in certain professional fields may be important, however, the essential goals of the universities and colleges should be student-centered, which means educating students to become well-rounded persons (Cardinal Newman, as cited in Cross, 2009; Kerr, 2009).

Van Amringe has noted that the ultimate purpose of the university should be "making men" instead of training scholars and professionals (as cited in Cross, 2009). The ideal of higher education should be to educate students as whole persons as well as world citizens (Nussbaum, 2009). Boyer (1990) also advocated the same notion, that the institutions of higher education need to prepare students for their future careers, living with dignity and purpose, generating new knowledge and using it for human well-being, as well as becoming a citizenry that can promote the public good.

Astin (1985, 1987, 1991) indicated two traditional approaches (reputational and resource-based) used to define excellence in higher education. The reputational view defines excellence as the rank of an institution in the prestige pecking order; while the resource-based approach views excellence in terms of the test scores of entering students, the size of the library and the student–faculty ratio. He noted, however, that these two approaches are flawed. He argued that these two approaches failed to focus directly on the central mission of most colleges and universities which is, "the education of [the] student," or to be more precise, "the fullest development of the student's abilities and talents" (Astin, 1987, p. 14). Therefore, he concluded that the talent development view which focused on the educational impact of the institution on its students would be the most appropriate approach to define excellence in higher education (Astin, 1987, 1990).

Consequently, whole-person development is the core mission of higher education. In order to help students to become well-rounded persons and to succeed at college, the entire college environment should be taken into consideration. Braskamp, Trautvetter and Ward (2008) stated that "creating a campus environment to foster student development takes a whole campus of whole persons to develop whole students" (p. 27). The four Cs framework (culture, curriculum, co-curriculum and community) needs to be created in the campus environment.

Culture is the set of artifacts, espoused values and basic assumptions that are held by the majority of the organizational members (Braskamp, Trautvetter and Ward, 2008; Keyton, 2005; Schein, 2004). The mission statement of each university is a formulation of artifacts and espoused values. However, if the mission is only espoused and not enacted, the organizational culture cannot be formed (Keyton, 2005; Schein, 2004). Only when the mission is enacted and systemically internalized will it guide the daily action of the members of the organization. Kuh *et al.* (2005) mounted a project called "Documenting Effective Educational Practice (DEEP)" that identified 20 colleges and universities which had high student engagement and graduate rates in the USA. They claimed that the gap between the espoused mission and enacted mission of these institutions is smaller than in most of the other schools. Thus, in forming the culture of whole-person development, the institutions of higher education should not only put it on their espoused mission but also bring it to life.

Curriculum should be educational (Kelly, 2004). It is considered as "the most important part of the sociocultural environment in helping students to meet a college's learning and developmental goals" (Braskamp, Trautvetter and Ward, 2008, p. 28). An educational curriculum needs to provide a wide variety of experiences for students, such as promotion of freedom and independence of thought, of respect for the freedom of others, of acceptance of a variety of views, of the enrichment of each individual's life, and so forth (Kelly, 2004). There are three forms of curriculum in schools, namely, the formal, informal and hidden curriculum (English and Larson, as cited in Mullun, 2007). The distinction between formal and informal curriculum is that the former refers to the formal teaching activities shown on the school timetable and the latter is out-of-class activities usually participated in on a voluntary basis (Kelly, 2004).

In higher education, the formal curriculum consists of general education and professional education which provide course credit hours. The hidden curriculum, Mullun (2007) has noted, is "latent but present" in the sense that "implicit cultural values" are not transmitted overtly (p. 13). For example, the values embedded in the environmental arrangement or the attitudes which are conveyed through student–faculty interaction. In other words, when discussing the curriculum of a university as a whole, the three forms of the curriculum should be addressed in order to nurture student development that is whole-person oriented.

In this chapter, due to curriculum design differences among professional disciplines, the formal curriculum of professional education will not be addressed. Instead, the curriculum design of general education will be discussed from the broader perspective because it is usually a graduation requirement for every undergraduate.

Co-curriculum is a little bit different from the informal curriculum. The activities of the informal curriculum are also referred to as extra-curricular activities, which suggests that they are separate from the curriculum (Kelly, 2004). Braskamp, Trautvetter and Ward (2008), however, indicated that the activities involved in the co-curriculum are needed to "help students more fully explore particular interests and connect their in-class and out-of-class experiences" (p. 29). According to this definition, the planning of the co-curriculum stresses the connection of the objectives of formal and informal activities. Co-curricular experiences occur in a variety of locations on campus such as the library, residence halls, student clubs, recreation centers and dining halls (Braskamp, Trautvetter and Ward, 2008, p. 28).

Community refers to the relationship within the context of the campus and the connection that colleges and universities have with the communities beyond the campus (Braskamp, Trautvetter and Ward, 2008, p. 28). Chickering and Reisser (1993) stated that one of the key factors influencing student development is campus communities which are friendly and provide various opportunities for students to form friendships. It is also critical that higher education institutions have good relationships with the surrounding communities as well as with society as a whole. Community service and internship are effective ways for fostering student learning and development as well as establishing good rapport with the community beyond the campus (Braskamp, Trautvetter and Ward, 2008; Eyler, Giles and Gray, 2000; Hammer, 2002; Sax and Astin, 1997; Tandon, 2008).

In sum, institutions of higher education are places for discovering new knowledge, disseminating knowledge, providing learning for students and helping them towards full development. In the university, students' learning and development are fostered by an overall experience of college life that includes general education and studying in professional fields, as well as exposure to the entire college environment.

The following sections will address student development as a whole, the role of general education in enriching whole-person development and the design of a general curriculum that fosters student learning and development.

Goals of higher education: whole-person education and student development

Whole-person education can be referred to as student development, and, broadly, the term is used to explain all of the various attempts to enhance the development of college students (Rodgers, 1980, 1990), both within the classroom and outside of it (Brown, 1989). There are four basic assumptions of student development theory with respect to the goals of higher education and the nature of the individual (Berg, 1983). The first assumption is that each individual has his or her own unique background, competencies and characteristics. The second is that each individual is a whole person who develops in many dimensions, including intellectual, emotional, spiritual, vocational, physical and lifestyle orientation. The third is that each person is a part of a whole, such as a member of a family, a community, a society or a nation. The last assumption is that "each person is capable of learning self-direction, seeks maturity and possesses the potential for full and effective living" (Berg, 1983, p. 10).

Watkins (as cited in Best, 2008) noted that the person as a whole is greater than the sum of its parts who presents various dimensions including intellectual, emotional, moral, political, physical and sexual selves. Bowen (1977) also claimed that "the development of the full potentialities of [the] human and of society" (p. 54) should be considered when setting the goals of higher education. Well-rounded graduates are better prepared to succeed in the constantly changing, competing industry and globalized world (Yin and Volkwein, 2010). Accordingly, whole-person education can be characterized as fully developing students' potential and preparing them to deal with the challenges in the world after university.

Development of a whole person is the main purpose and goal of higher education. However, in reviewing the literature on the goals of higher education, the development of the whole person seems to be the ultimate goal but is something implicitly attained through student development and learning by engaging students in various campus experiences (Astin, 1984; Chickering and Reisser, 1993; Cramer, 2007; Kuh *et al.*, 2005; Pace, 1984; Pascarella and Terenzini, 1991, 2005). Therefore, according to these authors, outcomes of higher education are usually discussed as the effects of the college on students or the educational attainment of college students.

These goals and outcomes of higher education, which are also shared by general education (Stark and Lowther, 1989), can be categorized as follows: the first goal is to enhance students' intellectual competence, including cognitive skills, subject matter competence and intellectual growth (Pascarella and Terenzini, 1991, 2005), cognitive learning (Bowen, 1977), the development of competence (Chickering and Reisser, 1993), critical thinking (Hawthorne, Kelsch and Steen, 2010; Rhodes, 2010; Stark and Lowther, 1989; Warner and Koeppel, 2009), problem-solving (Laird, Niskodé-Dossett and Kuh, 2009; Rhodes, 2010; Wraga, 1999) and intellectual skills (Hawthorne, Kelsch and Steen, 2010; Laird, Niskodé-Dossett and Kuh, 2009; Pace and Swayze, 1992). Moreover, the possession of oral and written communication competence is another goal of higher education (Hawthorne, Kelsch and Steen, 2010; Lehman, Ethington and Polizzi, 1995; Rhodes, 2010).

A third frequently cited outcome is the personal and social development of students, including attitudes, values and moral and emotional development (Bowen, 1977; Chickering and Reisser, 1993; Lehman, Ethington and Polizzi, 1995; Pace and Swayze, 1992; Pascarella and Terenzini, 1991, 2005). Career and vocational development is another focus of higher education (Bowen, 1977; Chickering and Reisser, 1993; Lehman, Ethington and Polizzi, 1995; Pace and Swayze, 1992; Pascarella and Terenzini, 1991, 2005; Stark and Lowther, 1989). Quantitative, science and technology skills have also been noted by several authors (Laird, Niskodé-Dossett and Kuh, 2009; Lehman, Ethington and Polizzi, 1995; Pace and Swayze, 1992; Pascarella and Terenzini, 1991, 2005; Rhodes, 2010; Stark and Lowther, 1989). Finally, appreciation of literature and arts needs to be encouraged by institutions of higher education (Laird, Niskodé-Dossett and Kuh, 2009; Lehman, Ethington and Polizzi, 1995; Pace and Swayze, 1992; Pascarella and Terenzini, 1991, 2005; Rhodes, 2010; Stark and Lowther, 1989).

In summary, there is a consensus regarding the six major goals of higher education: (1) intellectual competence, including cognitive skills, subject matter competence, intellectual growth, critical thinking, problem-solving and intellectual skills; (2) communication competence, including oral and written communication; (3) personal and social development, including attitudes, values, moral and emotional development; (4) career and vocational development, including career choice and professional identity; (5) quantitative, science and technology skills; and (6) appreciation of literature and arts. Although the sum of all outcomes in a student is not equivalent to the fully developed whole person, it can be said that the more students gain in their campus experiences the more likely they will develop toward becoming well-rounded persons. Consequently, the underlying assumption of these agreed-upon goals is that the primary goal of higher education is the development of the whole person.

Several psychosocial theorists believe an "optimal mismatch" triggers one's development (Chickering and Reisser, 1993; Rodgers, 1989; Stage, 1989). That is, "if a student feels challenged by a situation but also receives sufficient support to meet that challenge, he or she will likely develop" (Stage, 1989, p. 296). In this vein, Roark (1989) also noted that in order to foster student development, the institution should provide students with challenges and supports. She indicated that "a delicate balance is needed because too much challenge or disequilibrium causes the student to retreat, while too much support leads to failure to develop" (p. 314). As a result, higher education institutions should not only provide challenges for students to grow, but also set up support in the campus environment. Successful education is a process by which a student becomes a well-developed individual and a whole person.

There are several environmental conditions which encourage student development (Chickering and Reisser, 1993; Kuh *et al.*, 2005). These conditions include clear and consistent objectives, student–faculty contact, curriculum design, teaching strategies, friendships and student communities, cooperation among students, active learning, prompt feedback, high expectations, respect for diverse talents and ways of learning, as well as student development programs and services. Kuh *et al.* (2005), in their study of 20 DEEP institutions, identified six common conditions for these schools to perform very effectively. These include (1) a living mission and lived education philosophy; (2) an unshakeable focus on student learning; (3) environments adapted for educational enrichment; (4) clearly marked pathways to student success; (5) an improvement-oriented ethos; and (6) shared responsibility for educational quality and student success.

In order for students to succeed in college, the above conditions and campus environment should be established. It takes an entire curriculum and the concerted efforts of the campus community to attain this success. Although institutions are accountable for providing resources and facilities as well as designing programs and procedures that enhance and facilitate student learning and development, students also need to devote their effort and time (Pace, 1984; Astin, 1987). Hutchings (1989) has claimed that student development and learning is "a function of a college's teaching, curricula, and broader campus culture; but it is also significantly a function of student effort" (p. 14). Students themselves play crucial roles in their learning and development (Davis and Murrell, 1993).

In this chapter, the roles of students will not be addressed. More attention will be placed on curriculum design to foster student learning, especially on the general education which is required for all undergraduates. Student development concepts need to be embedded in general education. The following sections will discuss the role and contribution of general education and its curriculum design to the goals of higher education.

The meaning and role of general education

In reviewing the literature on the definition of liberal education and general education, these two terms are frequently used interchangeably in many articles and books. Brint *et al.* (2009) have noted that these two terms are now used interchangeably. However, in the early twentieth century general education and liberal education were understood differently. The reviewed literature shows that the general education movement was influenced by John Dewey, who emphasized knowledge integration for the purpose of participation in the problems of contemporary civilization, while liberal education focused on students' intellectual development and cultural appreciation in studying the heritage of Western civilization.

The general education movement gained a foothold in the USA from the 1920s to 1930s (Miller, as cited in Brint *et al.*, 2009), but the term general education in relation to college curricular requirements was adopted in the 1940s and 1950s (Rudolph, as cited in Brint *et al.*, 2009). General education refers to the courses or curriculum that all college students must take and pass in order to fulfill graduation requirements, regardless of the student's major or area of specialization (Bowen, 2004; Warner and Koeppel, 2009). Consequently, general education is required of all undergraduates and it should be central to the college's mission to show its importance.

In Taiwan, general education gained its statutory role due to the regulation issued by the Ministry of Education (MOE) in 1984. The MOE required every college and university to provide four to six general education credit hours for students. This was a milestone for the general education curriculum implemented in higher education institutions. In 2007, the MOE initiated a four-year national plan called the "Intermediate Range Program of General Education." The program provided grants for higher education institutions to reform their general education curriculum. It focused on increasing the required credit hours and on providing a school-wide general education curriculum, interdisciplinary learning, competence-based and problem-based learning in order to enhance students' critical thinking, problem-solving, integrative, creative and reflective abilities. The general education requirements in most higher education institutions have increased credit hours to 20 or even 25 percent of total hours needed for graduation. In Taiwan, the general education reform movement called for higher education institutions not only to recognize the importance of general education but also its central role in relation to each college's mission. The four-year plan ended in 2010, and another plan was initiated in 2011 which emphasized fostering students' competence for citizenship (Ministry of Education, 2011).

In discussing undergraduate education, Weaver (1991) refers to the first two years of lower-division coursework as "general education." The later upper-division years mainly consist of coursework in major and minor areas as well as professional study. General education, according to Erickson's (1992) definition, is a required and basic curriculum of "50 hours" of fundamental liberal arts courses and studies. Similarly, Patterson (1984) viewed general education as providing basic knowledge for more specialized learning and as serving to enhance a student's moral awareness and intellectual maturity. The fundamental purpose of general education is to help students become interdependent persons who can autonomously participate in their own life (Berkowitz, 1982). General education is also interdisciplinary, with the purpose of letting students have access to different disciplines and be able to integrate knowledge (Glynn, Aultman and Owens, 2005; Orillion, 2009; Scott, 2002).

According to the above definitions, general education is the basic and fundamental curriculum of undergraduate programs which provides students with broader knowledge for further learning in upper-division years and beyond, and which enhances their abilities for coping with their life. Erwin (1991) indicated that there are three common divisions of general education: (1) liberal studies, including interdisciplinary learning in natural and social sciences as well as in the humanities; (2) course learning skills consisting of writing, speaking, listening, reading as well as computing, numeric and library competencies; (3) developmental outcomes including cognitive development, critical thinking, ethical reasoning, maturity and identity.

Astin (1993) indicated that general education or liberal education needs to go far beyond just teaching the student to become a professional person; it should even encourage the student to grapple with some of life's most fundamental questions. This notion is congruent with Mackenzie and Evans's definition of general education as "a continuous program of life experiences for all [students]; life experiences that focus on common needs, common interests, common problems" (as cited in Wraga, 1999, p. 528). Boning (2007) reviewed the literature regarding the development of general education over the past 200 years in the USA. He concluded that universities and colleges placed more emphasis on the general education curriculum as it is an important pathway to enhance students' personal, intellectual and social abilities.

In summary, the purpose of general education is to develop human potentialities fully. Hence, whole-person development is embedded in the general education curriculum. The general education curriculum can be defined as the integration of knowledge for the purpose of solving the problems of contemporary society and of helping students to work toward becoming world citizens. It can be viewed as the basic and fundamental curriculum of undergraduate programs and also a graduation requirement for all undergraduates. It plays a major role in fulfilling the stated goals of higher education, as mentioned previously.

Boning (2007) has concluded that general education calls for more attention and importance in higher education. Scott (2002) has identified three sets of reasons why general education is needed more than ever in higher education institutions. The first is that enrollment policies have changed over time from recruiting elites to the general public, resulting in variation in student characteristics, abilities and aspirations (Brint *et al.*, 2009; Scott, 2002). Many of these students access college for the purpose of having a broader sense of "college culture" rather than pursuing a particular discipline or preparing themselves for a specific profession (Scott, 2002, p. 74). Taiwanese higher education has gone through a similar experience.

From 1895 to 1945, Taiwan was occupied by Japan. In 1945, with the end of World War II, Taiwan was restored to China. After the restoration, Taiwan's higher education institutions adopted the model of Chinese colleges and universities, which were influenced by the American educational model (Wu, Chen and Wu, 1989). From 1945 to 1949, the government of the Republic experienced a major upheaval. This change forced China to be divided into two entities: the People's Republic of China (mainland) and the Republic of China (Taiwan). In the winter of 1949, the Central Government of the Republic of China was relocated to Taiwan when the entire mainland was taken over by Chinese communists.

Taiwan's higher education experienced the first rapid growth stage with the relocation of the Central Government in 1949. The number of institutions increased from 7 in 1950 to 134 in 1996 (approximately a 19-fold growth), while student enrollment increased from 6,665 in 1950 to 751,347 in 1996 (approximately a 113-fold increase) (Ministry of Education, 1996). However, in 1996, the Ministry of Education promulgated a new policy that removed the embargo on upgrading and establishing four-year colleges or universities. By that time, Taiwanese higher education had gone through another rapid growth period. The number of institutions increased to 163 as student enrollment expanded to 1,343,603 in 2010 (almost double that of 1996) (Ministry of Education, n.d., b). The college admission rate was 49.24 percent in 1996 which increased to 94.87 percent in 2010 (Ministry of Education, n.d., a). This means that almost every high school graduate has access to higher education.

The second reason for emphasizing general education is the development of the post-industrial job market. Stable linear careers are no longer the case for most college graduates, entrance to the labor market is delayed and exit from that labor market is accelerated (Scott, 2002). Scott also noted that professional experts are also facing enormous challenges as "the production of knowledge [becomes] more widely distributed" (p. 74). As a result, in order to compete and survive in the post-industrial job market, transferable and adaptable skills need to be stressed. Scott claimed that "this emphasis may favor a revival of liberal [general] education" (p. 74).

The third set of reasons reflects the fact that general education can revive the significance of intellectual abilities, morality and absolutism (Scott, 2002). Shapiro (2005) has also noted that "liberal [general] education is directly connected to the nature of society we wish to sustain" (p. 90). He claimed that education should be concerned with what kind of persons we expect students to be, instead of what is taught and what they have learned.

General education is thus seen to connect to the central goals of higher education and the mission of the institution. It develops and educates students to be well-rounded persons. However, do the students really perceive its values? The answer is no. In the University of North Dakota, a team of ten faculty members conducted a six-year study of student perception of general education (Hawthorne, Kelsch and Steen, 2010). They administered a semi-structured interview to approximately 120 students once every semester regarding their perceptions and learning related to general education goals. The results were quite disappointing, because students perceived that general education was unimportant and they did not value its goals. They also found the most discrepancy between the perceptions of students and faculty regarding the special goals of "achieving a familiarity with [a] culture other than their own" (p. 25). They concluded that although the faculty valued the goal, they exerted very little effort to convince their students.

Another study by Miller and Sundre (2008) was conducted at a mid-sized southeastern university in the USA regarding students' attitudes toward general education versus overall coursework. The results showed that entering students had equal motivation toward all their coursework. However, by the time students became second-semester sophomores, the attitudes toward general education coursework as compared to other coursework have changed significantly. The motivation to learn in general education coursework was less than in learning coursework overall, even though the learning motivation also decreased toward other coursework. The researchers concluded that sophomores sought strategies to "just get by" in their general education course (p. 165).

In conclusion, general education is perceived as important and central to the goals of higher education and the development of whole persons. Yet how to trigger students' motivation and positive attitudes toward general education is the challenge for faculty members in designing curriculum and pedagogies. The design of the general education curriculum is addressed in the following section.

Curriculum designs in general education

Brint *et al.* (2009) conducted a study that analyzed the organization of general education requirements at four-year colleges and universities in the USA from 1975 to 2000. There was a total of 292 institutions from the College Catalog Study database surveyed. They distinguished four popular models for designing the general education curriculum over this 25-year period, that is, "core distribution areas," "traditional liberal arts," "culture and ethics," and "civic/utilitarian" (p. 605). The core distribution areas consisted of humanities, social sciences, natural sciences, mathematics and the arts. The traditional liberal arts included mainly the subjects of literature, history, philosophy and foreign languages. These two models were rooted in the nineteenth and early twentieth centuries.

The culture and ethics and the civic/utilitarian models are more recently developed conceptions. The former emphasizes courses related to Western and non-Western civilization and culture. The latter is organized by responding to state and employer interests in human capital development that includes government, business and technology courses. During the period studied, the core distribution areas model was the most prevalent form of general education (Brint *et al.*, 2009). The focus of course requirements related to the four models changed during the 25-year period. For example, the broader category of humanities weakened, while a more specific required course in English composition or English literature was gaining strength in many institutions; courses dealing with Western and non-Western civilization and culture, as well as those emphasizing moral reflection, took their place. The civic/utilitarian model made its appearance during 1980 to 1981 and focused on preparing students for the world of civic and business life. The study also found that there was no strong relation of particular types of institution with the four models. The trend toward changing the emphasis of general education models was due to a call for increased accountability from state legislatures, the accreditation requirements of the regional accrediting bodies and as the expansion of student enrollments with weak academic preparation and different career objectives. Shapiro (2005) also noted that "there never has been a 'right' curriculum (p. 95)," the best way to organize the general education is "a continued exploration of possibilities (p. 95)."

According to the above descriptions, there were different models of organizing the general education curriculum. Each model emerged from the context of the environment and had its own rationale. The curriculum model of general education may have changed due to the needs of contemporary society and student characteristics in higher education. Therefore, the design of the general education curriculum had to scan environmental needs and requirements, characteristics of student bodies and the mission and the goals of the institutions. As there has never been an agreement regarding the most appropriate curriculum (Shapiro, 2005), the following section discusses how to provide an appropriate general education curriculum that meets the mission and goals of the institution as well as the needs of students instead of the best way of organizing the curriculum.

Connecting the goals of general education to the mission of the institution

Mullen (2007) has identified four ways of approaching curriculum theory and practice, namely, curriculum as (1) a body of knowledge to be transmitted; (2) an attempt to achieve certain ends in students – the product; (3) process; and (4) praxis (p. 30). The first two refer to the content and outcomes that should be organized in and expected from the curriculum, while the last two emphasize the process of transmission (Mullen, 2007). There were different advocates regarding product-learning and process-learning in the curriculum, as well as hybrid views. Nevertheless, no matter what kind of philosophy undergirds the curriculum approach, the curriculum leaders or designers should focus on what is best for student learning and the goals that institutions need to accomplish.

There is no explicit statement regarding what the general education curriculum should consist of in terms of regional accreditation requirements. However, offering a general education program in colleges and universities is required and the program needs to "make sense for its student body and mission" (Warner and Koeppel, 2009, p. 242). Light and Cox (2001) have also argued that there are increasing pressures on higher education to educate students to possess a wider range of knowledge, skills and attitudes for solving future problems. As general education is required for all college and university students, it should not only fulfill the goals and mission of the institutions but also meet the needs of students and the interests of contemporary society.

Although there are six common goals of higher education as identified in the previous section, each institution must review and discuss the major goals in relation to its mission. In Ratcliff, Johnson and Gaff's (2010) study of the general education curriculum reform from 1990 to 2000, they found that most curriculum reform was in the mission orientation and 60 percent of respondents indicated that the goals of general education were closely related to the missions of the institution. They concluded that there were three reasons for reforming the curriculum: (1) connection of the goals of general education with the mission of the institution; (2) meeting the needs of students and faculty members to help students to gain the abilities and skills needed in a globalized society as well as providing more latitude to faculty to construct their courses; and (3) renovating courses that have become outdated. More and more academic leaders view general education as a dynamic curriculum in response to the changing needs of students, society and the expansion of knowledge (Ratcliff, Johnson and Gaff, 2010).

In designing general education for an institution, the curriculum leader or designer should address the goals of general education and its relationship to the mission of the institution. "Curriculum goals are defined as general, programmatic expectations without criteria of achievement or mastery" (Oliva, 2009). Therefore, the statement of general education goals is broad and needs to meet the educational expectations of students. Moreover, when the goals of general education are developed, faculty members should have come to a prior consensus regarding them. The study by Hawthorne, Kelsch and Steen (2010) found that "part of the reason students were so vague about and disengaged from the general education program was that faculty were far from clear about either its meaning or its purpose" (p. 26). As a result, it is important to communicate and clearly define the meaning and the purpose of the goals of general education among the faculty.

Assessing the needs of students

There are several needs assessments that should be conducted as part of the process of defining the goals of general education. As universities have a dynamic relationship with society, they are an essential supplier of products and services for contemporary society (Shapiro, 2005). Oliva (2009) has identified six levels of student needs regarding the design of curriculum. First of all, the curriculum should address human needs, for example, the needs of students as members of the human race or of the global society and the universal needs of humanity. Moreover, curriculum designers should assess the general needs of students in their respective nations and they should also recognize the changing needs of the country over time. The third level is assessing student needs particular to the state or region. For example, in Taiwan, local governments may have different requirements for their students. The fourth level is addressing student needs for the community served by the institutions. The fifth is the needs of students in a particular institution. These needs take into account the characteristics of the entire student body. Finally, the curriculum planner should examine the needs of individual students in a particular school.

Consequently, when addressing the variety of student needs, the goals of general education in higher education in a country will have something in common with human and national needs. However, there should be some goal differentiations among higher education institutions because of differences in respect of the region, the community, the school and the characteristics of the student bodies. Warner and Koeppel (2009) have noted that "general educa-tion should be individualized for each institution to accomplish its educational purposes" (p. 249). The following is an example of the reform of the general education curriculum in relation to the goal-setting process and meeting the various needs of students at Fu-Jen Catholic University in Taiwan.

The university is a private comprehensive university consisting of 11 colleges and having nearly 27,000 students. The Center of Holistic Education is responsible for the general program of the university. The center was established in 1990. Before the center was established, general education courses were spread out in different colleges. In 1990, general education was renamed whole-person education. The goals of the program were adopted from the school's mission and objectives. The curriculum consisted of 5 major sub-curricula with 32 required credit hours including languages and cultures, basic curricula, general education (as mentioned previously, called core distribution areas), physical education and military training. The field of languages and cultures includes Chinese literature, foreign languages and history and cultures. Students had to take 4 credit hours in each field for a total of 12 credit hours. The basic curricula were the two credit hours of introduction to university studies, which is similar to the first-year experience course in the USA, four credit hours on the philosophy of life and two credit hours on professional ethics. General education consisted of three discipline areas, namely, social science, humanities and arts, natural science and technology. Students had to take 4 credit hours in each area for a total of 12 hours. Physical education was required of all students, two hours each semester for the first two years with no credit hours. The military training course had no credit hours but was required for all freshmen.

In 1998, the center initiated curriculum reform as part of the overall curriculum reform of the university, national requirements, the re-examination of student needs and changes in the student body. The process of curriculum reform lasted two years and took numerous meetings in order to reach consensus. Students, faculty members, deans of colleges and top administrators participated in the reform process. The major requirement came from the Ministry of Education, which required every institution of higher education to establish basic abilities for their students as a threshold for graduation. In considering the characteristics of the student body, prior academic ability and the issue of globalization, three basic abilities – Chinese and English written communication and information literacy – were set in 1998 as the threshold for graduation for students who would enroll in the academic year 2010.

After establishing basic student abilities as a threshold for graduation, the goals of the whole-person education curriculum were clearly defined as "to nurture students to appropriate a broader foundation of knowledge and the basic abilities of adapting to society, as well as to form them into whole persons with the integration of body, mind and spirit." These goals are in accord with the major mission of the university to educate students to be whole persons. In relation to the goals, the curriculum was sub-divided into three sub-curricula including the basic ability curriculum, core curriculum and the curriculum of general literacy.

The basic ability curriculum consists of four credit hours of Chinese literature; eight credit hours of foreign languages with at least four credit hours required in English; and information literacy, where students have to take at least a two-hour-credit course related to information technology in their overall coursework. The core curriculum consists of the original basic curriculum plus physical education. The curriculum of general literacy is the original general education program with three discipline areas. In the basic ability and core curriculum courses, except for the courses in information literacy and some foreign languages, students have no choice with regard to the courses. However, students have more choices regarding the courses of the three discipline areas of the general literacy curriculum. There are always more than 75 courses for students to choose from. The new whole-person education curriculum is planned to be implemented for students who enroll in the academic year 2011.

The above example of general education reform shows that the goals of general education should be clearly defined and closely connected with the mission of the institution, as well as being transmitted to students and faculty members. Student needs have also to be taken into consideration when designing the curriculum.

Conclusion

When there are tremendous changes in society, job markets and the higher education student body, the expectations and accountability required of higher education institutions with regard to their role in educating students are much higher than before. Education is not just a matter of learning particular facts or techniques. Ideally, education is a process by which one guides students to reflect upon themselves as interdependent beings who exist in a historical and social context. As persons capable of thinking about who they are, choosing a purpose and a direction in life, and communicating and developing community with others, they are able to take what they have learned from others and build further on human knowledge. Hopefully, this educational process results in the ongoing development of persons who strive to be an integral part of the world.

In order for students to become fully developed persons, the development of whole persons should become the core mission of higher education. It takes the whole campus to accomplish this core mission. The culture, the curriculum, the co-curriculum and the community of higher education institutions should focus on providing congruent college experiences to foster the development of students and educate them to be civilized persons who can lead and live in contemporary society.

As general education is a requirement for all students, it plays a central role in meeting the mission and the goals of the institutions. There are different models to organize and implement the general education curriculum and there is no best way to formulate it. The appropriate way to construct the general education curriculum for each institution is to examine whether the goals of its general education are consistent with the mission of the institution and the needs of the students. Therefore, scanning the environmental changes and conducting needs assessment are crucial in designing the general education curriculum. The needs of students may vary according to the changes taking place in the nation, the region, the community, the institution and its student body, as well as in the individual student. As a result, the design of the general education curriculum is a dynamic process in response to the changes in the environment.

In conclusion, university and college graduates are the backbone of future society. As Shapiro (2005) has emphasized, "liberal [general] education is directly connected to the nature of [the] society we wish to sustain" (p. 90). Higher education institutions should seriously think about the kinds of persons they expect their students to become. Institutions need to allocate resources and devote their effort to construct a well-programmed campus and an appropriately designed general education curriculum to help students engage in the campus experiences and the learning activities so that they become fully developed whole persons and assume major roles in society.

References

Astin, A. W. (1984). "Student Involvement: A Developmental Theory for Higher Education." *Journal of College Student Personnel*, 25: 297–308.

Astin, A. W. (1985). "Involvement: The Cornerstone of Excellence." *Change*, 17(4): 35–39.

Astin, A. W. (1987). "Competition or Cooperation?" *Change*, 19(5): 12–19.

Astin, A. W. (1990). "Educational Assessment and Education Equity." *American Journal of Education*, 98: 459–478.

Astin, A. W. (1991). *Assessment For Excellence: The Philosophy and Practice of Assessment and Evaluation in Higher Education* (New York: American Council on Education and Macmillan).

Astin, A. W. (1993). *What Matters in College?* (San Francisco, CA: Jossey-Bass).

Berg, T. G. (1983). "Student Development and Liberal Arts Education." *NASPA Journal*, 21: 9–16.

Berkowitz, L. J. (1982). "Specifying the Objectives of General Education." *Journal of General Education*, 34(3): 210–23.

Best, R. (2008). "Education, Support and the Development of the Whole Person." *British Journal of Guidance and Counseling*, 36(4): 343–51.

Boning, K. (2007). "Coherence in General Education: A Historical Look." *Journal of General Education*, 56(1): 1–16.

Bowen, H. R. (1977). *Investment in Learning: The Individual and Social Value of American Higher Education* (San Francisco, CA: Jossey-Bass).

Bowen, S. H. (2004). "What's in a Name? The Persistence of 'General Education'." *Peer Review*, 7(1): 30–31.

Boyer, E. L. (1990). *Scholarship Reconsidered: Priorities of the Professoriate* (New York: John Wiley and Sons).

Braskamp, L., Trautvetter, L. G. and Ward, K. (2008). "Putting Students First: Promoting Lives of Purpose and Meaning." *About Campus*: 26–32, doi:10.1002/abc.244.

Brint, S., Proctor, K., Murphy, S. P., Turk-Bicakei, L. and Hanneman, R. A. (2009). "General Education Models: Continuity and Change in the U.S. Undergraduate Curriculum, 1975–2000." *Journal of Higher Education*, 80(6): 605–42.

Brown, R. D. (1989). "Fostering Intellectual and Personal Growth: The Student Development Role." In U. Delworth, G. R. Hanson and associates (eds.), *Student Development in Higher Education* (San Francisco, CA: Jossey-Bass), pp. 284–303.

Chickering, A. W., and Reisser, L. (1993). *Education and Identity*, 2nd edn. (San Francisco, CA: Jossey-Bass).

Cramer, G. L. (2007). "Fostering Student Success: What Really Matters?" In G. L. Kramer and associates (eds.), *Fostering Student Success in the Campus Community* (San Francisco, CA: Jossey-Bass), pp. 433–48

Cross, T. P. (2009). *An Oasis of Order: The Core Curriculum at Columbia College*, trans. M.-S. Xie (New Taipei City, Taiwan: Weber Publication International) (originally published 1995).

Davis, T. M. and Murrell, P. H. (1993). *Turning Teaching into Learning: The Role of Student Responsibility in the Collegiate Experience*, ASHE-ERIC Higher Education Report No. 8 (Washington, DC: George Washington University, School of Education and Human Development).

Erickson, M. E. (1992). "General and Liberal Education: Competing Paradigms." *Community College Review*, 19(4): 15–20.

Erwin, T. D. (1991). *Assessing Student Learning and Development* (San Francisco, CA: Jossey-Bass).

Eyler, J., Giles, D. E., Jr. and Gray, C. J. (2000). "Research at a Glance: What We Know about the Effects of Service-Learning on Students, Faculty, Institutions and Communities, 1993–1999." In Campus Compact (ed.), *Introduction to Service-Learning Toolkit: Readings and Resources for Faculty* (Providence, RI: Brown University), pp. 19–22.

Glynn, S. M., Aultman, L. P. and Owens, A. M. (2005). "Motivation to Learn in General Education Programs." *Journal of General Education*, 54(2): 150–70.

Hammer, D. M. (2002). *Building Bridges* (Boston: Allyn and Bacon).

Hawthorne, J., Kelsch, A. and and Steen, T. (2010). "Making General Education Matter: Structures and Strategies." *New Directions for Teaching and Learning*, 121: 23–33, doi:10.1002/tl.385

Hutchings, P. (1989). "Behind Outcomes: Contexts and Questions for Assessment." Paper presented at the American Association of Higher Education Assessment Forum, Atlanta, GA (ERIC Document Reproduction Service No. ED 311 777).

Kelly, A. V. (2004). *The Curriculum: Theory and Practice*, 5th edn. (Thousand Oaks, CA: Sage).

Kerr, C. (2009). *The Uses of the University*, trans. Y.-T. Yang (New Taipei City, Taiwan: Weber Publication International) (originally published 2001).

Keyton, J. (2005). *Communication and Organizational Culture* (Thousand Oaks, CA: Sage).

Kuh, G. D., Kinzie, J., Schuh, J. H., Whitt, E. J. and associates (2005). *Students' Success in College* (San Francisco, CA: Jossey-Bass).

Laird, T. F. N., Niskodé-Dossett, A. S. and Kuh, G. D. (2009). "What General Education Courses Contribute to Essential Learning Outcomes." *Journal of General Education*, 58(2): 65–84.

Lehman, P. W., Ethington, C. A. and Polizzi, T. B. (1995). *CCSEQ: Test Manual and Comparative Data*, 2nd edn. (Memphis, TN: University of Memphis, Center for the Study of Higher Education).

Light, G. and Cox, R. (2001). *Learning and Teaching in Higher Education* (Thousand Oaks, CA: Sage).

Miller, B. J. and Sundre, D. L. (2008). "Achievement Goal Orientation toward General Education versus Overall Coursework." *Journal of General Education*, 54(3): 152–69.

Ministry of Education (1984). *Rules in Implementation of General Education Courses in Universities* (Taipei City, Taiwan: Author).

Ministry of Education (1996). *Education Statistical Indicators: Republic of China* (Taipei City, Taiwan: Author).

Ministry of Education (2007). *The Intermediate Range Program of General Education* (Taipei City, Taiwan: Author).

Ministry of Education (2011). *The Grant Program of Cultivated Contemporary Citizenship* (Taipei City, Taiwan: Author).

Ministry of Education (n.d., a). Statistical Data of College Admission Rate. Online. Available HTTP: <http://www.edu.tw/statistics/content.aspx?site_content_sn=8956>

Ministry of Education (n.d., b). Statistical Data of Schools. Online. Available HTTP: <http://www.edu.tw/statistics/content.aspx?site_content_sn=8869>

Mullun, C. A. (2007). *Curriculum Leadership Development: A Guide for Aspiring School Leaders* (Mahwah, NJ: Lawrence Erlbaum Associates).

Nussbaum, M. C. (2009). *Cultivating Humanity: A Classical Defense of Reform in Liberal Education*, trans. S.-H. Sun (Taipei City, Taiwan: Chengchi University Press) (originally published 1997).

Oliva, P. F. (2009). *Developing the Curriculum*, 7th edn. (Boston: Allyn and Bacon).

Orillion, M.-F. (2009). "Interdisciplinary Curriculum and Student Outcomes: The Case of a General Education Course at a Research University." *Journal of General Education*, 58(1): 1–18.

Pace, C. R. (1984). *Measuring the Quality of College Student Experiences* (Los Angeles, CA: Higher Education Research Institute).

Pace, C. R. and Swayze, S. (1992). *Psychometric Supplement to the CSEQ Third Edition, 1990* (Los Angeles, CA: UCLA Center for the Study of Evaluation).

Pascarella, E. T. and Terenzini, P. T. (1991). *How College Affects Students* (San Francisco, CA: Jossey-Bass).

Pascarella, E. T. and Terenzini, P. T. (2005). *How College Affects Students: A Third Decade Research*, 2nd edn. (San Francisco, CA: Jossey-Bass).

Patterson, W. B. (1984). "Defining the Educated Person: From Harvard to Harvard."

Sounding, 66: 192–217.

Ratcliff, J. L., Johnson, D. K. and Gaff, J. G. (2010). *Changing General Education Curriculum*, trans. B.-C. Wu and Z.-Y. Zhan (Taipei City, Taiwan: Chengchi University Press) (originally published 2006).

Rhodes, T. (2010). "Since We Seem to Agree, Why are the Outcomes so Difficult to Achieve?" *New Directions for Teaching and Learning*, 121: 13–21, doi:10.1002/tl.384.

Roark, M. L. (1989). "Challenging and Supporting College Students." *NASPA Journal*, 26: 314–19.

Rodgers, R. F. (1980). "Theories Underlying Student Development." In D. G. Creamer (ed.), *Student Development in Higher Education* (Cincinnati, OH: American College Personnel Association), pp. 10–95.

Rodgers, R. F. (1989). "Student Development." In U. Delworth, G. R. Hanson and associates (eds.), *Student Development in Higher Education* (San Francisco, CA: Jossey-Bass), pp. 117–64.

Rodgers, R. F. (1990). "Recent Theories and Research Underlying Student Development." In D. G. Creamer and associates (eds.), *College Student Development: Theory and Practice for the 1990s* (Alexandria, VA: American College Personnel Association), pp. 27–79.

Sax, L. J. and Astin, A. W. (1997). "The Benefits of Service: Evidence from Undergraduate." *Educational Record*, 78: 25–32.

Schein, E. H. (2004). *Organization Culture and Leadership*, 3rd edn. (San Francisco, CA: Jossey-Bass).

Scott, P. (2002). "The Future of General Education in Mass Higher Education Systems." *Higher Education Policy*, 15: 61–75.

Shapiro, H. (2005). *A Larger Sense of Purpose: Higher Education and Society* (Princeton, NJ: Princeton University Press).

Stage, F. K. (1989). "College Outcomes and Student Development: Filling the Gaps." *Review of Higher Education*, 12: 293–304.

Stark, J. S. and Lowther, M. A. (1989). "Exploring Common Ground in Liberal and Professional Education." *New Directions for Teaching and Learning (Integrating Liberal Learning and Professional Education)*, 40: 7–20.

Tandon, R. (2008). "Civil Engagement in Higher Education and its Role in Human and Social Development." In Global University Network for Innovation (ed.), *Higher Education in the World 3: Higher Education: New Challenges and Emerging Roles for Human and Social Development* (New York: Palgrave Macmillan), pp. 142–60.

Warner, D. B. and Koeppel, K. (2009). "General Education Requirements: A Comparative Analysis." *Journal of General Education*, 58(4): 241–58.

Weaver, F. S. (1991). *Liberal Education: Critical Essays on Professions, Pedagogy, and Structure* (New York: Teachers College Press).

Wraga, W. G. (1999). "The Progressive Vision of General Education and the American Common School Ideal: Implications for Curriculum Policy, Practice, and Theory." *Curriculum Studies*, 31(5): 523–44.

Wu, W. H., Chen, S. F. and Wu, C. T. (1989). "The Development of Higher Education in Taiwan." *Higher Education*, 18(1): 117–36.

Yin, A. C. and Volkwein, J. F. (2010). "Assessing General Education Outcomes." *New Directions for Institutional Research, Assessment Supplement 2009*: 79–100, doi:10.1002/ir.332.

7 The impacts of liberal arts education on undergraduate programs

Fulfillment or frustration?

Li Manli and Shi Jinghuan

Introduction

Although traditional Chinese education was characterized more by holistic than subject-based learning, only in the last century has the Western philosophy and practice of liberal education become familiar in Chinese higher education circles. With increasing contacts between China and the United States in the first half of the twentieth century, American concepts of general and liberal education became popular in China. Colleges and universities founded by foreigners were especially likely to implement Western – often American-style – liberal arts curricula. For more than two decades after the creation of the People's Republic of China, however, the government followed a model of higher education that emphasized rigid subject-based knowledge plus moral-political studies.

However, in the last two decades, the Ministry of Education has strongly encouraged universities and colleges, especially some of the science-engineering intensive schools in China, to bring liberal arts courses back into their education programs. Liberal education is thought to provide engineering professionals with the necessary skills to practice engineers, skills such as critical thinking, effective communication, collaboration with others, appreciation of diversity and integration of knowledge from science and the humanities in order to solve problems. As a result, almost all college students in China experience general education (liberal arts education), at least in theory. The motivation for reform was the acknowledgement by both government and universities that narrowly trained graduates would not be productive in a rapidly changing job market nor would they have well-balanced personalities (Feng and Guo, 2007). In short, liberal education enhances professional practice. Therefore, each institution determines its curricular specifics depending on faculty interest, institutional priorities and academic strengths (Li, 1999).

The case studies of some of the leading universities in China provided in this chapter give a good sense of the range of academic and curricular structures employed in liberal arts education. In addition, many other institutions look to the top universities as models for their own reform programs, and sometimes wait to see what the leading institutions have done before developing their own general education curricula, and so these universities have an influence that goes beyond their own faculty and students.

In the reforms of the 1980s and 1990s, many Chinese universities revised their undergraduate programs to include general education as a crucial element to strengthen academic excellence. The term most often used is *wenhua suzhi jiaoyu* (cultural quality education), which harkens back to traditional concepts about the importance of educated individuals in Chinese society.

Although it is evident that liberal arts education has enhanced the academic program, we actually know very little about just how liberal education enhances academic programs. In order to address this gap in the literature, the question addressed in this study is how is the undergraduate curriculum transformed by liberal education in terms of credits, distribution and administrative approaches? This question will be answered by findings based on our observations.

Broader common courses in undergraduate programs

Currently in mainland China, the typical undergraduate program in higher education institutions has three components: (a) Ministry of Education compulsory courses, (b) *wenhua suzhi jiaoyu* courses and (c) courses required for the major. In some cases, students have free electives as well. Specialized courses for the major are provided by academic departments such as Chinese literature, mathematics or electrical engineering.

In this chapter, we observe that common courses have been extended by the introduction of the concept of liberal arts education. The common course refers to two components. One is the courses required by the Ministry of Education (e.g. political theory, military training, English language and sports) as Ministry of Education compulsory courses. The other is *wenhua suzhi jiaoyu* courses, which are determined by individual institutions. Different universities use different terms for this part of the curriculum; for example, some universities refer to *wenhua suzhi jiaoyu* courses as "general education elective curriculum," while others call these courses the "cultural quality curriculum." Both the Ministry of Education compulsory courses and the *wenhua suzhi jiaoyu* courses fall outside the students' field of concentration and have the primary goal of cultivating the whole person.

The Ministry of Education compulsory courses are the same at all institutions of higher education in China. The goals of *wenhua suzhi jiaoyu* are shared by all universities, but the implementation of the goals and the exact configuration of courses differ from one campus to another depending on faculty interests and institutional strengths. The case studies below demonstrate the philosophy and practice of *wenhua suzhi jiaoyu*, as well as the Ministry of Education compulsory courses, through curricular offerings, extra-curricular activities and organizational structure in different universities.

In most major universities in China today, undergraduate students must fulfill required credits in both Ministry of Education compulsory courses and in *wenhua suzhi jiaoyu* courses. Chinese academics consider these non-specialized, non-major courses as general education, even though that description is different from the definition used in other countries represented in this volume. Table 7.1 presents the undergraduate program of several leading universities in

Table 7.1 General education curriculum at three Chinese universities (by credits required)

Distribution of common courses	Course categories	Peking University	Zhejiang University	Tsinghua University
Ministry of Education compulsory courses	Common English series	8	9	6
	Political series	12	13.5	14
	Military sports series	6	5.5	7
Wenhua suzhi jiaoyu courses	Mathematics and natural sciences	2	3	2
	Social sciences	2	3	4
	History	2	3	1
	Language, literature and arts	4	1.5	2
	Philosophy and psychology	2	0	3
	Communication and leadership	–	1.5	–
	Technology and design	–	3	2
Total credits required for bachelor degree		140–50	116	175
Percentage of total in non-specialized, non-major courses		25–27%	33%	22%
Percentage in *wenhua suzhi jiaoyu* courses		8–9%	10%	7%

Sources: Course guides for undergraduate programs: Peking University (2008), Zhejiang University (2007), Tsinghua University (2006).

China. At Tsinghua University, for example, with its traditional strength in engineering and technology, non-major courses account for 22 percent of a typical undergraduate program, while at Zhejiang University the comparable figure is 33 percent. Overall, non-major education represents between a quarter and a third of the undergraduate program at the universities represented, which is not too different from the American experience.

Distribution of the common courses

As already noted, the Ministry of Education compulsory courses are mandated by the Ministry and implemented by all colleges and universities. The newer *wenhua suzhi jiaoyu* courses, designed to broaden students' knowledge and perspectives, are usually based on current faculty interests and available academic resources. For example, at Peking University, the *wenhua suzhi jiaoyu* curriculum offers more than 300 choices in five categories: mathematics and sciences; history; philosophy and psychology; social sciences; and language,

literature and arts. These courses are the responsibility of the relevant departments – physics, history, economics, art, and so on. Every student must take
at least two credits in each of the five categories, as well as the Ministry of
Education compulsory courses.

These reforms at Peking University draw on the institution's history as a multi-
disciplinary comprehensive university with well-known professors committed to
offering courses to cultivate students' broad educational experience. As early as
the 1920s and 1930s, students were encouraged to choose courses from different
disciplines outside their majors (Wang, 2005). In the early stages of reform in
the 1990s, Peking University set up a number of cross-school elective courses
that combined liberal arts with science. Many of the general education courses
are taught by top academicians and famous researchers at the university.

In contrast, Tsinghua University has created eight groups of courses: four
credits in language and art, at least one of which must be in the art curriculum;
history and culture; literature, philosophy and life; science and technology; technology and society; contemporary China and the world; arts education; and law,
economics and management. Students in science and engineering must earn at
least 13 credits in the 8 categories, while liberal arts students must take certain
courses in science and technology. In order to raise the quality of *wenhua suzhi
jiaoyu* courses, Tsinghua has strengthened the process of review before offering
the courses and has also given greater attention to students' evaluations of their
courses and professors.

Zhejiang University divides its approximately 300 courses into 10 categories:
ideology, military sports and language (the Ministry of Education compulsory
courses); basic computing, history and culture, literature and art, economics
and society, communication and leadership, science and research and technology
and design (the *wenhua suzhi jiaoyu* courses). All students must earn 3 credits
in history and culture, but they may choose among more than 40 courses in
this category, including Chinese philosophy, architectural history, PRC history,
Western art history, the Silk Road and Mogao Grottoes art and Chinese tea
culture.

Administrative approaches

Chinese universities bear the responsibility of creating their own approaches
to general education. Most institutions' current programs have followed the
successes of pilot programs introduced by the Ministry of Education in 1999,
usually coordinated by the undergraduate education staff in the provost's office.
Curricular offerings are enhanced on some campuses by two administrative
approaches: strengthening the educational impact of extra-curricular activities
and creating new management systems for undergraduate education.

For example, in 1994 Huazhong University of Science and Technology instituted a series of humanistic quality education lectures, which has since offered
more than 1,400 events with a total audience of more than 50 million people.
Many influential professors, scholars and political figures have given speeches in

this series, allowing students to benefit from their teaching style and knowledge, absorbing their positive thoughts and culture.

At Tsinghua University, student associations have flourished. In 2007, more than 100 student groups had about 20,000 members involved in such activities as sports, science and technology, arts, humanities and social sciences and commonweal. These organizations have developed into one of the important means of cultivating students' interests, encouraging healthy growth, providing space for self-education and developing an active cultural life on campus. At the same time, these student associations play an important role in the development of school values, moral education, the popularization of scientific knowledge and practice, employment guidance, creating a harmonious campus and voluntary social service. Coordinated with Tsinghua's *wenhua suzhi jiaoyu* courses, the associations create an atmosphere in which the students can grow.

Fudan University exemplifies the second approach – the establishment of new management systems for general education. Fudan takes the intellectual approach that general education first and foremost is an educational philosophy. Operationally, Fudan believes that general education is a system; the implementation of general education reform requires its own system for both curriculum and activities outside class. In 2007, Fudan University reformed its management system, promoting general education as the core and creating Fudan College as the mechanism for these reforms.

Fudan College is an undergraduate teaching unit as well as a student affairs unit with four residential colleges. All undergraduate students (including international students), regardless of discipline, are members of Fudan College, usually for one year but two years for students in the eight-year clinical medicine program.

The four residential colleges are the basic units of student management. They also continue the cultural tradition of the Chinese *shuyuan* academy while drawing upon the experiences of residential colleges in foreign universities. The four colleges are named after the school's most respected past presidents. Each college has a uniform, school song, unique logo and motto, separate residential buildings and a museum that showcases the former presidents' deeds to strengthen students' recognition of school culture and history. Students with different backgrounds, interests, talents, expertise and origins all live together, promoting multi-cultural integration and international exchanges while overcoming emotional alienation. This reform at Fudan is designed to encourage students to gain an education that fully and effectively combines the universal and the specialized, the curricular and the extra-curricular.

The most recent experiment in general education is at Zhongshan University (Sun Yat-sen University) in the south of China. Its new Liberal Arts College was established in 2009 with, as dean, Professor Gan Yang, a scholar well known for actively promoting general education in China (Gan 2006). The goal of the college is the cultivation of elites equipped with well-organized general knowledge and the creation of leaders in the fields of liberal arts, humanities and social sciences. Students are admitted through a highly selective process and live together at the Nanshan campus separate from the main campus of

Zhongshan University. The curriculum for the student during the four-year undergraduate program includes classical Chinese, Greek, Latin and other foundations of ancient civilizations.

According to the ideas of both the president of Zhongshan University and Gan Yang himself, the Liberal Arts College is not just a separate program for a small group of students, but a pilot project for the transformation of the whole university, leading to reform in the country's higher education system. It is too early to evaluate the program and to predict the influence it may bring, but there is no doubt that it represents a challenge to the entire university system. The continuing emphasis on innovation in undergraduate education, and especially in general education, clearly predicts more such reforms in higher education in China.

Contemporary challenges and perspectives

Higher education in China faces a series of challenges that have real implications for the long-term success of general education:

- *The challenge of social transition and marketization.* Like most other countries, China has looked to market forces to finance its higher education system. The recruitment and training of personnel reflect market demand, and students are increasingly attentive to the needs of the job market when selecting majors. The uncertainty and constant fluctuations of the job market have caused instability in higher education and have eroded the integrity of teaching and research. Many students and their parents favor the pursuit of a specialized education that equips the graduate with vocationally relevant knowledge and skills – with the result that such students neglect general education targeted at the cultivation of the whole person.
- *Making general or liberal education central to the undergraduate program.* While Chinese students are required to take a significant portion of their undergraduate courses outside the major, many do not believe that these courses improve their knowledge base, specific set of skills, and overall credentials and, as a result, do not take them seriously. In addition, in many universities, the general education curriculum lacks organic links and cannot be integrated into the total undergraduate program. Neither professors nor students consider general education courses as fundamental academic training but rather as an opportunity to expand knowledge and to learn a bit about everything; often these courses are relatively easy to pass. As a consequence, general education is too often seen as additional or marginal, the departments offering them do not take such courses seriously and at times neither do the universities themselves.
- *Providing organizational structures that link "universal" and "special".* The establishment of Fudan College and the Liberal Arts College in Zhongshan University represent systematic breakthroughs that are both pioneering and creative. These new organizational units provide an institutional guarantee for the students regarding both general education courses and the larger

goal of cultivation of the whole person. In the long run, general education in China's universities will continue to develop and reach a new stage.

References and further reading

de Bary, William T. (2007). *Confucian Tradition and Global Education* (Hong Kong: Chinese University Press).

Dello-Iacovo, Belinda (2009). "Curriculum Reform and 'Quality Education' in China: An Overview." *International Journal of Educational Development*, 29: 241–49.

Feng Huimin and Guo Mei (2007). "General Education Curriculum Reforming Advance in the Universities of China Mainland." *US-China Education Review*, 4(7): 23–25.

Gan Yang (2006). "Da xue tong shi jiao yu de liang ge zhong xin huan jie" [Two Key Links in the General Education in Universities]. *Du Shu*, 4: 3–11.

Li Manli (1999).*Tong shi jiao yu: yi zhong da xue jiao yu guan* [General Education: A View of Higher Education] (Bejing: Tsinghua University Press).

Wang YiQiu. 2005. "Tui Jin Tong shi jiao yu: Cui Sheng Yi Zhong Xin De Jiao Shi Mo Shi" [Advance Liberal Arts Education: Induct a New Model of Liberal Education Faculty]. *Journal of Peking University (Philosophy and Social Sciences)*, 42(5): 191–96.

8 Curricular designs for general education at the UGC-supported universities in Hong Kong

Hedley Freake

Introduction

Universities in Hong Kong are undergoing a period of unprecedented change. They are growing their enterprise by one third as the standard period of study for a bachelor's degree is being extended from three years to four years, commencing in September 2012. Leading up to this change, secondary education is also being extensively restructured, meaning that students entering university will be one year younger and have a different skill set in comparison to those currently in attendance. As part of these changes, the universities are developing new general education programs, in some cases building on a strong tradition, but in others starting from a very minimal base. This chapter will summarize the programs that have been developed and compare them with each other and with those operating in the United States. Particular attention will be paid to the general education programs at Hong Kong Polytechnic University (PolyU), which serve as a useful case study for general education reform.

Background

The University Grants Committee (UGC) administers public higher education in the Special Administrative Region of Hong Kong. It acts in an advisory role for the Hong Kong Government and delivers government funds to the eight eligible institutions (Table 8.1). These vary considerably with respect to mission, including very highly ranked research-extensive universities (Hong Kong University, HKU), those arising from polytechnic backgrounds with more focused strengths (PolyU), smaller liberal arts universities (Lingnan University, LU) and one institution, not yet formally a university, with the focused mission of training teachers (Hong Kong Institute of Education, HKIEd). The UGC determines the scope and size of major programs that these institutions offer and only 18 percent of school leavers in Hong Kong can find places. Thus entry is highly competitive.

These eight institutions are being required by the UGC to reinvent themselves and are moving from three- to four-year undergraduate degree programs. Radical as these changes are, they are arguably more limited and certainly secondary to even larger reforms of the preceding parts of the Hong Kong educational system.

Table 8.1 Student enrollments at UGC-supported institutions in Hong Kong

Institution	SD	UG	PG	Total
Chinese University of Hong Kong	–	11,213	2,187	13,300
City University of Hong Kong	900	8,617	704	10,221
Hong Kong Baptist University	–	4,786	262	5,050
Hong Kong Institute of Education	436	2,647	187	3,270
Hong Kong Polytechnic University	3,391	9,920	614	13,925
Hong Kong University of Science and Technology	–	6,151	1,057	7,208
Lingnan University	–	2,233	54	2,287
University of Hong Kong	–	10,492	2,424	12,916

Notes
1 SD = sub-degree programs; UG = undergraduate programs; PG = postgraduate programs (includes both taught and research programs).
2 Figures are for 2010/11 and are from the UGC: <http://www.ugc.edu.hk/>, accessed November 1, 2011.
3 Part-time students are not included.

In 2000, the Hong Kong SAR Education Commission published *Learning for Life, Learning through Life: Reform Proposals for the Education System in Hong Kong*.[1] This comprised a thorough review and proposals for reform of the entire education system, starting with early childhood education. In some ways, it is remarkable that such wholesale reform was considered necessary or even desirable. Students in Hong Kong have long scored close to the top of international assessments of abilities in science and mathematics.[2] Nevertheless, the Commission recognized the changing nature of the world economy and the unique position of the Hong Kong SAR at the junction of East and West and the bridge between the rapidly exploding Chinese economy and the rest of the world. According to the report, it was agreed that the aims of education for Hong Kong in the twenty-first century should be:

> To enable every person to attain all-round development in the domains of ethics, intellect, physique, social skills and aesthetics according to his/her own attributes so that he/she is capable of life-long learning, critical and exploratory thinking, innovating and adapting to change; filled with self-confidence and a team spirit; willing to put forward continuing effort for the prosperity, progress, freedom and democracy of their society, and contribute to the future well-being of the nation and the world at large.[3]

There were a number of principles articulated to underlie these reforms, including that they be student-focused, enhance educational opportunities, be holistic in design and encourage lifelong learning. While details of these proposals are beyond the scope of this chapter, it is worth describing briefly the changes envisaged at the secondary level and then the framework for reform supplied to the tertiary institutions.

Hong Kong secondary education, based as it was on the British system, comprised five years of study for all and then two additional years for approximately the top third of students who did well on their Year Five examinations. Thus most students left school at age 16 and those that continued studied a restricted and focused number of subjects in preparation for A-level examinations, which would determine their placement at university. Under the new proposals, the first three years of secondary education was viewed as the last part of a nine-year integrated basic education system. This would then be followed by three years of senior secondary education for all students that would be broader, more integrated and more interdisciplinary than the existing system. Though changes at the university level became operational in September 2012, the senior secondary changes were instituted three years earlier to prepare the entrants for the new university programs. In contrast to specialized A levels, students now study four core subjects, English, Chinese, mathematics and liberal studies. The latter novel subject integrates a range of liberal arts and science disciplines. This new curriculum is designed not only to prepare students for further study at universities but also directly for the world of work in the fast-changing and less predictable twenty-first century.

The Education Commission report did not require universities to expand their programs to four years. While it raised this as a possibility, it charged universities with determining the appropriate length for each of their programs of study. It did call for more flexibility, suggesting credit-based systems that would allow easier transfer between programs and institutions and multiple entry and exit points. Nor did it tell universities to develop general education programs, though it did argue against over-specialization and for breadth of study, pointing out that the world needs problem-solvers who have developed the ability to learn in new situations. Strong support for educational reform has also come from the business sector, which found Hong Kong graduates to be technically knowledgeable upon entry to the workforce, but with limited ability to develop over time and adapt to new situations. Other points raised by the Commission were that universities should use a range of approaches to suit different student needs and offer a diversity of programs that built on the strengths of each institution and offer variety and flexibility to students.

The UGC also established the 3+3+4 group, so named for the two three-year segments assigned to secondary education, followed by the four years of university study. This committee was charged with making recommendations to the UGC about a range of issues associated with the changes. These included the duration of undergraduate programs, design and funding of capital projects that would be required for university expansion, admission, curricular and pedagogical concerns and coordination and information-sharing among the institutions. The 3+3+4 group has been quite active and provided further direction and guidance to the institutions as they develop their new programs. One additional charge to the committee was to provide recommendations about how to deal with the "double cohort." The shortening of secondary education by one year means that two cohorts of students will graduate simultaneously from

Hong Kong high schools in 2012, the last group to complete the old seven-year curriculum and the first group to finish the new six-year programs. Universities will admit two classes of students concurrently, one to study for three years under the old degree programs and the second as the first group to enter the newly developed four-year programs. Thus the operation of these new programs will be made much more difficult thanks to the resource and logistical problems associated with this "double cohort."

The opportunities and also the potential pitfalls associated with this relatively open and non-specific call for university reform led to the genesis of the Fulbright Hong Kong General Education Program.[4] With funding from Mr. Po Chung that was matched by the UGC, the Hong Kong-America Center, which coordinates Fulbright activities in the region, developed a program to bring experts in general education from the United States to Hong Kong. The funding was sufficient to allow 20 scholars to come, each for 10 months, over the 4-year period 2008–12. Each Fulbright Scholar was selected and hosted by one of the eight UGC-funded institutions. In any given year, four to six scholars were present in Hong Kong and they worked as a team across all institutions.[5] This pooling of expertise was particularly effective in allowing the team to respond to the needs of their hosts and think creatively and synergistically together about the project at hand. While the Fulbright Project undoubtedly influenced the development of general education programs at Hong Kong universities, the role of its scholars was advisory. The true authors of the changes are to be found within the eight institutions themselves.

General education program goals

The eight UGC-funded universities in Hong Kong are quite diverse with respect to size and programs offered (Table 8.1) and also the extent to which they embraced general education prior to the current reforms. But all have now announced new four-year programs for undergraduate degrees and general education programs that are more or less revolutionary for the institution. The first way in which these programs will be considered here is how they describe themselves and what goals they have established.

The goals articulated for general education by different organizations and institutions within the United States are usually reasonably consistent. Higher-order intellectual skills that enable students to think critically, creatively and transferably are almost always mentioned. Developing the skills to examine problems from a wide range of perspectives, which involves both understanding the approaches used by different disciplines as well as integrating across disciplines, is usually considered important. Multicultural competency, ethics, citizenship and lifelong learning are often included. Appendix A lists the goals articulated for general education by the Hong Kong universities and they fall into this general pattern. Table 8.2 examines this a little more systematically by looking at which components of general education are included in the goals of the eight institutions. There are many ways to categorize the attributes in question and the ones here were selected based on what is usually expected to be an objective for general education, with modifications suggested by a reading of the Hong Kong institutions' goals.

All institutions include mention of breadth and higher-order thinking, albeit often expressed in slightly different ways. These are so central to general education that it would be surprising if they were not included. Six out of eight of the institutions think it important that students learn to see themselves as part of a larger community on a variety of different levels ranging from the local to the global. Notions of citizenship and responsibility are important. Six out of eight, though not necessarily the same ones, talk of developing value systems and ethics. Lifelong learning, literacy and communication and multicultural skills are the other goals mentioned by a majority of the universities.

Of interest is the extent to which universities expect their students to learn about Hong Kong and China. Surprisingly, only three mention it as a specific goal, although this low representation may be misleading, being related more to how the goals are expressed and how well the curriculum is aligned with them. For example, Hong Kong University does include "China, culture, state and society" as one if its areas of inquiry, without mentioning China per se in the goals of the core curriculum. It does have goals that could be interpreted to require a focus on China, for example "To cultivate students' appreciation of their own culture and other cultures," though this seems to be directed a little differently.

Goals addressing literacy and communication skills are listed by five out of eight of the universities, although this includes some that make reference just to oral communication rather than more broadly defined literacy. This reflects a larger pattern, where some institutions treat these skills quite separately from general education, while others integrate them together. An example of the latter is PolyU, considered in greater detail below, where the General University Requirements include those for English and Chinese.

Size and organization of general education programs

Higher education institutions in Hong Kong were given no mandate by the UGC about the scope and size of their general education programs. Thus universities were left to themselves to determine how large the program should be. In the United States, regional accrediting agencies recommend that about a third of the curriculum (or 40 credits) should be reserved for general education. Also, in Hong Kong, the Education Bureau suggests that the community colleges assign 60 percent of the credits in their associate degree programs to generic rather than specialized education. Given 60 credits for a typical associate's degree, this implies 36 for general education. In both cases language requirements would be included.

Credit assignments for general education programs at the universities in Hong Kong are shown in Table 8.3. Disregarding language requirements, they vary from 18 credits (HKU) up to 33 (Lingnan) with an average requirement for 25 credits. The fact that Lingnan has described the largest general education program is hardly surprising, given its identity as a liberal arts university.

Table 8.2 General education attributes specifically addressed by Hong Kong universities

Attribute	CUHK	CityU	HKBU	HKIEd	PolyU	HKUST	LU	HKU	Total
Breadth	X	X	X	X	X	X	X	X	8
Higher-order thinking	X	X	X	X	X	X	X	X	8
Civic/global responsibility			X	X	X	X	X	X	6
Ethics	X	X	X	X	X	X			6
Life-long learning	X	X			X	X		X	5
Literacy and communication	X	X	X		X	X			5
Multicultural skills	X	X	X				X	X	5
Chinese culture	X				X		X		3
Teamwork	X	X				X			3
Healthy lifestyle			X		X	X			3
Quantitative skills		X	X						2
Information literacy		X	X						2

Notes
CUHK   Chinese University of Hong Kong
CityU   City University of Hong Kong
HKBU   Hong Kong Baptist University
HKIEd   Hong Kong Institute of Education
PolyU   Hong Kong Polytechnic University
HKUST   Hong Kong University of Science and Technology
LU   Lingnan University
HKU   University of Hong Kong

Hong Kong Baptist University (HKBU) is perhaps the next closest to that type of institution and has the next largest program (29 credits).

The Lingnan program also includes a greater language requirement (18 credits) than any other institution, exaggerating this difference. Institutions differ with respect to how they describe their language requirements and the extent to which they are integrated into general education. In some cases they are viewed as a separate part of the curriculum, whereas PolyU requires not only nine credits of language courses (six English, three Chinese) but also suggests that content courses in other areas include reading and writing instruction and assignments of a specified nature.

Similarity in overall goals and size of general education programs conceal some variety in the way these curricula are structured. Overall, general education

Table 8.3 The size of general education programs in Hong Kong

Institution	Number of credits	
	including language	*without language*
Chinese University of Hong Kong	39	24
City University of Hong Kong	30	21
Hong Kong Baptist University	38	29
Hong Kong Institute of Education[1]	–	24
Hong Kong Polytechnic University	30	21
Hong Kong University of Science and Technology	36	27
Lingnan University	51	33
University of Hong Kong[2]	27	18

Notes
1 Language requirements for HKIEd are still being determined.
2 At HKU, undergraduate degree programs may require 240 credits over 4 years, including 36 credits from the common core. These values are twice what might be typically expected and so the numbers for the general education program have been divided by two for the purposes of this table.

programs range from those that ensure breadth by requiring students to select subjects from different disciplinary categories to those that mandate a core curriculum for all students that is integrated across disciplines. Most programs, both in the USA and Hong Kong, lie somewhere between these two extremes. Thus while they may require students to select courses from different categories, those courses are specifically designed for the general education program and the connections between them are made more or less explicit. All of the new programs in Hong Kong include some kind of distribution requirements where students are required to select a certain number of subjects from different categories (Table 8.4). Some are described in relatively simple disciplinary terms, e.g. HKUST (arts and humanities, social analysis, science and technology, quantitative reasoning), whereas others have more interdisciplinary names, e.g. HKIEd (truth, value and aesthetics, identity, community and culture, science technology and nature). While the names may differ, the broad disciplinary areas are apparent.

For some institutions, general education is simply the aggregate of these courses. Others have planned an additional core curriculum, though this is quite variable in nature (Table 8.4). Both HKBU and Lingnan list categories of required core courses, a structure similar on the surface to the distribution requirements. Presumably what makes them "core" is the removal of student choice from within a category. CUHK requires all students to take two core courses "In dialogue with humanity" and "In dialogue with nature." At one point, CityU proposed "Me and my university," a subject focused on helping students become more self-aware and develop the habits of mind needed for successful academic study. This type of first-year course is often found in universities in the USA, but was turned down by the CityU Senate. Now they have a single core course on Chinese civilization. The model proposed for HKIEd is notable in that it sandwiches its distribution requirements between two core courses, general education foundation and consolidation. While the exact nature of these courses is not yet clear, the opportunity to set the stage for university study and general education in the foundation course and then to make sure the connections have been made and the programmatic learning objectives have been achieved in the consolidation course is coherent and attractive.

Hong Kong Polytechnic University: a case study for general education reform

PolyU has operated a general education program of one kind or another since 1997, when two "broadening" courses were added to the curriculum. These courses were located in five different domains of knowledge and were seen as a required adjunct to PolyU's strength in applied and professional education. However, over time this curriculum was devalued, as the courses were reduced from three to two credits and offered only on a pass/fail basis. In addition one of the courses was required to be China studies, an amalgam of units each taught by a different instructor. General education was viewed as a minor and less important part of the curriculum.

As planning began at PolyU for the new four-year curriculum, it was agreed that general education needed to be expanded and strengthened. However, many at PolyU expressed another concern, which was that students would be entering the university one year younger and with less foundational disciplinary knowledge. Up until this point, programs accepted students who had taken A-levels in areas specific to each major field of study and provided them with a solid disciplinary preparation. To make up for this potential deficit in the new students, the first plans for the General University Requirements (GUR) at PolyU included 15 credits of what were called Broad Discipline Requirements (BDR). This curricular space was assigned to the various schools and colleges so that they could offer disciplinary courses that would be foundational for study in the major. This is arguably the antithesis of general education but was viewed as necessary and appropriate, given the perceived lack of knowledge among entering students. The counter-argument was made that if these foundational courses were necessary, then they should be considered part of the major field of study rather than general education. In addition, 72–96 credits were assigned to each major at PolyU. This number, which appears large by US standards, would seem to be sufficient to include any needed foundational courses.

If the BDR were not considered part of general education, then the curriculum as proposed appeared rather sparse. Students were to be required to take one course in each of four content areas (human nature, relations and development; community, organization and globalization; history, culture and worldviews; and science, technology and environment) for a total of 12 credits. However, changes in leadership at PolyU enabled rethinking of the proposed general education program. The BDR were formally assigned to the major fields of study. They are

Table 8.4 Summary of general education programs at Hong Kong universities

Institution	Core courses	Credits	Distribution areas	Credits	Other components/notes	Credits	Totals
Chinese University of Hong Kong	In Dialogue with Humanity	3	Chinese Cultural Heritage	3	Each college provides an additional 6 credits of general education courses.	6	24 (39)
	In Dialogue with Nature	3	Nature, Science & Technology,	3			
	English Language	9	Society and Culture	3			
	Chinese Language	6	Self and Humanities	3			
City University of Hong Kong	Chinese Civilization		Arts and Humanities		Students select 3 additional distribution courses.		21 (27)
	English Language		Study of Societies, Social and Business Organizations				
			Science and Technology				
Hong Kong Baptist University	Public Speaking	3	Social Sciences	3	Students must select a course from 4 out of the 5 distribution areas.		29 (38)
	History & Civilization	3	Arts	3			
	Numeracy	3	Communication/Visual Arts	3			
	Values & the Meaning of Life	3	Science/Chinese Medicine	3			
	Information Management Technology	3	Business	3			
	Physical Education	2					
	English Language	6					
	Chinese Language	3					

continued overleaf

Institution	Core courses	Credits	Distribution areas	Credits	Other components/notes	Credits	Totals
Hong Kong Institute of Education	GE Foundation	6	Truth, Value and Aesthetics	3	Students will select from a series of Foundation and Consolidation modules.		24
	GE Consolidation	3	Identity, Community and Culture	3			
			Science, Technology and Nature	3	Students select a total of 5 distribution courses		
Hong Kong Polytechnic University	Freshman Seminar	3	Human Nature, Relations and Development	3	Two of the distribution courses must be China Related (60% content)		21 (30)
	Leadership and Intra-Personal Development	3	Community, Organization and Globalization	3			
	Community Service-Learning	3	History, Cultures and Worldviews	3	Others required to emphasize reading (R) or writing (W) in English or Chinese		
	English Language	6	Science, Technology and Environment	3			
	Chinese Language	3					
Hong Kong University of Science and Technology	English Communication	6	Arts and Humanities	6	Students must select 2 additional distribution courses	6	27 (36)
	Chinese Communication	3	Social Analysis	6			
	Healthy Lifestyle	0	Science and Technology	6			
			Quantitative Reasoning	3			

Institution	Core courses	Credits	Distribution areas	Credits	Other components/notes	Credits	Totals
Lingnan University	Logic and Critical Thinking	3	Creativity and Innovation	3	Students must select 2 additional distribution courses	6	33 (51)
	The Making of Hong Kong	3	Humanities and the Arts	3			
	Understanding Morality	3	Management and Society	3			
	World History and Civilizations	3	Science, Technology and Society	3			
	English Language	12	Values, Cultures and Societies	3			
	Chinese Language	6					
University of Hong Kong	English Language (includes 3 credits in major)	6	Scientific and Technological Literacy	3	Students must select 2 additional distribution courses	6	18 (27)
	Chinese Language	3	Humanities	3	For HKU, a 6-credit course = 120–80 student effort hours and a degree = 240 credits. Their values have been divided by 2 here to parallel other institutions.		
			Global Issues	3			
			China: Culture, State and Society	3			

Note
Totals in parentheses include language requirements.

now replaced within the GUR by three new three-credit courses, designed to give PolyU students a common core learning experience. The first is "Freshman Seminar." These are to be offered within the broad disciplines and serve as an introduction to the majors but are also required to emphasize generic attributes like critical and creative thinking, global outlook and entrepreneurship. The second course is "Leadership and intra-personal development," which builds on the research and experience of an individual faculty member at PolyU. This course is designed to build self-understanding and self-efficacy in PolyU students as a means to developing their leadership skills. The third course, "Community service-learning," is still being developed. These courses appear to fit both the needs of incoming PolyU students, a large majority of whom are first generation to college, and the institution itself, with its mission of applied excellence.

One other point of note about the PolyU program is the extent to which general education is integrated with language instruction. As outlined above, in addition to the nine credits of language instruction (six English, three Chinese) general education subjects can be designated as teaching language reading (R) or writing (W) skills, in English or Chinese. Instruction in these courses is coordinated between the content instructor and the staff of the Language Centers. Students are required to take R and W courses in both languages amongst those they select to meet their GUR. Furthermore, there are requirements for courses within the major fields of study to emphasize both written and oral communication skills in both languages. This approach, where the writing skills are learned and developed in the context of relevant subject matter and subject learning is enhanced by the writing process, is likely to be doubly beneficial and therefore to be encouraged.

Overall, PolyU appears poised to effect an enormous transformation in its general education program. It is moving from a minor, non-graded and not well-regarded 4-credit program to a well-conceived 30-credit curriculum, integrated across the whole university. It builds well on the strengths of the institution and also incorporates many approaches for student engagement that have demonstrated efficacy. It can stand comparison with programs offered at US universities that have been practicing general education for decades.

Challenges to come

Higher education in Hong Kong has come a long way towards meeting the challenges posed by the 3+3+4 transition. All have conceived general education programs in a thoughtful and well-informed way that is designed to teach students the intellectual and practical skills required for the twenty-first century. However, the real work is just beginning, with the entry of the new students in September 2012. The expansion of higher education by one third, consequent to adding the extra year, is an enormous resource and logistical challenge, exacerbated by the arrival of the double cohort. Institutions have varied in the speed with which they have moved towards hiring the additional faculty that are required but clearly there will be many employment opportunities for academics in Hong Kong in the near future. Indeed, institutions may struggle to find well-qualified staff. However, what is needed is not just more of the same but rather faculty, new and existing, who are equipped to engage and challenge students in the general education classroom. Faculty development efforts targeted at strengthening interactive and interdisciplinary teaching skills are under way and will need to be expanded. In addition to preparing faculty, the students also will need more help. Traditionally in Hong Kong, students have entered a degree program and emerged three years later, having followed a set pathway. Some students will now enter without having selected a major. Even those that have will enjoy more program flexibility and the UGC has suggested that transfer between majors or even institutions should be possible. This requires the development of a new advising system to guide students along these pathways and also to help them make sense and good use of a novel general education program. One aspect not addressed in this chapter is the administrative structure required for a strong general education program. General education comprises a quarter to a third of the undergraduate curriculum, a very significant proportion that requires leadership at a high level to ensure it gets the appropriate resources and respect. Finally, this giant experiment in higher education in Hong Kong deserves detailed evaluation to determine the effects that it has on student learning. Assessment is needed to see which aspects are working well and producing the desired outcomes and which require modification. This is particularly crucial at a time internationally when others are suggesting shorter and more highly focused higher education programs.

Notes

1   <http://www.e-c.edu.hk/eng/reform/index_e.html>, accessed November 1, 2011.
2   OECD Programme for International Student Assessment Rankings. Online. Available HTTP: <http://www.oecd.org/edu/pisa/2009>.
3   <http://www.e-c.edu.hk/eng/reform/index_e.html p4>, accessed November 1, 2011.
4   <http://www.e-c.edu.hk/eng/reform/index_e.html p4>, accessed November 1, 2011.
5   <http://www.fulbright.org.hk/hkac/fulbright-hk-programs/fulbright-hk-general-education-program/>, accessed November 11, 2011.

The author of this chapter was part of the second cohort of Fulbright Scholars and was based at Hong Kong Polytechnic University from September 2009 through June 2010.

Chapter 8 appendix
Summary of goals articulated by Hong Kong universities for their general education programs

Chinese University of Hong Kong (http://www.cuhk.edu.hk/)

General education at CUHK is designed to:

- furnish students with a broad intellectual perspective for dealing with the unfamiliar;
- engage students in active reflections on perennial issues, prompting them to make connections between intellectual pursuits and personal life at work, at home and in the community;
- promote an understanding of Chinese cultural heritage and of other cultural traditions;
- develop in students attitudes and skills that are conducive to critical thinking, self-expression and communication with others;
- serve as a platform where students can extend their curiosity, read widely beyond their chosen discipline and develop attitudes and competence as independent learners and also as team players.

City University of Hong Kong (http://www.cityu.edu.hk/)

The intended learning outcomes of the general education program are:

- demonstrate the capacity for self-directed learning;
- explain the basic methodologies and techniques of inquiry of the arts and humanities, social sciences, business and science and technology;
- demonstrate critical thinking skills;
- interpret information and numerical data;
- produce structured, well-organized and fluent text;
- demonstrate effective oral communication skills;
- demonstrate an ability to work effectively in a team;
- recognize important characteristics of their own culture(s) and at least one other culture, and their impact on global issues;
- value ethical and socially responsible actions.

Hong Kong Baptist University (http://www.hkbu.edu.hk/)

The goals of the GE program are:

- communicate effectively as speakers and writers in both English and Chinese;
- access and manage complex information and problems using technologically appropriate means;

- apply appropriate mathematical reasoning to address problems in everyday life;
- acquire an active and healthy lifestyle;
- use historical and cultural perspectives to gain insight into contemporary issues;
- apply various value systems to decision-making in personal, professional and social/political situations;
- make connections among a variety of disciplines to gain insight into contemporary personal, professional and community situations.

Hong Kong Institute of Education (http://www.ied.edu.hk/)

At the end of the general education program, the students will be able to:

- analyze the connections among the contexts of human cultures and the physical and natural world through systematic inquiry;
- draw meaningful connections among the contexts of human cultures and the physical and natural world through systematic inquiry;
- apply intellectual skills developed in GE to tackle academic and practical issues;
- construct ethical and thoughtful responses to the challenges of responsible citizenship in Hong Kong;
- develop a global perspective which allows students to make informed connections and commitments to people, issues and cultures.

Hong Kong Polytechnic University (http://www.polyu.edu.hk/)

Students will:

- acquire the foundation knowledge and skills that underpin their major study;
- acquire the language and communication skills to facilitate their university studies;
- expand their intellectual capacity beyond their disciplinary domain so as to enable them to tackle professional and global challenges from a multidisciplinary perspective and in a holistic manner;
- gain an increased understanding of China (e.g. its history, culture and society, as well as its emerging issues/challenges);
- develop a more healthy lifestyle;
- develop a sense of ethical conduct as a citizen and a professional.

In addition, all GE courses should help students develop:

- literacy (substantial reading and extensive writing);
- higher-order thinking (systematic, critical and creative thinking);
- lifelong learning (active enquiry, learning-to-learn activities).

Hong Kong University of Science and Technology (http://www.ust.hk/)

Goals and objectives of the common core program:

- spark passion for learning, broaden horizons and liberate the mind;
- develop communication and analytical capacity and independent thinking;
- foster appreciation of arts and culture, social issues and scientific and technological precision;
- encourage inquiry and ability to work as a team;
- cultivate responsible, ethical and compassionate citizenship;
- ensure balanced physical and intellectual growth.

Lingnan University (http://www.ln.edu.hk/)

Compulsory common core:

- acquire a fundamental and indispensable knowledge base and a broad and balanced foundation;
- develop sound judgment, critical discernment and analytical abilities;
- learn how to think critically and tackle social, cultural, moral and ethical problems rationally;
- understand Hong Kong, other cultures and civilizations and be prepared to become future leaders of our increasingly globalized city;
- think, judge, care and, ultimately, act responsibly in this ever-changing world.

University of Hong Kong (http://www.hku.hk/)

Goals of the core curriculum:

- to enable students to develop a broader perspective and a critical understanding of the complexities and the interconnectedness of the issues that they are confronted with in their everyday lives;
- to cultivate students' appreciation of their own culture and other cultures, and the inter-relatedness among cultures;
- to enable students to see themselves as members of global as well as local communities and to play an active role as responsible individuals and citizens in these communities;
- to enable students to develop the key intellectual skills that will be further enhanced in their disciplinary studies.

Part III
Pedagogical approaches to general education

9 Science, the first humanity

John Freeman Babson

Man is the measure of all things.
Protagoras (*c.* 490–420BCE)

This chapter will look into the issue of what C. P. Snow (1960) called the "Two Cultures," the claim that somehow science is separate from and not representative of the humanities.[1] It will be found to be a false dichotomy, the perception of which is reinforced only through ignorance. The refutation of this claim will come in three parts. First, the historic and philosophic underpinnings of science will be briefly examined, which will not only show that it is rooted in the humanistic tradition but arguably in the modern sense it is the *first humanity*. Second, we will demonstrate that the scientific method is an exercise in humanistic thinking. Finally, a practical pedagogy for teaching general science in the Hong Kong classroom, developed over a ten-year period at Hong Kong Polytechnic University, will be described, whose meta-goal is the cultivation of human potential.

Humanitas

In the Spring of 1996, I found myself an Associate Professor in southern Japan teaching computer science and ecology. Following a public lecture sponsored by the college, I attended a small dinner party consisting of the speaker, the college president, an art historian, an English teacher and myself. In the early 1970s the speaker, an architect, Mr. Shinichi Okada, had been responsible for the design of the building housing the Supreme Court of Japan. A Yale graduate and internationally famous, he has won many awards for his work. Our president, like myself, was a physicist. During the conversation, we talked much about the Japanese aesthetic and eventually turned to the topic of *Mono no aware* or "aware" for short, the bittersweet awareness of the impermanence of all things. So far, so good, all could follow the conversation. At that point I made a reference to it as a Japanese or Buddhist example of the Second Law of Thermodynamics.[2] Immediately there was mutual incomprehension on the part of the art historian and the English teacher while the architect and physicists nodded agreement with the statement. Why this separation of understanding within such an educated gathering?

One of the problems of language, which we will see repeatedly in this chapter, is that a common word can be given different meanings by different groups. Such overlaid words can lead to long-standing ongoing confusion. One such word is *humanitas* or "the humanities" in English, the concept of which is absolutely central to the notion of a liberal (i.e. liberating) education. Some operationally use it as a collective term for disciplines or study areas which are *not* grounded in science such as philosophy, history and the arts.[3] Others, such as the author of this chapter, look to the essential spirit of *humanitas* and strongly argue for the inclusion of science. Arguing this and its profound impact on general education and its reform in particular will be the essential theme of this chapter.

A common characteristic of human civilizations is to be able to point back in mytho-history and identify a founding progenitor who laid the foundation for subsequent developments of that civilization. A particularly ripe time in human history for such developments was roughly 500BCE. In China you had Confucius, who was concerned with social harmony. In India you had Gautama Siddhartha (the Buddha), who taught only two things, "the cause of human suffering and how to relieve it." And in Ancient Greece you had Protagoras,[4] the pre-Socratic agnostic philosopher who promulgated the epigraph to this chapter. Even earlier, in the Middle East, you had Moses the lawgiver.

Our attention here will be concentrated on the Western tradition of the Greeks, for it is from this tradition and the likes of Protagoras that we get the notion of *humanitas*. Protagoras' sense of "things" was not everything but rather that which was of utility to our species, i.e. human-centered. The moon is very far away and perhaps not of much use. Then the moon would not count, but, on the other hand, if one were dependent upon moonlight, then in that limited sense man would be the measure of the moon.

All ancient societies of course had multiple progenitor founders, but this was particularly true of the Greeks, for whom the discourse of views were not just promulgated as in other societies but rather expressed dynamically through the three Ds of discussion, dialog and debate, with each participant sharpening his arguments in the interaction with others. This succession of different thinkers in aggregate gave rise to what might be called the Greek humanist ideal, which may be summarized as having three shared characteristics. First, it was *materialistic* in seeking rational explanations for natural phenomena. The working premise of the likes of Protagoras' near contemporary Pythagoras was that the universe was intrinsically *cosmos* (Greek: "order") in contrast to earthly *chaos*. Second, a major value was *free enquiry*, which could lead to the discovery of new possibilities. Asking questions was a "good." Third, it valued *humanity*, placing human beings at the center of moral and social concerns.

Examples would be Archimedes (material), Socrates (enquiry) and of course Protagoras (humanity). There was great emphasis on the individual in Greek and later Western societies in contrast to the more collective societies of the East and their greater insistence on social conformity. To the Western mind, many of the iconic Greek heroes, such as Socrates, were those who stood up to a conformity-demanding authority. This only gradually disappeared when Rome changed from a Republic (Latin: *res* "concern" + *publicus* "of the people") to an Empire, with its emphasis on collective power focused on an emperor (Latin: *imperator* "military"; akin to "imperative"). This was the beginning that led to a long dark period from which European civilization was not to emerge until the Renaissance.

Still, echoes of this were to survive for some time before the fall of Rome in 476CE and the beginning of the Dark Ages. One example is the last of "the good emperors," the Stoic philosopher Marcus Aurelius. He kept a reflection journal in "highly educated" *koine* (international) Greek later published as *Meditations* in which he wrote that one must live one's life in accord with Nature. The work is suffused with this recurring theme (Marcus Aurelius 2002).

Another is the late Roman notion of Martianus Capella, a lawyer in the fifth century CE in North Africa, of the Liberal Arts of the educated citizen in contrast to the Mechanical Arts of the slave. The Liberal Arts were divided into a qualitative-oriented lower division, the *trivium* (Latin: "three parts"; akin to "trivial"), and a quantitative-oriented upper division, the *quadrivium* (Latin: "four parts"), which were to subsequently form the foundation or "general education" of the medieval university student before specializing in one of the professions of theology, law or medicine. The "arts" of the *trivium* consisted of grammar, logic and rhetoric (emphasizing communication and discourse), while those of the *quadrivium* were arithmetic, geometry, music and astronomy (emphasizing what today we call science).

Need the reader be reminded that a major part of the teaching of Pythagoras was his connection between music and mathematics, echoes of which are to be found in the late medieval concept of the "music of the spheres"? Later, in the Renaissance, this connection, this sense of cosmos, was extended by Johannes Kepler in empirically teasing out his three laws of planetary motion from the data of Tycho Brahe.

Unfortunately with the fall of the Western Roman Empire and the subsequent political chaos, the individual was subsumed into the collective. The social glue of the time was the Holy Roman Catholic (Greek: "universal") Church. One was taught to not look to this life for relief but instead to look to the "afterlife." One obeyed without question the church and king if one wished to get to heaven. This is not to say great things were not accomplished during the Dark Ages: just look at the splendor of the cathedrals, some of which took over a hundred years to construct. Yet, and this is the key point, we do not know the names of the architects and master builders of genius. They are all anonymous. This is in sharp contrast to the subsequent period of the Renaissance, in which typically we recognize genius with a single name – Leonardo, Raphael, Michelangelo, Donatello, Copernicus, Tycho, Galileo, Kepler, etc.

The names that come down to us through the Dark Ages are those of the powerful – popes, kings and princes. Still, although the Greek ideal of the individual was suppressed, there were occasional hints of its return. A notable example of this was the pervasive development of "courtly love" which emanated from the court of Eleanor, duchess of Aquitaine. She inherited her duchy from her father, which made her an independent woman, a most unusual character for her times. Joseph Campbell (1988, pp. 231–38) claims that the whole tradition of courtly love, celebrated by the troubadours (Roma vs. amor), stems from her court. Her second husband was Henry II of England, with whom one of her sons was Richard *Cœur de lion* (the Lionheart).

The Dark Ages were the cauldron within which the ingredients that were to give rise to the modern world simmered just beneath the social surface. The subsequent Renaissance development of the humanities and humanism was to blossom out of this mud. Perhaps most of us relate to this period of rebirth through the explosion of the arts.

Yet right from the beginning, we find science intimately involved with this recovery of *humanitas* and its focus on the individual. Think of Leonardo (*da Vinci* of course). Can you separate his art from his science (or vice versa)? In both cases, he pushed the envelope in trying to better understand Nature. He also understood that much of what he was doing was taboo for his times and so he had to act in secret. One need only think of his human dissections, which through his direct observations of human anatomy allowed him to represent more realistically than ever before the human form – *humanitas*, both art and science!

One way to distinguish the difference between the arts and science is that when a question is posed in the arts, multiple answers are possible, even expected. How does the work affect you? Indeed, beauty is in the eye of the beholder. And of course each answer can in turn spur yet more questions. As such, it is possible, and it has probably always been the case, that an artist can hide within their work a deep criticism by simply allowing alternative interpretations to be publicly spun. Think of Goya and his representations of the Spanish royal family.

Science is different in that when a question is posed of Nature, and if asked in the right way, Nature answers it. One question gives rise to one answer, which then forms the platform upon which the next question is answered and so on *ad infinitum*. The questioner is of course human and probably asks the question out of some subjective experience or guess (a hypothesis), but the answer is more object than subject. Yet science in discovery is value-free. Nature dictates.

Now ask yourself the question, in the Renaissance re(dis)covery, through which broad avenue might it have been easier to effectively challenge (i.e. refute) authority, art or science?

Copernicus is a perfect example. After completing his foundational course in the Liberal Arts, he studied in the best of contemporary universities, Kraków, Bologna and Padua, variously mathematics, astronomy, philosophy (Aristotle and Averroes) and interestingly all three of the main disciplines of the day, law, theology and medicine – a true Renaissance man. As a cleric, law (especially canonical) and theology were his official vocation, while the practice of medicine was taken up so that he might be useful in preserving the health of senior clerics. Astronomy was his avocation (and passion).

The Ptolemaic (geocentric) explanation of the appearances, in other words the movement, of the planets (Greek: "wanderer") against this background of the "fixed" stars was very involved. This motion, known to observers of all of the ancient agricultural civilizations, is puzzling in that for the most part, a planet appears to move in a forward (*prograde*) direction but then, unexpectedly, reverses in direction for a period of time (*retrograde*), only to then move forward again inscribing an overall loop-to-loop motion. How do you explain this? This question, probably prehistoric, was to be debated for many millennia.

Ptolemy, building on the geocentric assumptions of Aristotle, proposed in his *Almagest* (*c.* 150CE) that planets have a complicated motion consisting of a combination of two orbital paths. The main one, a *deferent*, was a circular orbit about the earth (the center of course in the Christian interpretation of God's universe). This explained the prograde motion. The secondary one, an *epicycle*, was centered on the orbital path of the deferent. This explained the retrograde motion. According to Ptolemy, the actual motion of a planet was the combination of the two. This was to be taught in the West as canonical truth for over 1,300 years. In retrospect this is akin to mistaking the orbiting valve (earth) located on the rim of a bicycle tire, with the fixed axis (sun). The valve's view of a circling object about the axis is a loop-to-loop path.

There was predictive power in this version of astronomy – Columbus successfully navigated the Atlantic Ocean with it – but it was based upon observed repetition, which can be summarized in an empirical table, not upon a theoretical underlying construct that can be used to make a prediction through calculation.

Copernicus did not make observations that were markedly different from those of the ancients, for he saw the same patterns in Nature that they did but with different eyes. Galileo (1615) tells us that Copernicus was involved in the long-standing effort on the part of the church to enlist the aid of astronomer-clerics to rectify the Julian calendar (named after Julius Caesar, and proclaimed in 46BCE), which was incorrectly predicting Easter (upon which all of the rest of the church's feasts were dependent).[5] The problem was that should one continue reasoning along the lines of Ptolemy, epicycles on top of epicycles would be needed and an already complicated model would become even more complicated. God may work in mysterious ways, but he is not perverse. It ran against the grain. Midlife, Copernicus had his sudden insight;[6] he placed the sun instead of the earth in the center of the universe. As long as you assumed two motions for the earth, a daily rotation about an internal axis giving rise to day and night and an annual revolution about the sun, this much simpler model worked![7]

Further, Ockham's razor, which was much in favor in the early Renaissance, basically says that the simpler of two (equally comprehensive) explanations is the right one and Copernicus' explanation was much simpler.

Copernicus was smart. His close friends begged him to publish. However, he knew his times and the power of his church. He was to wait another half lifetime until he was on his deathbed before publishing. Thus he avoided the likes of the Inquisition. Today we may inhabit a world in which as an academic you either publish or perish, but in his case he understood that should he publish, he would perish. The subsequent stories of Bruno[8] and Galileo[9] testify to this observation (de Santilliana, 1955).

So in sum, what can we generalize about the stories of Leonardo, Copernicus, Bruno, Galileo and many other such Renaissance men? In each case, at some point in their lives, they stood alone with the vision of a minority of one, questioning revealed wisdom and some authority of their time. For me the summative image is that of Leonardo's 1487 *Vitruvian Man*. Named for the Roman architect Vitruvius, who in his compendium *De architectura* paid homage to the Greek ideal of "man as the measure of all things." Is architecture art or science? Obviously it is both. Who is Vitruvian Man? Why, he is you or I, each of us, modern man, an individual no longer subsumed by the collective! This is *humanitas*.

The scientific method

The brief history outlined above argues that modern science evolved from and completely developed within the humanist tradition, that a single insightful individual, originally a minority of one, standing up against the common thinking of the day, *may* be right and have something of real value to offer society as a whole (Bronowski, 1973; Kuhn, 1970). The test is not whether society as a whole shares this point of view but whether it accords with "the dictates of Nature."

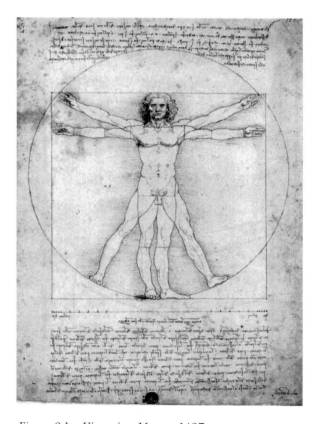

Figure 9.1   Vitruvian Man, c. 1487.

One refers to "the arts" in the sense that they have some characteristics in common. While they may be conveniently categorized as literary, representational, performance, etc. they all deal as noted above in an open-ended questioning process, which is highly subjective to the observer. There is an associated aesthetic.

The modern scientist, however, does not refer to "the sciences." While there are very distinct broad areas of investigation based in a natural hierarchy, notably in the pure sciences of physics, chemistry and biology, which in turn may be applied to natural sciences such as astronomy, geology, meteorology, oceanography and most notably ecology (more about ecology later), each needs to be studied on its own terms, the working assumption being that ultimately they are different pieces of a common jigsaw puzzle. The study of this puzzle is known as science, and it has a common method, the scientific method, by which questions are asked of Nature, and if asked in just the right way, Nature answers. It does not matter what the individual, scientist or not, or society as a whole may hold to be near and dear, Nature answers and within the limits of our ability to read the answer, Nature has answered the question.

In practice, of course, one can refer to "methods," but they can all be shown to be variations on a common theme, which continues to evolve to this day. This section will be devoted to an introduction to the scientific method, which in any science-oriented general education course ought to be a major objective of study. A working assumption in general education is that when a student takes a subject in a particular area, it is very likely that may well be the *last* such course they will ever take in that area. Thus to be an informed individual and citizen, they need to be given a reasonably rigorous introduction to the thinking patterns of that area. In science, this means the scientific method.

What makes science so different from other human activities is that it is a reliable means of *dialoging* with Nature. Through this process, our species comes closer and closer to understanding the structure of the universe and how Nature works.

Indeed, this questioning process is so fundamental that it completely transformed the philosophical discourse of the West, giving rise to the age of Enlightenment. In turn, it led to active challenging of the prevailing social fabric based in aristocracy and privilege and replaced it, through *revolution* (Copernicus' word[10]), with more democratic means of social organization. Finally, in the nineteenth century, the application of basic laws of science, uncovered through the scientific method, to the problems of technology, precipitated fundamental change in technological development. This accelerated the industrial revolution in a way that continues unabated 200 years later. In a very real, practical and historical sense, it can be argued that science is not only part of the humanistic tradition but that it led the revolution that gave rise to the modern world.

In the end, we shall find that the scientific method is a simple dialog between two long-standing worldviews – *empiricism* and *theory*.

Let's start with empiricism and turn to the *American Heritage Dictionary* (2006) for a typical definition (italics added for emphasis).

em•pir•i•cism *n.*

1. The view that experience, especially of the senses, is the only source of knowledge.

2.a. Employment of empirical methods, *as in science.* b. An empirical conclusion.

3. The practice of medicine that *disregards scientific theory* and relies solely on practical experience. – em•pir´i•cist *n.*

From this definition, we may infer two things. First, roughly speaking, empiricism is "knowledge gained through practical experience." Second, it may or may not be scientific, as we can see when we compare definition (2a) to definition (3).

Modern science is based in the premise that there are a few very basic ideas which we may variously call first, fundamental or theoretical principles or *default positions* since they are so fundamental to analysis (and thus *assumed* by default unless there is evidence to the contrary). Contrary to popular opinion, science is not a completely open exercise. Not everything imaginable is possible in science. Patent offices worldwide accept the default position of the Second Law of Thermodynamics (the *entropy* law) and as a consequence will not accept an application for a perpetual motion machine (even with a *working* model). These basic default positions, hard won over time, guide everything that is done in science. Theories are constructed out of them (Hardin, 1993, pp. 40–42).

Empiricism is a good example. A modern textbook in science, in introducing the scientific method, especially the empirical side of it, may present a series of steps something like the following:

1   *Making observations.* Observations may be *qualitative* (snow is white; ice is cold) or *quantitative* (water boils at 100 degrees C at one atmosphere of pressure; a certain crate weighs 35.7 kilograms). A qualitative observation does not involve a number. In contrast, a quantitative observation is called a *measurement* and does involve a number (and an associated unit, such as kilograms or centimeters).

2   *Formulating hypotheses.* An hypothesis is a *possible* explanation for the observation. Sometimes it is referred to as an *educated guess.*

3   *Performing experiments.* An experiment is something we do to test the hypothesis. We gather new information that allows us to decide whether the hypothesis is *not incorrect* – that is, whether it has not been falsified by the new information we have learned from the experiment.[11] Experiments always produce new observations, and this brings us back to the beginning of the process again.

(Zumdahl, 1990, pp. 5–8)

Thus, we see, we have in scientific empiricism a cycle of observation leading to hypothesis leading to experiment leading to further observation, etc. Pretty soon, if one does not watch out, one could cover the whole earth in data notebooks. Fortunately, scientific empiricism is not limited to an exercise of data-harvesting constrained by hypothesis-testing – it is more than that. Tycho Brahe collected data for decades on the motions of the planets.[12] Admittedly, it took Johannes Kepler an additional decade to reduce the data on the planet Mars. When he did so he uncovered a definite pattern in the data, which was in its full form to give rise to his famous three laws of planetary motion.[13] The logic in such pattern-matching is inductive, going from multiple specific incidents to uncover a general picture. For our purposes we shall refer to such a summary pattern found in the data as an *empirical law* (or "law" for short).

It can be argued that the empirical cycle, at least in some nascent form, has been around for a very long time. Certainly Archimedes (*c.* 287 to *c.* 212BCE) demonstrated some understanding of it when he famously solved the puzzle as to whether the goldsmith had cheated in making a votive crown for the king of Syracuse by substituting silver for gold – *eureka!*

There is another equally important aspect to the scientific method, *theory.* The word "theory" comes to us through the Greek and is related to the word "theorem." Pythagoras (*c.* 570 to *c.* 495BCE) developed his theorem roughly 300 years earlier and so this worldview is also quite ancient.

So let's look at that other side of the coin, theory. Again, we turn to the *American Heritage Dictionary* (2006) for a typical definition (again, the italics are added).

> the•o•ry *n., pl.* the•o•ries.
> 1.a. *Systematically organized knowledge* applicable in a relatively wide variety of circumstances, especially a system of assumptions, accepted principles, and rules of procedure devised to analyze, predict, or otherwise explain the nature or behavior of a specified set of phenomena. b. Such knowledge or such a system.

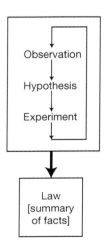

Figure 9.2 The empirical contribution to the scientific method.

2. Abstract reasoning; *speculation*.
3. A *belief* that guides action or assists comprehension or judgment.
4. An assumption based on limited information or knowledge; a *conjecture*.

From this definition, we may infer two things. First, roughly speaking, theory may be considered to be "systematic knowledge" as in definition (1a and b). Second, it may be speculation, belief or conjecture of some form as in definitions (2) through (4).

There is a lot of confusion about this in the public sphere. One hears of the *theory of evolution* being just "theory" and not proven "fact." Obviously, this is an appeal to the last three definitions and not the first. Generally, in science, the use of the word "theory" is more akin to that given in definition (1). Evolution, and particularly the process of natural selection, is so fundamental to the modern worldview of biology, that little of a meaningful nature can be said without it – it is as if one were to drop numbers from a discussion of arithmetic.

Closely akin to the idea of theory being systematic knowledge is the idea of *first principles* or *default positions* mentioned earlier. These are very simple *assumed* relationships out of which theoretical constructions are made. Another way of describing them is *common sense* and it follows that scientific theory is often an extension of common sense (Quine, 1957).[14]

Perhaps the description of theory by Garrett Hardin (1993) in his *Living within Limits* may help us out. He points out that there are exactly two rules of a robust theory:

> Rule 1: Take a simple idea.
> Rule 2: Take it seriously.

Another way of describing rule 2 is to say that you must follow the pathway to its logical consequences (obviously regardless which path it may take). That is the key ingredient, a simple idea adhered to seriously. A proper theory, one that *accords* with experience, is a *system*, which over time, through a cyclic process, gets better. Most importantly, a good theory makes predictions about physical phenomena that have yet to even be observed and connects up seemingly unrelated phenomena. This is a clear distinction from the mere empirical view of science. Our theory cycle then takes the form shown in Figure 9.3.

A theory is a *model* but not all models are theories. What is meant by a model is a mental construct of reality capturing the essential features at the intended scale of interest. For example, a map of the world will give you an accurate rendering of the coastlines of landmasses and the intervening oceans. Maybe it shows you major river and mountain systems. It certainly will not tell you anything about the subway systems of New York City or Hong Kong. As far as we know, among all of the species on this planet, only ours is capable of such a mental process – *humanitas*.

As we have seen, a theory is based in a few simple assumptions as to how the world works, then the logical consequences are worked out, from which predictions are made. Thus in a theoretical model, the structure that you see

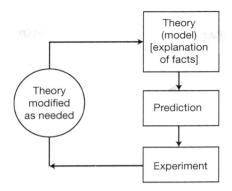

Figure 9.3   The theoretical contribution to the scientific method.

is derived from the assumptions. The logic is deductive, going from a general pattern to predict a specific incidence. Not all models are necessarily like this. Many (our map of the world for example) may contain a large amount of strictly empirical data (i.e. "mapping"). In science, most models are semi-empirical, in other words at their base are a set of theoretical assumptions which are then supplemented in the study of a particular phenomenon by empirical data, the history of which may be completely unknown, just its existence at the time of measurement determined. This is much like taking note on a certain day the amount of money in your bank account without knowing anything about the history of deposits and withdrawals.

As we have seen, the scientific method is made up of two ancient worldviews, empiricism and theory. So why is it accurate to claim that science is only about 400 years old, going back only to the time of Galileo? The answer is that it was the likes of a Galileo[15] who put these two worldviews together in a *dialog*. Both approaches, when used to study a particular phenomenon must ultimately be in agreement. They are akin to a double-entry bookkeeping system. Everything must add up.

If they are not in agreement, either something is wrong in the empirical measurement or the theoretical assumptions. This is what makes modern science "modern." One returns to the laboratory or the blackboard to get it right. When in agreement, it means that Nature has revealed another of her secrets. This answer then becomes the foundation upon which further investigation is possible. Progress in scientific understanding of a matter is like the movements of a ratchet. Each click locks in the previous work and advances the motion. All of this, of course, is very transparent. Publishing in journals, someone else wanting to further understand or challenge something is free to repeat the investigation.

The practice of science within human society involves many dialogs. The pure scientist dialogs with Nature and provides the applied scientist with the laws of Nature. In turn, the applied scientist provides the instrumentation used by the pure scientist as well as the technological devices used by society

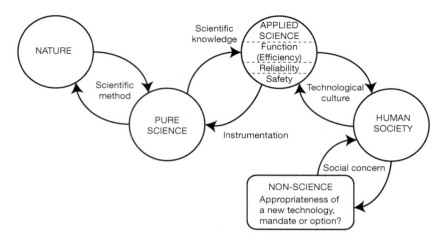

Figure 9.4   Some of the various dialogs associated with the scientific method.

as a whole. There are any number of such dialogs with respect to this such as functionality, reliability, safety and sustainability. Finally, we can identify one of the major problems of our day. How do you put in place a means to determine the *appropriateness* of a technological option? This of course is a question of values and not a question that can be answered solely by science. Since the nineteenth century, we have tended to equate "progress" only with material progress, which is closely linked to technological development. Currently, we tend, as a default in society, to treat all technological advances as if they were a *mandate* rather than an *option*. Much of the current ecological crisis stems from this failure. It should be obvious, that to fulfill the humanist vision the proper teaching of basic science and in particular the scientific method is absolutely essential to a true modern education.

The above, while truly illustrative of the power of science to dialog with Nature, is not the whole story. The astute observer may criticize this description of the scientific method for being *linear* or overly *deterministic*. However, historically this was the dominant view in science going into the twentieth century and an enormous amount of progress in terms of our understanding of the laws of Nature was accomplished by way of it. The industrial revolution is just one consequence of this. It is more accurate to say that the scientific method is a work in progress and most of the work of the past century has been a move beyond such strict determinism into the realm of *systems thinking*, also known as the *ecological paradigm*. Historically, quite a number of different thinkers from many different fields have contributed to its development, Jay Forrester (engineering, business), Margaret Mead (anthropology), John von Neumann (physics, mathematics), Norbert Wiener (robotics, mathematics), Richard Feynman (quantum mechanics) and Eugene Odum (ecology) among many others. One of the obvious points that should be made is that as an approach to knowledge, it is inherently interdisciplinary (Meadows, 2008, and Richmond, 2004) and provides a natural cross-disciplinary language.[16] Perhaps this is most easily visualized through ecology, where everything is understood to be *inter*-dependent. In other words, this paradigm is non-linear.

A *system* is a collection of parts (components, concepts, etc.) that in some sense work together. This new entity, the system, is more than the mere aggregate of its parts but typically exhibits *emergent* characteristics that are not easily predicted from just the study of its constituent parts. This sense of working together is what is meant by *synergy*.

For example, certain subatomic particles (the study realm of physics), the proton, electron and neutron, under the right conditions will spontaneously form an atom whose properties are different from its component particles. In turn, atoms can combine to form molecules (the study realm of chemistry). Certain complex carbon-based "organic" molecules give rise to the peculiar chemistry of earth known as life (the study realm of biology). Further, through evolutionary processes, organisms change, being influenced by and influencing their environment, giving rise to ecosystems (the study realm of ecology).

One thing should be immediately obvious from the above example. A system at one level can be a component of a system at another level. Typically there is a natural hierarchy associated with systems. Human engineering mimics Nature. Thus a bus which has many subsystems for components such as a seating system, a money-collection system, a propulsion system, a steering system, a braking system, an air-conditioning system, an emergency escape system, etc. is in turn a component of a public transportation system, etc.

The emergent properties of a system come not from the components but out of the complex of relationships between any two of them. Consider for example a system with only four components (C_i). In total there are six possible relationships (R_{ij}) among them. As one linearly adds components (4, 5, 6, 7, 8 ... 10 ... 20 ...), the count of relationships goes up exponentially (6, 10, 15, 21, 28 ... 45 ... 190 ...). Not all possible relationships are of equal strength. Systems-modeling is the art of mapping out the important relationships, identifying the essential or salient features to be explored, and comparing the calculated result to the bio-physical reality being modeled.

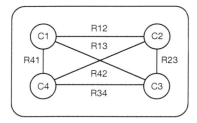

Figure 9.5 A simple system with only four components (C_i) can possibly have six relationships (R_{ij}) among them.

So what is really important is the *relationships*.

In a linear system, such as outlined above, there is a distinct relationship in a one to one mapping in which a *cause* leads to a resultant *effect*:

cause → effect.

An example would be a simple pendulum, a mass hanging from an effectively weightless line attached at the other end to a fixed point. With the line still stretched taut, the mass is displaced to one side and then released. The pendulum swings with a regular period. The measurable (and actually predictable) period is the effect of the combined forces of constraint (along the line) and gravity, which collectively are the cause. More precisely, the period is the *dependent* variable (effect) while the length of the line and the strength of gravity are the *independent* variables (cause). This sort of phenomenon is easily modeled in such a linear way.

Much can be learned with such a tool but not everything is so simple (or linear).

In systems thinking, the distinction between cause and effect is blurred in the sense that both may have a bit of both characteristics (see Richmond, 2004, and Meadows, 2008, for detailed discussions of this). This is feedback. In other words, they are *inter*-dependent:

cause ↔ effect.

Here part of the effect is fed back to the cause, which in turn drives the effect, and so on *ad infinitum*. It is inherently non-linear.

In a typical systems model, there are two kinds of feedback depending upon the "sense," positive or negative, of what is fed back. A positive feedback system is one in which the effect is fed to the cause in the *same* sense. Thus the output (effect) increases over time, in fact it increases exponentially. A common term for this is the "snowball effect." All explosions are characterized by this. Avalanches, compound interest, inflation, consumer growth economies and unchecked human population growth are all examples of this. They all reinforce or magnify a trend over time. From a systems view, they are *destabilizing*. If you had a marble and an inverted bowl, the marble would roll off:

cause ↔ + effect.

In contrast, a negative feedback system is *stabilizing*. It comes about when the effect is fed to the cause in the *opposite* sense. Here, the marble would roll back and forth within the bowl eventually dampening down to a standstill:

cause ↔ − effect.

Unfortunately, we run into the problem of daily use of language again. In physics, "negative feedback" is a good thing for it lends stability to a system.

However in everyday and social science use, the same words communicate a less than positive attitude in terms of criticism ("don't give me that negative feedback ..."), which may be a bad thing.

Actually, the simple pendulum is also an example of negative feedback from the point of view of energy. At the bottom of a swing, the energy is pure kinetic (i.e. energy of motion) which through inertia carries the swinging mass uphill against gravity. At the peak of a swing, the mass comes to a stop and the energy is all potential (i.e. energy of position), and reversing direction the mass falls due to gravity. The potential energy is the cause of the buildup of kinetic energy, which in turn is the cause of the buildup of the potential energy. The sense of such a feedback loop is negative (it reverses direction) and the motion stabilizes about a set point, the bottom of the swing.

Most complex systems are a combination of both positive and negative feedback loops allowing for dynamic change within the system while the system as a whole does not run away. As pointed out above, systems manifest emergent properties. Typically these are not predictable from the properties of the individual components. Educationally the beauty and point of all of this is that such complexity can be readily modeled using a personal computer!

To summarize, in a very real sense, when the scientist enters their laboratory, observatory, or study site or stands before a blackboard, he or she is approaching the Oracle attempting to divine Nature. The scientific method is a far more reliable and less ambiguous guide for human society than the Oracle of Delphi ever was. In the modern world, we ignore the Oracle of Science to our great detriment. How can a modern person make the claim that they are "educated" if they do not have at least a working knowledge of the scientific method? Perhaps even deeper, how can one claim to have had a truly *humanistic* education, when science is such a perfect example of the humanist approach, without being at least minimally conversant in science and its method? In a world of exponentially exploding technology driven in large measure by an understanding through science, how can one competently help solve problems, both personal and societal, without a fundamental understanding of the thought process of science?

Pedagogy and learning to learn

Having made and supported the claim that science is not to be viewed as separate or in contrast to the humanities but instead fundamentally a product and driver of the humanistic tradition, we then looked at its way of relating to the world, the scientific method. In this final section, we will now take up the question of pedagogy and how the way of thinking called "science" can be taught in the general education classroom.

Experience shows that in Hong Kong students tend to come to enter the university with three major hurdles to overcome. First, like freshman students virtually anywhere, the *study habits* that they have developed in high school are generally not appropriate for effective university study. This is particularly true in Hong Kong where the secondary education culture is so greatly focused on beating the test rather than on learning to engage material for deep understanding. With "3+3+4" the planned reduction from two major public exams (the HKCEE and HKALE), preparation for which takes up three to four years out of seven to just one exam (the new HKDSE) at the end of Form 6 is intended to be an improvement but one has doubts. Liberal studies is supposed to introduce other aspects of assessment than just exams but it is superimposed on a pre-existing and deeply entrenched exam culture. Without uprooting that culture, how can one expect fundamental change? One often hears the use of language that describes either liberal studies (or general education in the university) as if it were just another subject to be mastered rather than an alternative approach to education. Real change will have to come about in the university setting.

Second, this same educational system does not emphasize reading and writing so too many students enter the university with *inadequate literacy*. This is true in their native Chinese yet alone in English. The problem of deficient literacy is compounded by the use of a second language but it is fundamentally an attitude first nurtured in their native language. Again, much of this can be blamed because of the exam culture orientation. The attitude is "if it is not on the exam, it is not worth pursuing."

Third, coming from a Confucian background, there is a general tendency to not engage in an effective questioning process. I have experienced this in common over the decades with students in Korea, Hawai'i, Japan, and Hong Kong. In such a system, the teacher may be venerated and is certainly not questioned. In practice, instead of engaging in *questioning* the attitude is to "shut up and listen to honorable teacher." Well at least pretend to listen.

Thus I plan activities not just to engage course content but to encourage behaviors which are designed simultaneously to overcome these three obstacles. I design a course to empower students by leading them on a journey whose overarching goal is for them to discover their capabilities. I attempt this through a cyclic process of *enquiry, awareness,* and *reflection.*

Let's start with *enquiry*, something which is natural for science, but which by no means has a monopoly. My first lecture is designed to give students an

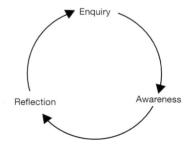

Figure 9.6　The *EAR* cycle (are you listening?).

understanding of what we hope to accomplish together during the course of the semester (i.e. the "thing") and how we will go about it (i.e. the "process"). As an example of enquiry, I identify some of the most common teaching and learning activities (TLAs) that they will encounter during the semester, most notably lecture, tutorial, self-study, team-study and examination (among others). I am then liable to randomly approach a student and ask them to describe in their own words what they understand a lecture to be. Typically I get a structural response such as "it is a meeting of the whole class." After thanking them and making a complimentary comment such as "OK, that's certainly part of it," I then use that response to open up greater *awareness* of opportunities for success and failure and with that some understanding of expectations. For example much of their self-study and team-study will be devoted to reading and discussion of that reading so I tell my students that in coming to lecture they have a choice to come either confused or confused.

Are you confused?

The "good" kind of confusion occurs when a student makes one or two preliminary or "quick" reads of the assigned material before attending lecture. In Hong Kong, there is a prevailing student culture that avoids reading. This makes it very hard to teach something of any substance if the student expectation is to only engage the material while physically in the classroom, with little or no advanced preparation. Thus, central to all of my classes is some mandatory reading. Lectures adhere closely to this material but I do not shoot for coverage. Instead, I focus on the fundamental parts and what experience and student feedback over the years have made me aware of as the perceived hard parts, with the rest of the material left for students to pick up on their own and in peer discussion (team-study).

I consciously model for them in class how to go about the process of doing a "quick" read and not getting bogged down in a time- and energy-consuming process. Probably well over 95 percent of my students are working in English as a second language, and obviously reading can be an extra challenge at first, especially if they are not accustomed to substantive reading in their first language. So we need to practice it. Having said that, however, by having something substantial to read which they know well will be a major part of what is to be assessed, it gives them a means by which to study on their own at their own pace without necessarily having to keep pace with the lecture should their command of English not be quite up to it.

The approach is simple. I tell them to experiment a bit with respect to the amount of time they devote to a quick read so that it will not be unending, perhaps 45 minutes or an hour. What does not work is a detailed read in which the student spends a huge amount of time looking up words in a dictionary and writing tiny little Chinese characters between the lines. Too often, especially if the word has a technical meaning, the dictionary will mislead. Some of the books I use have a built-in glossary and students are to use that. Others do not, so I supply students with a weekly handout, in advance, which includes such a glossary. Demonstrating the approach in the lecture, I get them to read the first sentence of every paragraph then jump to the next paragraph to do the same. I tell them to carefully read each subtopic heading as well as all table and figure captions. This way they are introduced to the flow of the text, the most important ideas and much of the specific vocabulary. Should they have time, they are to make a second pass the night before the lecture doing exactly the same as before, only this time adding the last sentence of every paragraph.

I then pose a question to the class, a chance for some *reflection.* "In coming to lecture with such preparation, will you be an expert on the material?" "Of course not, but you will have some idea as to what the lecture is about and how it fits in with everything else." Thus, when I am lecturing the student will be in a position to gain something meaningful from the lecture because unconsciously and occasionally consciously there are liable to be many unanswered questions in mind that will begin to be answered by the lecture. After the lecture, ideally within 36 or 48 hours, the student is finally directed to do a detailed reading of the material, which is now so much easier because she or he has been exposed to the material two or three times already. Gradually meaning is constructed.

Contrast this with the "bad" kind of confusion in which the student does not do any of this simple preparation work and finds themself instead trying to follow a lecture on material which they have no idea about, presented by a lecturer probably talking too fast in a foreign language! After three weeks they are overwhelmed and give up. That is not a recipe for success.

Because Hong Kong is such an extreme exam culture, I cannot ignore the problem it presents to effective education, so I use the exam experience itself as a major TLA. To begin with, I do not subscribe to the use of a comprehensive final exam. This can be a very good assessment tool in more advanced studies, challenging students equipped with high literacy to integrate everything they have experienced during the course of the semester. But with exam-cram-oriented freshman students lacking adequate literacy it does not really assess anything. Instead I make use of continuous assessment to expose students to effective study habits. Part of that continuous assessment consists of three multiple-choice/ short-answer midterm quizzes. The potential disadvantage of such an exam is that it may be difficult for the student to show an ability to apply their understanding to a novel situation, although this is not entirely impossible, depending upon how you word the questions. However, since the quizzes are only part of the overall assessment, other opportunities exist to evidence understanding. The overwhelming advantage is that I can grade the quiz in a short time and give feedback to the students. Typically the first quiz is given in the fourth week after an introductory lecture and two lectures devoted to the scientific method.

Thus by the fifth week, approximately a third into the semester, I can identify students who may be having difficulty studying and encourage them to come and see me for a one-on-one conversation. I find those meetings some of the most important educational experiences of all, for there we can explore together just how the student has gone about the process of studying. Many misperceptions are set aside and a dialog begun, which continues for the remainder of the semester and in some cases for years afterward. Often the discussion will be a review of their attitude and approach towards reading and a reiteration of how it and the lecture support each other, with active questioning throughout. To help this along, in terms of the quizzes, I count only the best two out of three. This way exam-oriented students have been given the equivalent of a mock exam and they will be comfortable with the format for the remainder of the semester. The silly concern, that the good students will skip the last quiz and only need to study about two-thirds of the material, I have found in practice to never materialize. Since they are good students, they seem compelled to show up. I am far more concerned about the struggling student.

Tutorials, of course, are smaller class settings. I use these aggressively to further the insight that mere lecture and reading alone will not easily provide. Students are divided early in the semester into small study teams. They will at some point facilitate a peer-run tutorial discussion but more importantly they are expected to meet outside the classroom at least once a week for an hour or so (during lunch?) to discuss everything and anything concerning the class. As a team they fill in a simple form which tells me who met when and where and what was discussed. Most importantly, they are encouraged to write out questions they may still have after discussion. These are collected weekly in lecture. Especially when I find that the same question appears on multiple forms I will make a point of including a response to it in the following lecture. Participating students find these peer discussions very useful for what one student may have understood another may not (Wieman, 2007). They have been particularly useful in working with mainland Chinese students, who, coming from single-child families, are not as accustomed as Hong Kong students to working together.

Contrary to what is often done in tutorials, I do not emphasize presentation skills. I am sure that this is well covered elsewhere. Instead I emphasize depth of understanding and thus self-empowerment. In my astronomy class, students are assigned yet another chapter in the book which will not be covered in lecture. It is expected that everyone has attempted to read the chapter and the facilitating student team, after a brief five-minute topical introduction, spends the rest of the hour throwing out review questions to the sitting teams to respond to in a competitive/cooperative environment. In my ecology class, which is typically taught in the Spring semester so that attending students have had at least one semester of university experience under their belts, we work instead on computer models of ecosystems in which once the facilitating team has introduced the canonical model the sitting teams get to struggle with a series of "what if ..." questions based in changes to the model, gradually building up something of a systems-thinking intuition. In sum, the entire tutorial experience is one of deep participatory enquiry, not boring presentation – very active!

To further encourage questioning, individually on a weekly basis, students are expected to fill in a form, which familiarizes them with the process and utility of questioning.[17] One such form is called the Learning Review Table. It consists of three columns. The first is used to write down a question on that week's lecture that the student is sure they know the answer to. The second is to write down a question they do not know the answer to. The third is to write down a question which goes beyond what the student has been exposed to. Later in the semester I switch to the Questioning Guide, in which a student is expected to write down a topical question and then after a spell assess it in terms of two criteria. The first scale is from mere recalling information to integrating information. The second scale is from mere focus on a topic to going beyond (not off) the topic. Finally they are to rephrase their question so as to improve either or both criteria. Handed in weekly, these make up part of the student's participation grade.

Much is made in educational circles of *active learning* and lectures in particular are given a very bad press. It is as if the lecture is the absolute epitome of how not to go about the process of education and is to be avoided at all cost. Well, it is true that a lecture can be deadly boring and used as a dumping ground to claim "coverage" of a seemingly unintegrated laundry list of topics. In contrast, my wife, who comes from Hong Kong but completed all of her university education clean through her PhD in the USA, often comments that it is hard to beat a good lecture, one that *engages* your mind. I find the wholesale criticism of the lecture format another false dichotomy. It all depends upon attitude and preparation.

The reality check is that whether we like it or not, administrators love lectures because they are cheap, one teacher and a hundred (or many more) students. So in practice, how do you instill active learning in such a seemingly passive environment? I would say the first part is to communicate the connection outlined above between preparatory reading and the lecture. Some will do it and some will not, but after the first quiz and a series of one-on-one conversations with students who obviously did not, I get much higher participation.

There are some simple structural things that can be done. For example, it is a really good idea to open a lecture, especially as students may still be drifting in a bit late, with a question-and-answer session. If there are no questions, fine, but at least the students know that the opportunity was afforded them. Next, I make sure that there is a brief review of the previous lecture, perhaps just a couple of slides. If at all possible, include a break halfway through. You need it and so do your students. You will get fewer students spontaneously heading for the rest room if they can anticipate that there is a break coming and thus less interruption of the class. It is also another opportunity to service student questions.

As long as the material is being covered in a rigorous way (i.e. the brain needs to be engaged) there is nothing wrong with making it entertaining. In science, this is particularly easy to do through the use of simple demonstrations. Often I turn these into a magic show of sorts, having a "pretty assistant" come up on the stage to help me out. There are a lot of opportunities for humor. Much is made of technological innovations to help out in the lecture environment, of "blended learning" and the like, but what I find really useful in practice is the use of the Personal Response System.[18] It has been around now for about a decade and consists of three major components. First, there is a logging program running on the teacher's laptop computer. Second, there is a receiver, which communicates with the logging program. Finally, each student is issued a "clicker" that on response uniquely identifies the student. Similar to an infrared TV controller, the student chooses a numerical or letter answer to a question posed and the logger program captures this and summarizes the overall class results. Students see a display that indicates participation but not the answer selected. Once a run is made, the system automatically displays a statistical summary of the answers. This gives both the lecturer and students real-time feedback on understanding.

There are quite a number of games that can be played with this to good effect often opening up dialog among students in the lecture.[19] Typically I will run three such sessions during a two-hour lecture. It should be obvious again that there is great emphasis here on questioning. The logger program keeps track of all of the individual responses, so should a student be having consistent difficulty the lecturer has something to dialog with the student about.

To summarize, I visualize the mass lecture general science class as having three legs. First and foremost in terms of content, I emphasize the *scientific method*. It is the basis of all thinking in science and its evolving development and application are a direct example of *humanitas*. Second, there is a *content focus* such as astronomy, ecology or the like in which throughout the rest of the semester, with the aid of the scientific method, the principles and major discoveries of the subject matter are explored. Students become empowered with respect to science as a way of thinking. Finally, underlying the entire study, understanding full well that most of my students are under-equipped for effective university study, is the conscious introduction of literacy and study-habit reflection – *lifelong learning*, which potentially empowers students for the rest of their university career and beyond.

It should be obvious that such an approach to general education subject design is not necessarily exclusive to science. Altogether, here the class is a system for cultivating human potential.

To conclude, the meta-goal of all education is empowerment and the very word "education" tells us this. It comes to us from the Latin *e* (out of) + *ducare* (lead, channel, duct), meaning "to lead out." Thus the notion is that one is led out of a smaller world into a larger one. Mastering a teaching one is *empowered* to apply it to the challenges of life. In the best humanist tradition, science is not an exception to the human potential movement; it is a perfect example of it, one among others. The only reason why in the minds of some science is separate from the humanities is taught ignorance, the result of an education system that teaches such a separation. It certainly is not fundamentally or historically true. We need to stop teaching what is not true! In a world increasingly dominated by technology, which is driven by science; this is not only foolish, it is dangerous. Major reform is needed here, but it ought to be simple.

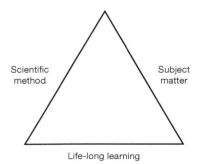

Figure 9.7 Summary of a general education science class.

Notes

1 Snow's concern stemmed from the observation that the British educational system over-rewarded Latin and Greek studies in contrast to science and engineering, just the opposite of what is common today throughout the world.

2 The "entropy" law, which says that in a closed system, i.e. one in which matter and energy cannot enter or leave, the system spontaneously moves in the direction of ever greater disorder. This is what gives us the sense of "time's arrow." Entropy is the measure of disorder. The Second Law is considered to be one of the most fundamental tenets in all of science.

3 Perhaps the confusion goes all the way back to Caesar's contemporary Cicero (106–43BCE), who as a Roman orator emphasized a sort of expanded (what would much later be called the) *trivium* adding poetry, history and moral philosophy to grammar and rhetoric while dropping logic and ignoring the *quadrivium* (see below). However, even Cicero wrote a poem on visiting Sicily praising the humanity of the mathematician-physicist Archimedes, in sharp contrast to his compatriot the tyrant Dionysius the Elder (Jaeger, 2002).

4 Not to be confused with Pythagoras, who is also a good candidate for a Greek progenitor.

5 This was only settled in 1582 with the promulgation of the modern calendar of Pope Gregory XIII.

6 Modern psychologists call such a sudden realization the "Copernican effect."

7 You just need to explain, which Galileo did, why no one "feels" those motions. Such an explanation was the beginning of modern science and of physics in particular.

8 Burnt alive at the stake on 17 February, 1600 for among other things advocating the Copernican model.

9 He was twice tried (in 1616 and 1633) by the same Holy Roman Inquisition which had tried Bruno again ostensibly for advocating the Copernican model. The second time he was condemned to life in prison (mitigated to house arrest due to his advanced age), with all of his written and future works placed on the Index of Prohibited Books along with the work of Copernicus.

10 The title of Copernicus' great work is *De revolutionibus orbium coelestium* [On the Revolutions of the Celestial Spheres], giving rise to the modern use of the word "revolution."

11 Karl Popper (1934) was one of the first to point this out. In the pure sciences, you cannot really prove anything but you can disprove a hypothesis. All you need to do is find one exception. A hypothesis, potentially open to experimental attack in some cases for centuries, such as the notion that gravity is an attractive force, is liable to eventually be accepted as a theoretical principle. The language and thinking of science is far more conservative than that of banking.

12 He was convinced that Copernicus must be wrong about the motions of the earth but as one of the truly modern minds in science, he felt that careful observation of Nature would settle the matter.

13 Kepler used Brahe's extensive data to show that Copernicus was right about the motions of the earth after all! It is not the opinion of the individual that counts but rather the very nature of Nature.

14 "Science is not a substitute for common sense but an extension of it" (Quine, 1957, p. 229). Further, Quine claims that the scientist "is indistinguishable from the common man in his sense of evidence, except that the scientist is more careful" (p. 233).

15 This sense of "dialog" goes right to the heart of the matter. Galileo's famous oblique defense of Copernicus (1632) was titled a *Dialogue Concerning the Two Chief World Systems* [*Dialogo sopra i due massimi sistemi del mondo*] which Italian colleagues of mine claim was written on par with some of the works of Shakespeare. The pope's reaction to this was to send him to the Holy Roman Inquisition for the second time.

16 In our modern complex world, it is rather rare when a problem neatly falls solely within the narrow confines of a single discipline. Systems thinking allows practitioners of different disciplines to effectively work together. In fact it is so fundamental and useful that I predict that in this century it will eventually be as ubiquitous in the education system as algebra is today.

17 These were developed about a decade ago as part of the Hong Kong Polytechnic University's Learning to Learn Project (see http://www.polyu.edu.hk/learn-to-learn/teacher/_frontpage/index.html).

18 See http://www.einstruction.com/products/student-response-systems/cps-ir for a current example of such a system.

19 When you insist on its use, it is also an efficient means of taking attendance.

References

The American Heritage College Dictionary (2006). 4th edn. (Boston: Houghton Mifflin).

Bronowski, Jacob (1973). *The Ascent of Man* (Boston: Little, Brown).

Campbell, Joseph (1988). *The Power of Myth* (New York: Doubleday).

de Santillana, Giorgio (1955). *The Crime of Galileo* (Chicago: University of Chicago Press).

Galilei, Galileo (1615). *Letter to the Grand Duchess Christina.*

Hardin, Garrett. (1993). *Living within Limits: Ecology, Economics, and Population Taboos* (New York: Oxford University Press).

Jaeger, Mary (2002). "Cicero and Archimedes' Tomb." *Journal of Roman Studies*, 92: 51–52.

Kuhn, Thomas (1970). *The Structure of Scientific Revolutions*, 2nd edn. (Chicago: University of Chicago Press).

Marcus Aurelius (2002). *Meditations*, trans. Gregory Hays (New York: Modern Library) (written *c.* 180–170BCE).

Meadows, Donella H. (2008). *Thinking in Systems: A Primer* (White River Junction, VT: Chelsea Green).

Popper, Karl (1934). *Logik der Forschung* [The Logic of Scientific Discovery]. (Tübingen, Germany: Mohr Siebeck).

Popper, Karl (1972). *Conjectures and Refutations: The Growth of Scientific Knowledge*, 4th edn. (London: Routledge & Kegan Paul).

Quine, Willard Van Orman (1957). "The Scope and Language of Science." *British Journal of the Philosophy of Science*, 8: 1–17.

Richmond, Barry (2004). *Introduction to Systems Thinking* (Lebanon, NH: isee systems).

Snow, Charles Percy (1960). *The Two Cultures* (Cambridge: Cambridge University Press).

Wieman, Carl (2007). "Why Not Try – A Scientific Approach to Science Education?" *Change* September/October: 9–15. Online. Available HTTP: <http://www.cwsei.ubc.ca/index.html>

10 Bridging two cultures

Designing Chinese medicine as a general education course

Fan Ka-wai

Introduction

In 2012, Hong Kong's university system will change from a three-year to a four-year curriculum, so each student will have to take more credits – including general education credits – to fulfill the graduation requirements. Accordingly, general education (GE) will play an increasingly important role in students' college careers. While each university defines and designs GE courses differently, to implement their respective missions and promote their values, generally speaking these courses should not be too specialized and should be suitable for students from any discipline. GE courses help students acquire the skills or abilities essential to university-level learning.[1] Stanford University introduces students to a broad range of fields and areas of study within the humanities, social sciences, natural sciences, applied sciences and technology. Research on GE course design thus emphasizes that such courses should offer diverse and sometimes interdisciplinary perspectives.

In his well-known *The Two Cultures and the Scientific Revolution*, C. P. Snow argues that two cultures – the sciences and the humanities – have been formed in modern society, with a great gap between them.[2] Similar gaps divide Chinese and Western cultures, even after a century of attention to communication between the two cultures.[3] However, bridges should and can be built to reduce these gaps. In my opinion, teaching Chinese medicine as a general education course can achieve both goals, bridging science and the humanities as well as China and the West.

Course goals: bridging two cultures

When students hear the term "Chinese medicine," they may well assume that the course is about diagnosing and treating diseases, and taught by medical doctors. This is understandable, as many students only know Chinese medicine as a medical system rooted in China and used by Chinese people. However, Chinese medicine can also be profitably examined from historical, anthropological, sociological and other perspectives. As a general education course, the aim of "Chinese medicine" is assuredly *not* to train students to treat diseases or to become Chinese medical doctors. Instead, the course should appeal to students with a broad range of interests and disciplinary training. As mentioned above, the primary course aim is to communicate between science and the humanities, and between Chinese and Western culture, by using interdisciplinary tools and techniques. According to the US National Science Foundation, interdisciplinary courses seek to "integrate information, data, techniques, tools, perspectives, concepts, and/or theories from two or more disciplines." Trinity Western University (British Columbia, Canada) likewise suggests that interdisciplinary study should "encourage dialogue across traditional academic boundaries." Specifically, in the proposed course students from the sciences, arts or social sciences may express viewpoints from their own disciplines in the classroom, and share their ideas with classmates from different disciplines.

Proposed pedagogical approach: problem-based learning

How can we achieve this mission? One option is the problem-based learning (PBL) model. Many studies demonstrate that PBL is an effective way to teach students from multiple disciplines.[4] As designed by Dr. Howard Barrows, the PBL curriculum consists of carefully selected and designed problems that demand from the learner acquisition of critical knowledge, problem-solving proficiency, self-directed learning strategies and team-participation skills.[5] In my proposed design, PBL would allow teachers to present students with a series of problems, and encourage them to share their respective viewpoints through teaching and learning activities.[6] A dialogue-focused pedagogy would work best here, rather than a standard lecture.[7] At the same time, though, after discussion students would have to search for and analyze further information individually, and express their findings and opinions in subsequent classes. This process will actively involve students in their learning.

Any interdisciplinary course requires a knowledgeable teacher, and this course is no exception. However, since no one knows everything, for the course to cross traditional disciplines, a team of teachers should be formed from different departments. It would hardly achieve the course aims if only one professor was to teach his own knowledge in the classroom, but two or more teachers presenting their knowledge through dialogue would be more effective. Students should also be encouraged to participate in the class, because the dialogue should not just go one way, and they can exchange viewpoints from different disciplines at the same time.

Proposed course contents

The course contents would be divided into three parts: basic concepts and knowledge of Chinese medicine; Chinese medicine in everyday use; and Chinese medicine in the world. All three parts should be connected to students' experience. Asking good questions – not too difficult, and not too easy – is central to the PBL method. Ideally, these questions should lead students to think about the set readings or other information collected from the Internet. Open-ended questions are necessary, and students from different disciplines may be grouped together in order to discuss questions.

Basic concepts and knowledge of Chinese medicine

In the first part of the course, I plan to inspire students to think about the nature of Chinese medicine. It is inevitable that students have to know some basic concepts and have some basic knowledge. The first question, then, is what is Chinese medicine? This question is very difficult to answer. Chinese medicine is a medical system which has been practiced from ancient times to the present. Actually, students in Hong Kong already know that herbs and acupuncture are the most important and common ways to treat diseases in Chinese medicine. However, they do not know what a Chinese medicine student should learn. Fortunately, there are three universities in Hong Kong that currently offer coursework in Chinese medicine: the Chinese University of Hong Kong, the University of Hong Kong and the Baptist University of Hong Kong. Students should start by visiting the program websites and integrating the information about program requirements. Obviously, students will note that Chinese medicine students take three kinds of courses: conventional medicine or Western medicine (including anatomy, pathology and pharmacology); Chinese medicine; and clinical training.

As these requirements demonstrate, Chinese and Western medicine are two different medical systems. Students should thus discuss two issues: (1) Why does a third of a Chinese medicine program cover Western medicine? (2) Western medicine is based on scientific, medical and clinical research. Is Chinese medicine based on the same approach? During their discussion, students will find out that Chinese medicine is based on philosophical systems (the theories of Yin–Yang, five phases and Qi); they will learn about the view of the body (Zhongfu [internal organs system], meridians and acupoints) in Chinese medicine; the causes of diseases, diagnosis treatments, and so on. The basic concepts and treatment methods in Chinese medicine are different from those in Western medicine. So, a further question is: can we use Western medicine to understand Chinese medical concepts? Why or why not? Furthermore, if we think science represents Western culture and Chinese philosophy represents Chinese culture, is Chinese medicine integrated within two cultures?

Students should also consider that a hundred years ago there was no need for a Chinese medical doctor to learn about Western medicine. This leads naturally into a discussion of the history of the transmission of Western medicine in China. Specifically, Chairman Mao Zedong proposed a very important national medical policy, which was to integrate Chinese and Western medicine after 1949.[8] Because of this policy, Chinese medical doctors have to learn both Chinese and Western medicine, and sometimes doctors of Chinese medicine and Western medicine work together to diagnose a patient. More specifically, the history of the development of Chinese medicine in Hong Kong may also be helpful for this discussion. After 1949, the Hong Kong colonial government stressed the need for developing Western medicine, but at the same time, it adopted a policy of non-intervention in the practice of Chinese medicine. Since competition with Western medicine, which enjoyed quasi-official status, was severe, the social status of Chinese medicine practitioners plummeted and they were subject to discrimination. In short, Chinese medicine was left alone to run its course.[9]

Of course, the historical view of Chinese medicine goes back farther than 1949. From ancient times to the present day, learning Chinese medical canons, such as *Huandi nanjing*, *Shang han lun* and *Shennong bencaojing*, have been the most critical way to learn Chinese medicine. These medical canons, written a thousand years ago, are included in the curriculum and regarded as important reading materials. This fact raises another question for discussion: why are these ancient medical canons studied when learning Chinese medicine? It also implies that medical students should have a good knowledge of ancient Chinese. Again, the Chinese medicine program websites will be helpful here.

In summary, students should understand that "Chinese medicine" may be viewed in terms of several disciplines, including medical science, history and philosophy. Likewise, traditional scientific subjects including biology and chemistry are also applied in Chinese medicine, but students should think about what aspects of these subjects are applied.

Chinese medicine in everyday use

In 2006, the State Council of the PRC announced that herbal tea was included on the list of National Level Intangible Cultural Heritage. Indeed, students in Hong Kong may have seen Chinese medicine clinics, and they may even have consulted Chinese medical doctors. Even those who have not visited them, though, likely drink herbal tea (涼茶). Since herbal tea is a particularly visible part of Chinese medicine throughout the world, the second part of the course will concentrate on discussing issues related to it. Herbal tea has been popular in Guangdong province for a thousand years. Many kinds of herbal tea are popular in Hong Kong, such as 24 herbs tea, 5 flowers tea, Canton love-pes vine tea, chrysanthemum tea, and so forth. Because of the hot and humid climate in Guangdong, Cantonese people are used to drinking herbal tea to expel heat and humidity from the body. Drinking herbal tea is part of the wisdom of traditional Chinese medicine. It is also believed that drinking herbal tea is good for general health.

One useful exercise here might involve cataloging how many kinds of herbal tea are popular in Hong Kong. In Hong Kong, students can buy cans or bottles of herbal tea in supermarkets and convenience stores, or they can drink it at a Chinese herbal tea shop. Students would have to record as many kinds of herbal tea as they can find. They may also note that different kinds of herbal tea may have different effects on the body. They should also do some research among their classmates and friends on how often they drink herbal tea and what kinds of tea are most popular. Through this activity, students learn the basic skills of conducting a social survey; those in the social sciences, of course, can offer their classmates more specific knowledge on how to gather and use survey data.

Students are always interested in why herbal tea is classified as a National Level Intangible Cultural Heritage; a combination of lecture and videos can give further details. Herbal tea is big business in China, and its sales volume is higher than that of Coca-Cola. In mainland China, herbal tea is defined as a food. Therefore, herbal tea companies in China cannot claim that herbal tea can heal any disease. However, students can investigate what strategies these companies use to promote their products. Students should search the websites of these companies in order to analyze the advertisements and slogans. How do these companies use Chinese medical concepts to promote herbal tea? Social science and business-oriented perspectives will be particularly valuable here.

The most important issue for students to consider in this part of the course is that Chinese medicine is still part of Chinese culture.[10] Many Chinese medical concepts are still used today. Furthermore, it is very common in Hong Kong for healthcare products to promote Chinese medical concepts, or to be made from Chinese herbs. Chinese medicine is a valuable resource for business in Chinese societies, including mainland China, Hong Kong and Taiwan. The question is, how do you use it?

Chinese medicine in the world

Do only Chinese people learn about and use Chinese medicine? Many students have never considered this issue. How can English-speaking people understand Chinese medicine? These questions lead to the third part of the course. To start discussion, students will examine two websites: the National Center for Complementary and Alternative Medicine (Maryland, USA), and the homepage for the *American Journal of Chinese Medicine*. As students will learn from the first site, in the USA Chinese medicine is classified as "complementary and alternative medicine." Why might this be so? Similarly, the second site reveals how medical experts and scientists conduct research on Chinese medicine in such fields as herbology, the effectiveness of acupuncture and *Taichi*. Students from college of sciences should participate actively in this part, because they can help explain the scientific methods and terms related to biology, chemistry and biochemistry. There is no need for students to read research articles in detail, as the teacher can provide supplementary materials.

Acupuncture, which gained attention in the USA after former President Richard Nixon visited China in 1972, can be a useful discussion topic here. At the time of Nixon's visit, acupuncture was regarded as an amusing treatment method. But now, many US states and European countries accept acupuncture as an "official" treatment and license qualified acupuncturists to provide services. There are many acupuncture associations in the USA and Europe. Students need to investigate these associations on the Internet in order to learn about their missions and activities and to prepare for in-class discussions on how Americans use Chinese medicine to treat diseases. Some scientists and medical experts refuse to adopt any Chinese medical concepts or methods to treat diseases, and students should explore the positive and negative effects of using Chinese medicine.[11] In my view, a person's personal experience of Chinese medicine is a critical factor in developing an attitude toward it. Upon completion of the course, students should rethink the opening question: "What is Chinese medicine?" Chinese medicine is not just a medical system, and many students will find that it is not far removed from their own lives.

Logistical challenges

This course is designed to communicate with different students from different disciplines through discussions on Chinese medicine. It offers several interdisciplinary benefits, as outlined above, and should also include training in oral presentations, effective writing and critical thinking. I believe that students will learn these skills through dialogue with teachers and with their classmates. Because of the interdisciplinary nature of the course, it is difficult to find a textbook that matches well with its content. Fortunately, *A Comprehensive Guide to Chinese Medicine* (ed. Ping-Chung Leung, Charlie Changli Xue and Yung-Chi Cheng) covers many aspects of the course.[12] I recommend it to my students and to anyone interested in teaching this course.

To move forward with this course design, though, two potential logistical difficulties should be kept in mind. First, as mentioned above, an interdisciplinary course requires a team of knowledgeable teachers. As far as I know, departments or offices of general education in Hong Kong universities do not organize such teams on their own, so course organizers would need to do so independently. It can be a challenge to find a group of teachers who are interested in and have conducted research on Chinese medicine or related topics, from different disciplinary angles, all in the same university.

Second, students have to do independent and self-directed study before coming to the classroom. PBL requires that students work cooperatively in small groups to provide solutions or insights to problems. My ideal design groups two or three students from different disciplines together. Each group will work as a team to collect the information, read the materials and present its members' viewpoints. Of course, real enrollment situations may not always match this ideal design, because students have the freedom to take any GE course. If too many students come from the same college or field, my ideal design may not be workable.

Conclusion and next steps

Using the proposed general education course on Chinese medicine as an example, this chapter has shown the vast and varied support needs for an ideal interdisciplinary course. Today, Hong Kong universities are placed in a very competitive environment. They need to attract more good students, to upgrade their rankings in the lists of top universities in the world and to obtain more resources. It hardly seems worth allocating more resources or staffing to develop general education, even though students need to take more general education courses, especially since designing a good general education curriculum is not an easy task.

Given these pressures, I want to close by raising three points for further discussion. First, I believe that general education should not consist of a set of unrelated courses. A university should reflect on the purposes of general education, and on what vision they use to design GE courses. Otherwise, GE will ultimately become a set of disorderly and confused courses to be carved up by different departments. Second, what is the role of a university's office of general education? Should it only organize the GE courses offered by different departments, or should it bear more active responsibility? What should it do or not do? Third and lastly, universities should offer very clear explanations of the purpose and value of GE courses. Otherwise, students will keep complaining that GE courses are simply not interesting, and regard them as just another school requirement – or worse, as a burden on their college careers.

Notes

1 The website of the National University of Singapore states, "First, they are general in the sense that they aim at those aspects of knowledge and abilities that we expect of educated individuals in general, not the knowledge and abilities that are required in the specialization in a particular discipline or profession. Second, they aim at education in the sense that they seek to inculcate higher-order qualities of the mind and intellect that make a person educated, as opposed to the practical know-how and abilities that might be useful in one's daily life or contribute to success in career." Similarly, Harvard University's website states, "The Program in General Education introduces students to subject matter and skills from across the University, and does so in ways that link the arts and sciences with the 21st century world that students will face and the lives they will lead after college."

2 C. P. Snow, *The Two Cultures and the Scientific Revolution* (Cambridge: Cambridge University Press, 1964). Snow's book has been in print for well over 50 years. The debate about the two cultures is very much alive. See Lawrence M. Krauss, "An Update on C. P. Snow's 'Two Cultures'." *Scientific American*, August 2009, p. 39.

3 Wang Jisi and Zou Sicheng, "Civilizations: Clash or Fusion?" *Beijing Review*, 39(3) (1996): 15–21.

4 See Barbara J. Duch, Susan E. Groh and Deborah E. Allen (eds.), *The Power of Problem-Based Learning: A Practical "How To" for Teaching Undergraduate Courses in any Discipline* (Sterling, VA: Stylus Publishing, 2001).

5 Howard S. Barrows and Wee Keng Neo Lynda, *Principles and Practice of a PBL* (Singapore: Pearson-Prentice Hall, 2007).

6 For details see <http://www.studygs.net/pblhandbook.pdf>.

7 Nicholas Burbules and Bertram Bruce, "Theory and Research on Teaching as Dialogue." Online. Available HTTP: <http://faculty.ed.uiuc.edu/burbules/papers/dialogue.html>.

8 Volker Scheid, *Chinese Medicine in Contemporary China: Plurality and Synthesis* (Durham, NC: Duke University Press, 2002); Kim Taylor, *Chinese Medicine in Early Communist China, 1945–63: A Medicine of Revolution* (London: RoutledgeCurzon, 2005).

9 P. L. Lee, "Perceptions and Uses of Chinese Medicine among the Chinese in Hong Kong." *Culture, Medicine and Psychiatry*, 4(1) (1980): 345–75.

10 Zhang Yuhuan and Ken Rose, *Who Can Ride the Dragon? An Exploration of the Cultural Roots of Traditional Chinese Medicine* (Taos, NM: Paradigm Publications, 1995).

11 According to a survey, the majority (70%) of medical students at the Chinese University of Hong Kong reported no change in attitudes towards Chinese medicine after studying Western medicine. The attitude was positive in 41%, neutral in 52% and negative in only 6%. The investigators concluded that most students are not aware of any possible side-effects in Chinese medicine. Kam-Lun Ellis Hon *et al.*, "A Survey of Attitudes to Traditional Chinese Medicine among Chinese Medical Students." *American Journal of Chinese Medicine*, 33(2) (2005): 269–79.

12 Ping-Chung Leung, Charlie Changli Xue and Yung-Chi Cheng, *A Comprehensive Guide to Chinese Medicine* (Singapore: World Scientific Press, 2003).

Websites

American Journal of Chinese Medicine: http://www.worldscinet.com/ajcm/ajcm. shtml

Baptist University of Hong Kong, School of Chinese Medicine: http://scm.hkbu. edu.hk/en/home/index.html

Chinese University of Hong Kong, School of Chinese Medicine: http://www.cuhk. edu.hk/scm/chi/home.html

Harvard University, General Education: http://www.generaleducation.fas.harvard. edu/icb/icb.do

National Center for Complementary and Alternative Medicine: http://nccam.nih. gov/

National Science Foundation, "What is Interdisciplinary Research?": National Science Foundation http://www.nsf.gov/od/oia/additional_resources/interdisciplinary_research/definition.jsp

National University of Singapore, General Education: http://www.nus.edu.sg/gem/about_what_is_ge.htm

Stanford University, General Education Requirements: http://www.stanford.com/dept/registrar/bulletin/4877.htm

Trinity Western University, "Definition of 'Interdisciplinary' in TWU's MAIH Program": http://twu.ca/academics/graduate/humanities/program/definition. html

University of Hong Kong, School of Chinese Medicine: http://www3.hku.hk/chinmed/index.html

11 Concepts and practice in teaching general education math

Wang Lixia

Introduction

In response to the demand for diverse talent in the twenty-first century, China has started to implement quality education (general education) at universities and colleges since 1990s. Since then, quality education in math (general education math) has begun to get more and more attention, gradually becoming a hot conversation topic.

As a university math teacher with 20 years' experience, I believe general education math is an educational concept with rich connotations which can be realized through various forms. This chapter introduces my experience of integrating the history of math and mathematical culture into the main math courses (especially the sequence on probability theory), and offering an elective course titled "History of mathematics" to math and applied math majors as well as a common elective course titled "Eastern and Western mathematical cultures" for all students on campus. It is intended to start a conversation on the core spirit, key objectives, teaching philosophy, curricular design and pedagogical approaches related to general education math.

The core spirit and key objectives of general education math

The content and methods of math education should clearly be closely related to the core spirit and key objectives of math education. In order to explore the spirit and objectives of today's university math education, we need to first explore the definition of math, review the history of math education and explore the relationship between math and today's society.

What is mathematics?

Undoubtedly, math is science in the first place. However, math itself is also a historical and developmental concept whose meanings change with the times.

On the whole, math only involved the concepts of number and shape before the nineteenth century. In fact, before the sixth century BC, math was mostly the study of "numbers." Greek math, emerging in the sixth century BC, focused on the study of "shapes." Thus, math had become the study of numbers and shapes. From then to the seventeenth century, the objects of mathematical study stayed essentially the same. But the seventeenth century was a major turning point for math. Throughout the seventeenth and eighteenth centuries, mathematicians focused on motion and change. Of course, mathematical description of motion and change is still not inseparable from number and shape. Thus, Engels in the nineteenth century gave the following definition: "Pure math has the spatial forms and quantitative relations of the real world as its object."[1]

In the early nineteenth century, the content of math began to change essentially. Mathematicians realized that the objects of mathematical thought should not be limited to number and shape. In addition, mathematicians' interest in math itself grew more intense than ever before in history. Abstract algebra, non-Euclidean geometry and rigorous analysis emerged one after another. The degree of mathematical abstraction entered a higher stage and math was often seen as a deductive system of logic which is unrelated to specific things – this is the pure math tendency in its modern sense.

Entering the twentieth century, with further expansion of the field of mathematical research, the application of math was no longer confined to physics, astronomy and engineering, but expanded to banking, social sciences, medicine and many other fields. In this context, a number of influential mathematicians from the former Soviet Union realized in the 1950s that contemporary math was the science of all possible quantitative relations and interdependencies.[2] The word "quantity" used here has a rich modern meaning: it not only includes spatial forms and quantitative relations in the real world, but also all the possible spatial forms and quantitative relations (such as high-dimensional space and infinite dimensional space in geometry, group and domain in algebra, functional and operator in analysis, etc.). Afterwards, mathematicians further understood that, in essence, the objects of mathematical studies were various "patterns." So from the 1980s, math is generally considered a science concerned with "patterns" and structure:

"The field [math] has been described as the science of patterns. Its purpose is to reveal the structures and symmetries observed both in nature and in the abstract world of mathematics itself."[3] Here the word "pattern" has extensive implications, including the patterns of number, the patterns of shape, the patterns of motions and change, the patterns of reasoning and communication, the patterns of behavior, and so forth. These patterns can be real as well as imaginary, and quantitative as well as qualitative. The above definitions have meant the gradual disappearance of the boundaries between the historical and application domains in the study and application of math.

Math and today's society

It is widely accepted that the spiritual core of modern math is the rational spirit inherited from ancient Greek civilization. Noted British historian Arnold J. Toynbee (1889–1975) once pointed out that it was such a rational spirit that provided the essential element of an industrial culture for Greek civilization.[4]

For ancient Greeks, math was not only knowledge, but a reliable methodology to obtain knowledge, a language that could describe the world scientifically and a key to uncovering the myth of nature. Math thus occupied the highest position in the structure of knowledge.[5]

Intellectual activities based on reason and math led to the development of a knowledge system and the pursuit of truth, thus making math a major force in Western civilization that pushed forward both the materialistic and spiritual development of mankind. In fact, math not only plays a central role in the fields of astronomy, physics and engineering, but also has a far-reaching and profound impact in almost all fields of human intellectual activities, including philosophy, religion, politics, economics, painting, music, architecture and literature.

In the twenty-first century, where society has entered the information age guided by science, technology and a knowledge-based economy, the role of math has become even more important than ever before. This is because, first, almost all the research areas have become more and more interdisciplinary, while new research fields are constantly being created. In addition, various disciplines, including the social sciences, are trying to complete the transformation from qualitative description to quantitative analysis, thus increasingly expanding and deepening the area of mathematical application, and even enabling a gradual shift for math from a supportive to a dominant role in many professions. Second, the information industry plays a more and more important role in society and math forms the core technology of the information industry. Finally, scientific and technological development and social transformation have impacted people's lifestyles, and, to some extent, made people's thinking more rational and quantitative, and, therefore, mathematical.

On the one hand, this situation shows how the role of math education is becoming more important for universities and colleges; on the other, it has also posed a challenge to the traditional mode of math education, because we not only need to require science and engineering students to learn more mathematical knowledge, but also need to extend math education to all academic disciplines, including the humanities and arts. So how can we provide appropriate math education to students of different majors?

The core spirit and key objectives for general education math

Modern math is often compared to an exuberant tree with many branches which are continuously throwing out new ones. According to the classification by the American journal *Mathematical Reviews*, today's math has about 60 second-level disciplines, and more than 400 third-level disciplines, plus countless further classifications. With such a huge knowledge system, professional mathematicians' specializations are increasingly restricted to one or two specific areas. Therefore, the university cannot teach students all the mathematical knowledge they may use later. By teaching basic math courses, what we could do is to help students learn scientific ways of thinking, enhancing their understanding of math and their ability to apply math so that they can better adjust to their future work and life and acquire the capacity to pursue further study and build up new knowledge.

Noted mathematician David Hilbert (1862–1943) once pointed out: "Mathematical science is in my opinion an indivisible whole, an organism whose vitality is conditioned upon the connection of its parts."[6] French mathematician Henri Poincaré (1854–1912), the so-called "last mathematical generalist," stated, "The true method of foreseeing the future of mathematics is to study its history and its actual state."[7] I think these statements tell us that teaching math should aim to improve students' mathematical literacy, guiding them to look at math from a holistic, integrated, historical and developmental perspective.

In sum, I believe that an ideal math education should be a kind of general education which includes three dimensions: mastery of the theoretical system, improvement of application ability and nurturing of mathematical literacy. As the three dimensions may mean different things to students of different majors, it is necessary to design math courses that cater to different students.

Curricular design of general education in math

Principles and guidelines

I have taught at several universities and most of my students are non-math science and engineering majors. Many of them do not like math or even hate it, but they have to take it seriously for the sake of examinations and admissions. Although they have spent a lot of time and effort on math, their learning experiences are passive, painful, undirected and uncomprehending. Faced with this kind of student, I think constantly about how to enable them to learn math pleasantly and effectively, and help them understand math and improve their math literacy.

Through many years of practice, I have learned that applying the concept of math general education to the teaching process can solve some of these problems to a certain extent. As for the principles and guidelines for curricular design in math general education, I think there are essentially four points, as follows:

1 Micro/macro observation. I believe that in teaching any course (especially math) we should try to guide students to observe both the micro and macro situations, i.e. to understand and learn the subject from both the holistic and individual perspectives, endeavoring to keep the general goal in sight while taking care of the details, and focus on micro analysis and macro structure. That is to say, students are taught to focus on the overall situation and details as well as interconnections of the various parts.

2 Exploration of origins. I believe that students would find math boring and difficult and even get lost, "seeing only trees without the forest," if I simply taught math in an orderly manner within the logical system framework. However, if I can trace the origin of the problems and clarify the evolution and development of ideas and methodology, the teaching process becomes much more lively and interesting, and it will be much easier for students to understand the ideas, methodology and conclusions. Just as American mathematician Hermann Weyl (1885–1955) said, "Without the concepts, methods and results found and developed by previous generations right

down to Greek antiquity, one cannot understand either the aims or the achievements of math in the last fifty years."[8]

3   The unity of knowledge, methodology and enlightenment. Han Yu, a poet of the Tang dynasty, said: "The teacher should advocate the doctrine, impart professional knowledge and answer questions." As a math teacher, I believe this quotation actually highlights the three ultimate goals for math teaching: first, to "impart professional knowledge," meaning to teach students knowledge, and to let them "know how"; second, to "answer questions," meaning to analyze problems and find the solutions, to let them "know why," and draw inferences about other cases from one instance; and, finally, to "advocate the doctrine," meaning to enable students to integrate knowledge and methods, and analyze, understand and refine them at a higher level and with a broader perspective so that they are enlightened and inspired. The first two goals can be considered as being about "knowledge and methodology," but the last is about "enlightenment." Obviously, the last objective is contingent on achieving the first two; enlightenment will be empty talk without the first two objectives. But without the last goal, students' understanding and knowledge of math cannot be elevated to the level of general knowledge. In short, the three objectives are interdependent. Therefore, the three dimensions should be fully integrated to constitute a whole process of math education.

4   Think out of the box. This means to study math from the perspectives of philosophy, history, culture and methodology, guide students to take an organic, holistic and progressive view of math, understanding its changes over time, especially in terms of its research content as well as the evolution and development of its methodology, experiencing the interactions of mathematical culture with other cultures and understanding the mode of mathematical thinking and its value and power.

Curriculum design

The four points described above serve both as my principles and guidelines in designing the curriculum and as self-imposed requirement for teaching math. Obviously math courses designed for students from different academic departments would have different emphases within these four broad principles. Specifically, in my own university, students can be grouped into three broad categories: science and engineering (non-math majors) students, math and applied math majors and liberal arts majors. For these three groups of students, I have developed the following three respective kinds of math general education courses:

1   Students of science and engineering (non-math) majors. These students represent the largest group in the student body at my university. They have a number of required math courses. So, based on the four principles outlined above, I have fully integrated the history and culture of math into the traditional math curriculum.

2   Math and applied math majors. They represent a small minority student group. Each year there are only 45–60 of them. I have tried to develop electives on the history of math to increase their mathematical literacy.

3   Liberal arts students. Math courses were not offered to these students in the past. To provide them with an overview of modern math, help them understand its essence and methodology, recognize its extensive application and appreciate its power and value, I have developed a public elective course (free elective): "Eastern and Western mathematical cultures." (In fact, many science and engineering students have also chosen this course.)

Pedagogy for general education math

Tracing the origins and unifying education and skills: teaching main math courses under the concept of general education

Since the teaching hours for undergraduate math courses are quite limited, how to implement the concept of general education, introduce mathematical culture (including math history, ideas, methodology and its relationship with other disciplines or even social life) into the teaching process and benefit teaching activities effectively on the premise of not adding hours, reducing content and lowering requirements is a topic worthy of intensive study.

My experience mainly comes from teaching probability theory (including probability theory, mathematical statistics and stochastic processes). After years of practice, my main approach is to maintain the original course structure, but I have adopted a few basic principles in course delivery as follows:

1   Divide the teaching content based on logical structure and historical process.

2   Arrange teaching content according to cognitive laws: giving examples before theory; showing applications after theory; conjecturing before verification; and conducting analysis before summary.

3   Fully integrate mathematical culture and history into the original curriculum, and systematically summarize the formation and development of related ideas and the main contributions of important historical figures based on their origin and trends, and highlight the clues to their spatial and temporal evolution and the linkages between the various elements based on a strictly structured theoretical system.

4   Select more famous mathematical problems in history as examples, demonstrate the development of mathematical ideas and methodology and guide students from simple subject learning to understanding mathematical methodology by means of introducing, analyzing and solving problems. As Leibniz stated, "The art of discovery may be promoted and its method known through illustrious examples."[9]

5   Select some comprehensive and practical examples to discuss at the end of each topic, analyze the thought processes in resolving these examples before providing keys to students, thus helping them thoroughly understand what they have learned and developing their ability to apply math skills.

6   Summarize, deduce and interpret abstract ideas with the help of various kinds of background knowledge, and guide students to achieve a higher level of math learning and further enhance their mathematical literacy.

Judging by classroom atmosphere, attendance records, after-class discussion, student questionnaire by the Office of Academic Affairs and final exam (independent graders and blind reviews) results, this teaching is well received by students and contributes to accurate understanding and flexible application of the knowledge by my students (see Table 11.1).[10]

Keeping both the big picture and observing all the details, covering all the fronts, finding the reasons to explain change, and moving to the next level: the elective course on the history of math for math majors

For senior math majors who have taken math courses, it is very important for them to stand on a higher ground, step out of the math "box," examine math from a broader perspective, understand math from an essential, comprehensive, contextual and developmental perspective, get to know the changes and development of math over the ages, especially research content and ways of thinking, and develop an appropriate view on the value and power of math. So, in the Fall of 2004, I offered an elective course titled "History of mathematics," with two study hours per week for senior applied math majors. I adopted a "semi-open" teaching approach for this course. Instead of having fixed teaching materials, students are given a reading list for each class and the teaching methods have been adjusted several times.

As we know, most college seniors are busy applying to study abroad, taking entrance exams for graduate school or looking for jobs; it is hard for them to concentrate on coursework. When I first started teaching, I adopted the

Table 11.1 Test score results for "Probability theory and stochastic processes"

Class / total number	Test score results					
	Excellent (number/ ratio)	Fail (number/ ratio)	Good (number/ ratio)	Fine (number/ ratio)	Pass (number/ ratio)	Median
(1) / 155	4 / 2.58	55 / 35.48	11	39	38	62.66
(2) / 153	1 / 0.65	50 / 32.68	15	45	42	63.78
(3) / 150	2 / 1.33	41 / 27.33	23	41	43	66.00
(4) / 153	11 / 7.14	31 / 20.78	30	50	31	70.85

Note
The test was more flexible but yet more difficult; class 3 and 4 are the test group, class 1 and 2 are the control group.

traditional classroom approach of lectures. But I soon found that many students were doing their own thing while listening to my lectures. They only raised their heads to laugh when hearing interesting stories and then went back to memorizing English vocabulary or doing math exercises. It is ironic that after class, when I was expecting students to come and ask questions about my lectures, I was embarrassed to find they needed my help only with exercises from algebra and analysis courses.

I believe the history of mathematics course, set up for math majors, should not be about "celebrity news" or "math anecdotes," but should be an organic and systematic discussion and analysis of the history of math in China and overseas from the philosophical, historical, cultural and methodological perspectives. Moreover, the course should enable students to have a new understanding of mathematical theory in terms of its essence, comprehensiveness, connections and developments, recognize the evolution of mathematical concepts and the development of mathematical methods, appreciate the interaction of math with other cultures and explore the general pattern of scientific thinking. To be honest, based on my limited knowledge and ability, I feel the history of mathematics is a very difficult course to teach. It took me much more time to prepare than other courses. So the students' casual attitude made me very disappointed.

I decided to change my way of teaching. After several adjustments, the final approach I have adopted is to give students a list of topics at the beginning of each semester so that they may pick one topic they are most interested in and prepare for it individually or in collaboration with others. When the course has proceeded to a particular topic for which the students have opted, I will ask them to give a 30-minute presentation, followed by questions and answers. At the end of the session, I will add to, synthesize or clarify the information, depending on the specific situation.

Based on the feedback over recent years, this teaching method is quite effective in motivating students to engage in self-study and class participation. Many students will take the initiative to seek my advice on their presentation topics, supporting materials, ideas and viewpoints. Students have a much stronger sense of class participation and are inclined to ask questions. To encourage independent learning and active class participation, course evaluation is designed as follows: attendance and performance 20%, homework 20%, presentation 20% and study report (term paper) 40%.

This course, which focuses on improving students' professional math literacy, has been benefiting the largest number of applied math majors. Over the years, more than 60 percent of the total number of students have taken this course. General feedback from students indicates that the course has broadened their horizons, introduced them to a comprehensive and deeper understanding of mathematical ideas, and provided a better assessment of the dynamic development of math and a more personal relationship to the subject. Many students suggested offering the course earlier in their college years. In addition, later student feedback indicates the training they received in the course has also been helpful for their thesis work and defense.

Beauty plus application, essence plus spirit: the free elective course of "Eastern and Western mathematical culture"

In the Spring semester of 2008, after four years of teaching the history of mathematical culture and with support from the Office of Academic Affairs, I offered a new elective course, "Eastern and Western mathematical culture," for all undergraduate students. The course was enthusiastically received by students, and there was an official enrollment of 193 students. It was a diverse group from 9 colleges and 83 classes of all 4 years. Since then, I have continued to offer this course every Spring semester, and there are about 200 students taking it every year.

For this elective course, I still hope to present math from the perspectives of philosophy, history, culture and methodology. However, since the students' mathematical background varies tremendously, it is particularly important to select the teaching content cautiously, thinking carefully about the introduction, demonstration and narrative so that every student can understand. With this in mind, I have based my teaching on the principles of "beauty, applicability and easiness." For the teaching content, I have selected the origin and development of important mathematical ideas, key roles played by prominent mathematicians, major branches of modern math, and relationships between math and other science and even social life. Teaching materials should be as broadly based as possible and be reasonably interesting. The learning outcomes are set to enable students to understand and appreciate math from various perspectives and angles, recognize the changes in math over times, sense the interaction of mathematical culture with other cultures and understand the power and value of mathematical thinking. After repeated practice and weighing different options, the current basic teaching content of the course is as follows (some adjustments are made each year according to students' situation):

1 Dawn in the valley – math origin and early development
2 Western rationalism – ancient Greek math and modern civilization
3 Oriental charm – traditional oriental culture and medieval oriental math
4 Corridor leading to light – Christian culture and European mathematics in the Middle Ages (476–1400)
5 Descartes's dream – efforts for math mechanization and the birth of analytic geometry
6 Highest triumph of the human spirit – establishment of calculus
7 A glimpse of "analysis time" – external forces driving math development
8 The number of space – elegant geometry
9 Math and time – history of non-Euclidean geometry
10 From the seven-bridge problem to Poincaré's conjecture – stories about topology
11 Flaws of math – stories of the three math crises
12 Does God play dice? – stories of random math
13 Approaching non-linear – history of soliton and fractal
14 Fluttering waves – math stories in mass communications and confidential communications
15 Let's talk about math – math and me.

Although the teaching content, outlines and approaches are decided before class starts, adjustments still need to be made to content and methodology according to specific situations. Overall, the course still operates on a semi-open approach, but due to the class large size, I have mainly used the traditional lecture mode for this class, with attention to interactive questions and answers. For some topics, I have asked students to do presentations and organize discussions. The final result consists of three parts: 30% for attendance and performance, 30% for homework and 40% for book report or research paper.

Although a few students have reported difficulties understanding the concepts and ideas of modern mathematical disciplines, such as non-Euclidean geometry, topology and others, judging by the interesting book reports and enthusiastic participation in class, all the basic learning outcomes are successfully achieved. In addition, the course has won great endorsement by students based on their learning experience reports and surveys.

Conclusion

Mr. Chen Fangzheng once said that science was involved in the three encounters between modern China and the West.[11] And the tone was always set that in the collision of two great civilizations the West had an upper hand due to its scientific advance. Perhaps because of this, over the past century (except for the period of the "Cultural Revolution"), the Chinese government has always made science and education a priority. Taking university education as an example, we know St. John's University, founded by the American Episcopal Bishop S. I. J. Schereschewsky in 1879, was China's first university in the modern sense. Following the three peak periods of development starting from the late Qing dynasty and the early Republican period (late nineteenth century to the 1920s and 1930s), the early period of the People's Republic (1950s) and the period of opening-up and reform (after the 1980s) up to 2007, China now has 742 regular four-year undergraduate institutions, 1,109 vocational (specialized) colleges, 317 independent colleges and 18 branch campuses in total.[12] Although social conditions are very different, there are some broadly shared goals of higher education for the three periods: "national salvation through science" for the first period, "catching up with America and surpassing England" for the second period and "reviving China through science and education" for the third. Thus, compared with Western universities' tradition of exploring nature and self-development, Chinese universities, since their establishment, have had to shoulder more national responsibilities and are, therefore, far more practical.

As we all know, for thousands of years, all civilizations have had their own tradition of math education. In today's information age, guided by science, technology and the knowledge-based economy, the role of math is bigger than ever and the importance of math education is also unprecedented. However, since the twentieth century, as American mathematician R. Courant pointed out: "The teaching of mathematics has sometimes degenerated into empty drill in problem-solving, which may develop formal ability but does not lead to real understanding or to greater intellectual independence."[13] As far as I know, at China's regular undergraduate colleges (I do not know much about other types of institutions of higher education), these problems are endemic and more serious in traditional math education. This situation is detrimental to the urgent goal of developing the cross-disciplinary and creative talents badly needed by the society. Nor will it be favorable to the nourishment of general practitioners and high-quality citizens in dealing with their jobs and life in the future. In this regard, I think implementing a math general education program in various forms according to students' specific situations is an important and effective way to solve the problem.

Notes

1 Friedrich Engels, "On Anti-Dühring." In *The Selected Works of Marx and Engels* (Beijing: People's Press, 1972), vol. 3, p. 77.
2 A. D. Aleksandrov *et al.*, *Mathematics, Its Content, Methods, and Meaning* (New York: Dover Publications, 1999), p. 63.
3 National Research Council, Committee on the Mathematical Sciences: Status and Future Directions, *Renewing U.S. Mathematics: A Plan for the 1990s* (Washington, DC: National Academies Press, 1990), p. 39.
4 M. Klein, *Mathematics in Western Culture* (Oxford: Oxford University Press, 1953), p. 105.
5 Ibid., p. 471.
6 Jeremy Gray, *The Hilbert Challenge* (Oxford: Oxford University Press, 2000), p. 282.
7 Emily Grosholz and Herbert Breger (eds.), *The Growth of Mathematical Knowledge* (Dordrecht: Kluwer, 2000), p. 267.
8 H. Weyl, "A Half Century of Mathematics." *American Mathematical Monthly*, 58(8) (1951): 523–53.
9 Raymond George Ayoub (ed.), *Musings of the Masters: An Anthology of Mathematical Reflections* (Washington, DC: Mathematical Association of America, 2005), p. 203.
10 As a way of summarizing my work in this area and drawing upon many years of research and teaching experience, I edited a textbook, *Probability Theory and Mathematical Statistics: Theory, History and Application*, published by Dalian University of Technology Press, 2010. The book was well received. For example, Professor Ye Zhongxing, Associate Dean of the School of Science, Shanghai Jiaotong University, made the following positive comments on my book: "The book breaks the traditional mode of writing and editing textbooks, and reflects the editor's pursuit of 'tracing the source and clarifying the trends' and 'showing the whole picture while giving details.' It's carefully planned, well focused, highly informative, coherent and well organized with ample and appropriate examples and exercises. In addition, the postscript for each chapter is a particular delight, adding further appeal to the book. The prose is smooth and lively, meeting both the teaching requirement and cognitive rules, and helping to stimulate students' interest in learning and promote innovation among them. It is a very special and outstanding textbook for science and engineering colleges." The textbook has been nominated by Dalian University of Technology Press for the Chinese University Press Outstanding Textbook award.
11 Chen Fangzhen, *Inheritance and Rebellion: Why Modern Science Emerged in the West* (Hong Kong: Sanlian Press, 2009).
12 Ministry of Education, "List of Certified Institutions of Higher Education for Student Enrollment."
13 Richard Courant, Herbert Robbins and Ian Stewart, *What Is Mathematics? An Elementary Approach to Ideas and Methods* (Oxford: Oxford University Press, 1996), p. 178.

12 How to train faculty to teach general education curricula

Liang Jia-chi and Wang Lin-wen

It goes without saying that general education curricula in undergraduate education are important for students to develop different perspectives. Students in general education programs should receive a generous orientation to intellectual expectations, acquire skills of thought and expression and integrate ideas from across disciplines to illuminate interdisciplinary issues, and so on. The problem with general education, however, is that teachers often are ill prepared. Research indicates that teachers are frequently not knowledgeable about a variety of teaching innovations and strategies, and that they identify more with their disciplinary interest and less with general education (Bakutes, 1998; Cranton, 1994; Heppner and Johnson, 1994). In addition, traditional pedagogical approaches in higher education do not work effectively with most of today's students, whose learning styles challenge teachers to employ more diverse and interactive teaching strategies. Unfortunately, there is no teacher training program at the college level to help faculty members to design and practice courses for general education. Facing a lack of adequate preparation in education, junior faculty members usually play multiple roles – teaching, research, service. Consequently, they spend little time on improving their own learning and teaching (Davis, 1993). Thus, some college faculty members simplify the teaching materials of introductory or lower-level courses for use in general education courses. Even worse, some college faculty and students treat classes in general education as easy-earned credits that require little effort in learning or even teaching.

In view of the lack of pedagogical training for faculty, the director of general education must provide direction and oversight to faculty members in general education, import various resources from outside schools and establish principles of responsibility and accountability for all curricula. In other words, the director needs to be responsible for helping faculty members establish a coherent rationale and positive attitude toward general education and improve campus culture in the following ways: (1) high-level administrative commitment and support, so that faculty will feel that the administration places a high value on teaching; (2) faculty involvement and shared values with the administration; (3) teaching demonstration as a part of the hiring process; (4) frequent interaction among faculty; (5) adequate learning resources, including opportunities for workshops, seminars, training programs, etc.; (6) supportive chairs; (7) connecting evaluation of teaching to tenure and promotion decisions (Feldman and Paulsen, 1999). A friendly campus culture can have a positive impact on instructors' motivations. Teachers must realize that general education is more than offering students breadth of knowledge and simple exposure to different fields. Questions they should consider might be, for example: how does general education function in the undergraduate program; what is general education preparing students for? Such questions have to be answered prior to curriculum design and implementation. Once the right attitude has been established, the director can then take it to the next level and strengthen the teachers' teaching skills and abilities. And once the director has encouraged faculty to engage in continuous learning and development, implementing curriculum quality control will be the next essential issue for general education.

Promoting the PCK of faculty

In the past decade, research focus on teaching has shifted from teachers' skills to teachers' knowledge and beliefs. Thus it is necessary to understand how teachers construct meaning in the classroom (Doyle, 1990). Pedagogical content knowledge (PCK) is a revolutionary concept that concerns taking particular topics of study and creating representations that are comprehensible and meaningful to learners. For Shulman, PCK should include content knowledge, general pedagogical knowledge, curricular knowledge, knowledge of learners, knowledge of educational contexts and knowledge of the philosophical and historical aims of education (Shulman, 1987). Furthermore, Magnusson, Krajcik and Borko (1999) conceptualize PCK for science teaching with five components: orientations toward science teaching; knowledge and beliefs about the science curriculum; knowledge and beliefs about students' understanding of specific science topics; knowledge and beliefs about assessment in science; and knowledge and beliefs about instructional strategies for teaching science. Based on these studies, for the general education field we suggest reducing the conceptual and contextual complexity of teaching into five elements: (1) knowledge of the essence and spirit of general education; (2) breadth and depth of knowledge in a specific discipline; (3) knowledge about students' learning attitude and their understanding of specific topics; (4) knowledge about using appropriate teaching methods; and (5) knowledge about using appropriate evaluation systems and methods (Figure 12.1).

First, faculty in general education should realize the spirit of general education. Courses in general education are not regarded as a "foundation" for teaching only most fundamental ideas on which specialized study might build. As teachers, we hope our undergraduate students will not only possess a broad base of knowledge, but also think logically and critically, communicate clearly, work collaboratively, implement ethical speculation, realize civic responsibility and social participation and have cultural and global vision. Teachers in general education should know how to cultivate these abilities, otherwise, they will obtain nothing from a great many classes in distribution requirements. In addition, teachers should not rely on adequate knowledge in teaching topics, but should also be encouraged to integrate materials, reshape courses and connect with other disciplines. After all, in order for students to become active

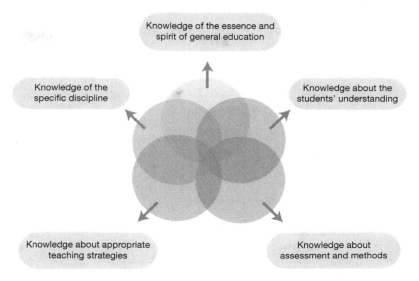

Figure 12.1 PCK of faculty in general education.

participants in the classroom, effective teaching requires innovative, purposeful, research-informed lessons.

Though it may seem unimportant at first glance, students' prior knowledge and learning attitudes influence the design of course curriculum and classroom management. For example, because many students consider classes in general education as mere "nutrient credits," teachers have to take the time and energy to cultivate positive attitudes towards learning. In addition, that some students begin higher education with apathetic feelings towards general education courses has serious implications for how effectively they will engage with the learning tasks set before them. Thus teachers need to make efforts to design learning contexts that help students to develop more sophisticated approaches to learning. The purpose of teaching is not to revise students' past experiences and conceptions, but to influence their future approaches. Therefore, faculty members need to continuously implement new teaching approaches and authentic assessment methods. For example, problem-based learning, action learning, performance-based assessment and portfolio assessment are advanced educational concepts, since faculty with no educational training have no idea about these new approaches. Faculty members need to know that the aspects of student learning assessments include self-referenced based on self-reflection, criterion-referenced based on levels of learning, norm-referenced based on comparisons with learning of others and peer-referenced based on peer appraisal (Light, Cox and Calkins, 2001); assessments must be aligned with the learning objectives, teaching methods and activities employed in the learning context. Unsuitable assessment methods and teaching strategies impose irresistible pressures on students to take the wrong approaches to learning tasks. Therefore, faculty members should participate in seminars and workshops to broaden areas of expertise and to learn new teaching approaches, since the general education college should provide the support and resources to construct a quasi-in-service system for the development of faculty members in general education.

The development of junior faculty in a quasi-in-service system (CLIPPER) for general education

Tensions arise in the professional track for higher education from the requirement that faculty focus on teaching more undergraduates, supervising more graduate students and publishing more papers. It is clear that while teaching is the core value in higher education, there is no way to improve students' capabilities or attitudes when teachers are so focused on writing high-index papers. Though knowledgeable in their own field, faculty members without pre-service professional training in teaching probably have great difficulty teaching and communicating efficiently with students. A lack of ongoing professional development and assessment among faculty leads to continued ineffective teaching. In addition, the faculty's beliefs and expectations about teaching and learning can limit change in teaching practices (Cuban, 1990). Some research in inquiry teaching, conceptual development and preconceptions has led to more innovative strategies for college classroom instruction in science courses (Driver, 1986; Sigel, 1985). Efforts to improve college teaching in professional development generally include workshops, written descriptions of effective practice, expert or peer consultation and mentoring and funded course development (Sunal *et al.*, 2001). In Taiwan, some faculty in the general education college are teaching-oriented teachers who offer many required and elective courses in the general education program. Thus, how to develop a quasi-in-service system for cultivating junior faculty becomes an important issue for the general education program. Figure 12.2 shows the framework of a proposed system, named CLIPPER, which was developed by the authors for cultivating junior faculty in the general education college.

The CLIPPER system encompasses seven perspectives: Community, Literature, Inspiration, Paradigm, Practice, Engagement and Resource. In former times, a "clipper" was a fast sailing ship used for traveling over long distances; some consider the era of clipper ships "the golden age of sailing." We have named this system CLIPPER not only because the seven perspectives make up its acronym, but also because we hope that through the system, junior faculty can start quickly and progress continuously in lifelong learning. The seven perspectives of CLIPPER are described as follows.

Community: "Community" addresses the importance of fostering a coherent teaching team empirically related to the educational impact around a vision for general education. General education programs need to foster conversations and interactions among faculty members by scheduling seminars, discussion series, lunch for conversation hour, and so on. In addition to practical teaching, the community can discuss curriculum reform, revise guidelines for basic requirements, exchange experiences and rethink classroom management issues; they can even implement co-teaching and apply the curriculum improvement project

Figure 12.2 A quasi-in-service system (CLIPPER) for developing junior faculty in general education.

supported by Taiwan's Ministry of Education. General education programs can also encourage junior faculty to participate in general education associations or societies outside of schools. It is essential to understand the faculty's efforts and to exchange teaching experiences across different universities, and so these activities help teachers to move beyond their own experience and expertise.

Literature: "Literature" addresses the importance of using books to elaborate on the history and revival of general education, the essential aims of general education and the traditional schools of thought. By referring to historical models, faculty in general education can learn and could reflect on self-teaching styles, curriculum design and even how to improve tensions between core curriculum and distribution requirement. From a historical context, faculty should rethink which kind of general education is useful, and how to develop an appropriate and distinctive general education program for a different educational system. Some academic journals in general education attempt to bridge the gap between research and practice. These are appropriate resources for junior faculty to apply theory to practice in the classroom. The general education college may periodically distribute literature to faculty members describing specific types of innovative practice.

Inspiration: "Inspiration" addresses the importance of creating insight from various seminars, workshops and performance-based shows, especially at national or international conferences. Many different colleges in Taiwan have held general education conferences that discuss a variety of topics, including how to implement effective teaching, how to implement authentic assessment, how to prepare problem-based learning or action learning, how to plan a curriculum framework, how to plan the map of curricula, how to plan life education in general education, and so forth. By attending these events, junior faculty can obtain inspiration and encouragement. Research reminds us that multi-day workshops with follow-up and monitoring results in significant positive changes in faculty attitude, knowledge, instructional behavior and interaction with students (Herr, 1988). Therefore, continued learning and development for faculty is crucial.

Paradigm: "Paradigm" addresses the importance of learning from the successes of other teachers. Teachers with excellence awards are models for junior faculty learning. These paradigm teachers not only have sophisticated teaching strategies, but also have endless enthusiasm and extraordinary educational ideals. Through one-to-one interactions, these teachers can offer expert advice to junior faculty. Both senior and junior faculty members have positive attitudes toward these mentorship interactions. Certainly, teaching commitment and positive attitudes must be honored and utilized to improve and promote faculty; otherwise junior faculty may be stuck in research performance.

Practice: "Practice" addresses the importance of reflection on practice. Teachers need to continuously update teaching materials, revise curriculum plans, elaborate classroom management strategies and improve student performance. In order to do so, teachers must assimilate student feedback, such as from their questions, facial expression, attitudes, group discussions and individual reports. In addition, research has found that instructional intervention helps faculty to become aware of their own classroom behaviors by analyzing them with other alternatives, and implementing action research to create change (Murray, 1985). Analysis of self-recorded teaching tapes has been reported to be another effective method (Weimer and Lenze, 1994).

Engagement: "Engagement" addresses the importance of participation in education improvement programs. For example, the curriculum improvement projects run by Taiwan's Ministry of Education focus on promoting quality of curriculum and teaching. With financial support and human resources, faculty obtained additional help from teaching assistants, and implemented courses like action-based learning, problem-based learning and fieldwork. Faculty involved in such projects revise teaching ideas, materials and strategies based on suggestions from a judging panel in interim and final reports. That teaching development involves the use of grants in a comprehensive approach will be a catalyst for pedagogical and curricular change in the long term (Eble and McKeachie, 1985).

Resource: "Resource" addresses the importance of increasing public resources in general education. In Taiwan, there is the general education database (GEDB) for sharing excellent courses with interested faculty (http://get.nccu.edu.tw/). GEDB is derived from the MIT OpenCourseWare idea, and it goes further to gather teachers' course materials, PowerPoint presentations, audio recordings and topics for group discussion. As a free resource, GEDB will be a very efficient public resource for junior faculty. There are also open course websites, such as NETEASE (http://v.163.com/open/), which is a video learning platform with dozens of open courses translated from renowned international schools.

Generally speaking, continuing professional development in general education encompasses three types of activities: (1) self-directed learning experience; (2) formal professional development programs; and (3) organizational development strategies (Cranton, 1994; Caffarella and Zinn, 1999). Self-directed learning experiences are as a result of preparing class materials, teaching classes, designing courses, revising curriculum, supervising dissertations and conducting research. Formal professional development programs entail professional meetings, workshops and conferences at the regional, national and international level. For example, university centers for teaching development may hold a series of workshops for promoting teaching quality; they may also offer mentoring programs that set up teams by assigning individual mentors to each new faculty member. As for organizational development, this means a systematically planned change effort for organizational issues and needs. For example, there are activities aimed at changing the culture of a college, or efforts to alter organizational structures and teaching approaches.

The three types of activities in continuing professional development mentioned above are all covered in the CLIPPER system. Faculty members who participate in workshops engage in "Inspiration," or self-directed learning experiences. "Inspiration" also occurs when the general education college holds a conference for promoting problem-based learning, which relates to formal professional development programs. Teachers engage in the "Paradigm" perspective when they join in performance-based shows or search the teaching websites of award-winning faculty. These all are self-directed learning experiences. Formal professional development program occurs within the mentor–mentee system where senior faculty help junior faculty to delve into research and teaching. Self-directed learning experience is the essence of the "Practice" perspective, as teachers develop strategies by teaching and gaining feedback. If the center for general education needs systematic reform in its course portfolio, it is necessary to require faculty members to offer teaching records, reflections, students' performance records, assessments and classroom improvement strategies. This kind of demand is part of organizational development strategies.

Because not every faculty member keeps up with the current trends and demands in self-directed learning, professional development programs or organizational development strategies, teaching reform is necessary. That is, the general education college should encourage all teachers to immerse themselves in the seven perspectives of the CLIPPER system because it is essential for faculty to understand that continuous improvements to curriculum and teaching are part of their day-to-day work. However, the general education college should take responsibility for offering additional support for substantially new curricular initiatives to ensure successful implementation of major reforms, and should create an appropriate culture and climate for faculty members to work cooperatively. In addition, the general education center should be accountable for monitoring faculty members' performance in teaching. Lastly, the work which faculty members do in general education, often the most challenging and interdisciplinary kind of teaching, should count significantly in promotion and tenure decisions.

General education program in Taiwan

In the wake of a lack of social responsibility and humanitarian caring in college graduates, and a deficiency of resources and attention in general education, the Ministry of Education in Taiwan recently implemented the General Education

Program, 2007–2010 to improve general education in higher education. The main objectives of the program are to establish general education paradigms, to construct public resources, to improve course quality, to integrate learning paths for professional and general field studies, to encourage high-quality teachers to get involved in the project, to encourage more students to participate in class and to strengthen the atmosphere of general education (Ministry of Education Advisory Office, 2011). The three essential methods by which the Ministry planned to achieve these are: (1) using general education-centered higher education; (2) constructing a public resource platform; and (3) subsidizing high-quality course projects. As a result, these reforms had a significant effect on cultivating a climate in which universities take general education issues more seriously.

The general education-centered higher education project is a school-based application system. Having received grants, a school must follow through with its reform plans, such as by constructing a core curriculum in general education, planning action-based or problem-based learning courses in general education, building an integrated program which covers professional courses in general education, developing the university curriculum map, constructing digital materials of high-quality core courses in general education and building a platform that allows teachers to upload students' learning portfolios. A total of 13 universities received the national subsidy to implement the project, and obtained positive results. For example, among these 13 universities, 229 action-oriented or problem-solving-oriented courses and 151 digital courses were offered.

Subsidizing high-quality course projects is the most effective means of increasing individual participation. The main goals of the project are to promote high-quality teaching models in general education courses and to help faculty in general education to design better courses in order to improve the quality of courses in general education. Courses that received the national subsidy could employ teaching assistants to help teachers create a more interactive learning environment that spurs students' critical thinking, logical analysis and communication abilities. These courses also had the funds to take students for field trips to explore specific issues, implement fieldwork and develop reflective action. In addition, subsidized courses were able to build websites dedicated to teaching transparency, which includes course outlines, teaching schedules, teaching materials and notes, learning silhouettes, learning outcomes, lecture records, action learning records, learning resources and recommended readings. The impressive results of this project can be observed by the gradually increasing number of applications to these courses year by year. Within a 7-semester period, the number of applications for subsidized courses rose from 108 in the first semester to 418 in the final semester. Also, teachers have applied for the project in 90 percent of universities, and teachers have received a subsidy from the project in more than 60 percent of universities. These results show that more teachers in general education are willing to design better courses, and build interactive learning or student-centered environments.

In addition to guidelines from the top education authorities, there are various strategies for cultivating teachers for general education based on the specific features of each university or institute. At Yuan Ze University, for example, there are eight indicators of student competency in general education: (1) sensibility and interpretive comprehension; (2) critical thinking and innovation; (3) logic and scientific thinking; (4) humanity and environmental care; (5) ethical thinking and practice; (6) cogent expression and collaborative teamwork; (7) civic responsibility and social participation; and (8) cultural learning and global vision. Faculty members are expected to design curricula around these indicators. Every course uses two indicators as the main competency capabilities for constructing curriculum materials, teaching strategies, learning tasks and assessments. For example, a course on "Environmental protection and literature of nature" focuses on "humanity and environmental care" and "civic responsibility and social participation" as the two primary capabilities for developing the curriculum. The teacher uses readings in the literature of nature and case discussions about the dilemma between economic development and environmental protection in Taiwan for facilitating students' sense of humanity and environmental care; the teacher also uses an action plan for caring for the environment in the final report to encourage students' social participation.

In discussion we have found that the understanding of and appreciation for classic books is important for undergraduate students. And so, in addition to the required Chinese, English and history courses at Yuan Ze University, there are multiple activities, reading certifications and elective courses for exploring classic books. The 50 Classics program is designed to improve undergraduate students' writing ability by cultivating strong reading habits. The program is a self-directed reading course in which undergraduate students read books and earn "points" that allow them to graduate from pre-designed levels, which include classics from Eastern and Western literature, as well as other ancient and modern texts. The effectiveness of self-directed reading depends on the check system, which means students can only earn points and progress if they pass the teachers' certification. In order to challenge students and encourage them to explore the different flavors of these books, a teaching task force meets routinely to discuss curriculum design, teaching approaches, assessment methods and students' performance. There is also a school-wide teaching seminar held every month for all teachers to exchange ideas about how to improve course quality; guest speakers, including distinguished college professors, have also been invited to share their experiences with teachers.

Conclusions

Societal demands, organizational demands and student demands pressure institutions to find ways to improve the quality and effectiveness of instruction. As classrooms become more student-focused, faculty development in general education faces the enormous challenge of providing more opportunities to faculty members to access and link the world to the classroom. Linking faculty responsibilities more closely to the aims and missions of the general education college means that the director of general education must have strong leadership and make faculty more accountable for their students' learning outcomes. That is, a good general education program should help faculty members to become more comfortable with the diverse needs and desires of students, while also teaching faculty different approaches to make instruction more inclusive. Of course, the most important thing is to provide faculty with support for continuous learning, to keep faculty vital, productive and working together as a community, and to lead faculty to reflect on their teaching so as to make stronger connections between teaching strategies and their disciplinary knowledge and skill.

General education challenges the boundaries and structures of traditional knowledge claims within the university. Strong general education recognizes that faculty members are the most important resource in general education, and therefore emphasizes ways of learning, the value of teaching, moral-political involvement and connection between in- and out-of-classroom experiences. Through the process of refining courses, many faculty members have found new insights, renewed energy and enthusiasm and satisfaction in teaching. As a result, taking general education reform seriously may be the best form of professional development for faculty. In addition to self-directed learning experiences, support from professional development programs and organizational development strategies, self-evaluation and formal assessment from external agencies may result in more effective teaching, better courses and more refined conceptions of requirements. Thus, to maintain continuous reform, general education programs need to construct institutionalized assessments, including standardized tests, questionnaires for student feedback on teaching, student interviews, focus groups and surveys of current students and alumni. In the future, using portfolio-based approaches to assessment will be the trend for teaching and learning. Faculty members in general education need to use the portfolio-based approach for recording the process of curriculum modification and development, and for collecting information on students' learning progress. In the final analysis, the relationship between general education and academic majors is an ongoing negotiation, so general education programs must offer faculty in professional majors the opportunity to transcend specific disciplinary limits. A balance is expected to help undergraduate students benefit from both academic majors and general education curricula. Thus, a strong general education program must have central educational values and commitments. And having the clarity of vision to make improvements at each decision juncture increases the chances that general education curricula may remain true to their original intentions over time.

References

Bakutes, A. (1998). "An Examination of Faculty Development Centers." *Contemporary Education*, 69(3): 168–71.

Caffarella, R. S. and Zinn, L. F. (1999). "Professional Development for Faculty: A Conceptual Framework of Barriers and Supports." *Innovative Higher Education*, 23(4): 241–54.

Cranton, P. (1994). "Self-Directed and Transformative Instructional Development." *Journal of Higher Education*, 65(6): 726–44.

Cuban, L. (1990). "Reforming Again, Again, and Again." *Educational Researcher*, 19(1): 3–13.

Davis, J. (1993). *Better Teaching, More Learning; Strategies for Success in Postsecondary Settings* (Phoenix, AR: American Council on Education and Oryx Press).

Doyle, W. (1990). "Themes in Teacher Education Research." In W. R. Houston (ed.), *Handbook of Research on Teacher Education* (New York: Macmillan), pp. 3–24.

Driver, R. (1986). *The Pupil as Scientist* (Philadelphia, PA: Open University Press).

Eble, K. and McKeachie, W. (1985). *Improving Undergraduate Education through Faculty Development* (San Francisco: Jossey-Bass).

Feldman, K. A., and Paulsen, M. B. (1999). "Faculty Motivation: The Role of a Supportive Teaching Culture." *New Directions for Teaching and Learning*, 78: 71–78.

Heppner, P. and Johnson, J. (1994). "New Horizons in Counseling: Faculty Development." *Journal of Counseling and Development*, 72(5): 451–53.

Herr, K. (1988). "Exploring Excellence in Teaching: It Can Be Done!" *Journal of Staff, Program, and Organization Development*, 6(1): 17–20.

Light, G., Cox, R. and Calkins, S. (2001). *Learning and Teaching in Higher Education* (Los Angeles, CA: Sage Publications).

Magnusson, S. J., Krajcik, J. S. and Borko, H. (1999). "Nature, Sources, and Development of Pedagogical Content Knowledge for Science Teaching." In J. Gess-Newsome, and N. G. Lederman (eds.), *PCK and Science Education* (Dordrecht: Kluwer Academic Publishers), pp. 95–132.

Ministry of Education Advisory Office (2011). Report on the Outcome of the General Education Program 2007–2010. Online. Available HTTP: <http://hss.edu.tw/>.

Murray, H. (1985). "Classroom Teaching Behaviors Related to College Teaching Effectiveness." In J. G. Donald and A. M. Murray (eds.), *New Directions for Teaching and Learning: Using Research to Improve Teaching* (San Francisco: Jossey-Bass), pp. 57–69.

Shulman, L. S. (1987). "Knowledge and Teaching: Foundations of the New Reform." *Harvard Educational Review*, 57: 1–22.

Sigel, I. E. (1985). "A Conceptual Analysis of Beliefs." In Sigel (ed.), *Parental Belief Systems: The Psychological Consequences for Children* (Hillsdale, NJ: Erlbaum), pp. 345–71.

Sunal, D. W., Hodges, J., Sunal C. S., Whitaker, K. W., Freeman, L. M. and Odell, M. (2001). "Teaching Science in Higher Education: Faculty Professional Development and Barriers to Change." *School Science and Mathematics*, 101(5): 246–57.

Weimer, M. and Lenze, L. F. (1994). "Instructional Interventions: A Review of the Literature on Efforts to Improve Instruction." In K. Feldman and M. B. Paulsen (eds.), *Teaching and Learning in the College Classroom* (Needham Heights, MA: Ginn Press), pp. 653–82.

Part IV

Outcome assessment for general education

13 A personal view of the evaluation of the humanities and social sciences in higher education

Huang Chun-chieh

Introduction

In recent years, one of the most noted trends in higher education in Taiwan has been the implementation of the university evaluation system and the resulting changes in the content of college education. The evaluation of universities and colleges is very complicated and multifaceted. Although such systems have been applied in Europe and Australia for many years, they still cannot avoid the criticism and shame brought to researchers and institutions of advanced learning. Furthermore, the existence of such systems makes it difficult for institutions to avoid surveying the substance of education as a result of stressing quantitative evaluation standards[1] as well as the problem of academic politics.[2] Since Taiwan has begun to push evaluation systems for universities and colleges, the above-mentioned problems, which have appeared frequently overseas, have begun to appear, though with a different intensity and speed. Among these evaluations, the most difficult, and yet the most important, is the evaluation of research performance in the humanities and the social sciences.

The purpose of the present chapter is to discuss the following issue: how should the academic performance of scholars of the humanities and the social sciences be evaluated? In order to probe this issue more deeply, we shall first look into the criteria and content of a "top university." On the basis of a definition of "top university," we discuss the evaluation criteria for research results in the humanities and the social sciences. We conclude by emphasizing the importance of publication of books as a yardstick for evaluating the research of the humanities and social sciences.

The standards and content for determining a "top university"

The so-called "top university": a redefinition

IN 2006, Taiwan's Ministry of Education (hereafter MOE) budgeted NT$50 billion (US$1.67 billion) for the following five years in the hope that at least one university in Taiwan would enter the world list of "top 100 universities." In formulating this new policy, certainly domestic educational and academic factors were considered, but the foreign academic background was weighted more heavily. In recent years, every country in East Asia has started allocating special budgets to improve higher education. For example, the Japanese government is promoting and investing a vast budget into the COE program (Center of Excellence), the South Korean government enacted the BK21 project (Brain Korea 21st Century), the People's Republic of China also has its "211 Engineering" project, while in the meantime pouring vast funds into Beijing University, Qinghua University and other renowned universities. Under the pressure of international and regional competition in higher education, the MOE's promotion of the "Aspiring for the Top University" program can be regarded as an essential measure to cope with this serious international competition.

Based on the resolution of the Legislative Yuan, the MOE has urged that the 12 universities that are granted special budgets be reviewed annually. The evaluation standards were set by the MOE and the institutions. These are firm standards; since they are fairly objective, it is possible to make comparisons between universities. From the standpoint of the administration of the MOE, concrete measures can be carried out easily and so the results can be reported to the Legislative Yuan.

Problems with the current criteria

However, in examining these evaluation criteria for "top universities" set forth by the MOE in detail, we discover that they have the following problems:

1   Quantitative criteria are favored at the expense of qualitative criteria. Regarding the 12 universities which were selected to receive the special grant by the MOE, the evaluation criteria are entirely quantitative, e.g. the number of talents cultivated, the number of international publications, the number of internationally outstanding instructors and researchers, the increase in the number of concrete cooperations between domestic and foreign universities and research institutions, and so forth. No substantial criteria are being considered in the evaluation. This sort of shortcoming inevitably leads to abuses and the long-term ills resulting from the "trap of quantitative thinking." Partly to rectify this sort of quantitative comparison among universities around the world, the *Times Higher Education Supplement* (London) stresses the overall reputation of a university and its impact on the long-term development of human civilization.

2   Emphasis on technological R&D at the expense of research and education in the humanities and social sciences. The criteria set by the MOE, such as "training of talents in advanced technology or in special areas and talents used in related industries," "number of international publications," "number of cooperative projects between academia and industry," and so forth, were all formulated in terms of technological development. In contrast to the attention technological sciences have received, research and education in the humanities and social sciences were overlooked. However, this sort of imbalance will cause the university to lose balance in its scholarship

and consequently become a crippled, rather than an "aspiring to the top" university. We merely need to look at examples of genuine top universities to see that they also have top-notch colleges of humanities and social sciences, and thus to understand what has gone wrong with these evaluation criteria.

3   Viewing the university's research function as far more important than its educational function. The MOE criteria reflect the rise of the so-called research-oriented university, which emerged in Germany in the nineteenth century. Within this growing trend, universities increasingly stress research over education and advocate "increasing the number of outstanding foreign instructors and researchers," which from their point of view is a way to anticipate the "anxiety about internationalization" that is now manifested in academic communities in East Asia.

Although these trends induced by the MOE's evaluation criteria provide a basis for comparison and are easily applicable, yet, if these standards were applied thoroughly, the "aspiring for the top university" project would end up with what Mencius (371–*c.* 289BCE) called, "climbing a tree to seek fish," and "the consequence will be disaster." Under the pressure of the criteria set by the MOE, the university faculties will mentally become unable to avoid transforming into a productive machine for SCI (Science Citation Index) or SSCI (Social Science Citation Index) papers. Apart from that the university will be reduced to a factory cultivating reserve forces to benefit the vested-interest class in capitalist society; its economic function would be as an R&D factory for high-tech enterprises. And in the end, the university would become "a body without a soul," an animated corpse.

Under the guidance of the MOE's evaluation criteria, especially in the administrative operations of universities that receive the special grants, many phenomena that have been dormant for years are now developing rapidly. Some of the most obvious ones are as follows:

1   University administrative operations emphasize mechanism over atmosphere of inquiry. In adapting to the evaluation criteria, many universities adopt standards of quantification, standardization and commodification to measure their faculty's performance in research.[3] This phenomenon has reached the point where, under multiple layers of mechanized control, the university's austere character as a sanctuary for seeking truth and cultivating moral conduct can no longer be felt. As a result, relations among faculty members as well as amity between students and faculty at the universities become more faint and indifferent than ever. Some university leaders downplay this by saying that a modern university forms a "mosaic" of combined multicolored porcelain tiles, and that under the slogan of "academic autonomy" in each college and department, feudal lords still exist just as in the old days, administering colleges and departments.

2   University administrative operations emphasize "operability" over "inoperability." Under the objective format of democracy on the college campus, all sorts of university affairs, such as teaching evaluation, faculty evaluation,

teaching or research awards, and so on, must be handled in accord with the formalisms of justice, fairness and openness. In order to meet with these standards, everything is settled by a committee formed by representatives from every department. In most cases, the committee votes to determine whether a proposal passes or not. On the surface, this appears to be very "rational," but beneath the surface lies its "irrationality." The space for rational discourse among faculty members has been squeezed and shrunk under high pressure. In other words, in the current university conduct of affairs, "operable" factors have squeezed out the "inoperable" factors. This approach is certainly well adapted for the performance criteria set by the MOE. However, the program of "aspiring for the top university" should embrace culture and spirit, instead of leaving them behind and ceasing to interact with them. Recently, Professor Chu Ching-yi (朱敬一) concluded that "the key link in aiming to be a top university in the world does not lie in these namable and describable tangible items but rather in the unnamable and indescribable internal culture."[4] His emphatic expression of the "unnamable and indescribable inner culture" comes close to my point about the "inoperable" atmosphere and spirit. We both refer to the "tacit" spiritual force, which undoubtedly is the key link in "aiming to be a top university."

The features of a "top university"

On the basis of the above discussions, we can take a fresh look at the features of a "top university." As far as I am concerned, these should include at least the following three facets:

1   A top university should make an effort to create new knowledge. Since the nineteenth century, the research function of the university has been greatly strengthened. From then on, the specific function of a university as an arena for creating knowledge has received special attention. Since the end of the Second World War, technological R&D has advanced rapidly, and natural science departments have expanded. For this reason, the university's creation of new knowledge has concentrated on seeking "definite" knowledge as its goal. Scientists believe deeply in the so-called "definite" knowledge that can be "verified" quickly through a sequence of scientific procedures. However, quite to the contrary, many disciplines in the humanities and social sciences and the most impressive writers often follow a trend toward the "indefinite" as their goal, considering that "comprehension" involves a sort of eternal, endless process, and that "truth" cannot be grasped completely by quantitative means. This sort of learning that takes "comprehension" or "interpretation" (and not merely "narrative") seriously is overshadowed in modern universities that are dominated by the research methods and *modus operandi* of natural sciences. Viewed from this perspective, the scope of the university's "creation of knowledge" should be suitably expanded and redefined, so that the university might adopt a humble attitude in facing the length and breadth of the unknown world.

2   The top university should participate in students' life development and growth. While focusing on the creation and transmission of new knowledge, the university never finds energy to spare for bearing the educational responsibility of assisting students' life development and growth. In the educational and research activities of modern universities, students, as the learning subjects, study the important contents of knowledge including those of the humanities, the social sciences and the natural sciences. Very few students encounter introspective reflections concerning "the value and significance of life." Consequently, educational activities at modern universities involve "external chasing" far more than "internal reflection," and the students' consciousness of values remains unwoken.

Ever since the May Fourth Movement of 1919, university campuses in mainland China have been imbued with an intellectual atmosphere which vilifies religion. Indeed, according to the observation of Cai Yuanpei 蔡元培 (1868–1940) at Beijing University in 1911, the intellectual atmosphere was an "aesthetic education in lieu of religion."[5] Thus, when the MOE underestimates the conditions for the university students' life development and growth by promoting this NT$50 billion special budget, it thereby accelerates this negative trend, which warrants our serious attention.

3   Faculty and students of a top university should be equipped with the intellectual acumen and moral integrity to criticize cases of unfairness and injustice in our social, political and economic life. In Chinese educational tradition, intellectuals bore the spiritual mission of taking the empire as their responsibility and emphasized using the fruits of their learning to benefit the empire. The education conducted at modern universities, however, follows the trend of objectifying and generalizing knowledge for instruction and, more recently, commodifying and packaging knowledge. In recent years, the government has viewed special budgets as a way to manage university education in Taiwan. This is certainly convenient for administrative operations – but it also makes the universities that are privileged to receive the funds become "as silent as a cicada in winter" regarding political problems. That is to say, these universities have become impotent in expressing the outrage of the moral conscience of the intellectual community. This is to stifle and muffle the spirit of a top university deeply and pervasively. In the last 12 or 13 years, every university in Taiwan has tried to evaluate faculty teaching effectiveness in a rather objective way, and that is to let students grade the teaching performance of the faculty members. An evaluation system based on this sort of standard can certainly remind faculty members to make improvements to the perceived weaknesses in their teaching; however, at the same time, the side-effect of undermining the teacher's position in the educational process is very likely to reduce him or her to the position of a sales clerk in a department store of knowledge.

All in all, the goal of the "aspiring to the top university" program is positive. However, we should first offer a strict and clear definition of "top university." What content would be conducive to a mutual enrichment of inner spirit and outer conduct? Learning and living should be integrated into one. With that principle in mind, we can start a new direction for instruction and learning. According to the definition of "top university" proposed above, the humanities and social sciences should be the most crucial link, since education and research in those disciplines enable us to recombine "fact" and "value," to integrate knowledge back into the students' life development and growth and to develop them into intellectuals with critical acumen.

Evaluation criteria for research results in the humanities and social sciences

In the ideal of a "top university" adumbrated above, the humanities and social sciences would be the most crucial link. Yet, the problem remains: how should we establish evaluation criteria for research results in the humanities and social sciences? This is a serious question that requires profound reflection.

The problem with the current evaluation criteria

At present, the Chinese academic community takes the number of English-language papers published in SSCI- and A&HCI-listed journals as the sole criterion of evaluation. The strength of this kind of standard is that it encourages linkage with the English-speaking academic community. Moreover, it offers an easy standard for comparison and enhances the international visibility of research results. Indeed, in some humanities fields, such as contemporary philosophy, journal articles are the most suitable way to present new theses and arguments and to make contributions. Therefore, I do not oppose faculty in the humanities and social sciences choosing to write journal articles.

Nevertheless, this practice of taking the number of papers published in SSCI- or A&HCI-listed periodicals in English is causing some serious problems. First of all, this sort of approach to evaluation involves the "fallacy of formalism": taking the number of papers published in SSCI- and A&HCI-listed journals to serve as the sole standard of evaluation, regardless of theses, arguments or references proposed by each paper. Second adopting this standard based on the number of papers published in SSCI- and H&ACI-listed periodicals in English cannot avoid the appearance of a fawning submission to the "hegemony" of the humanities and social sciences in the English-language academic community. Needless to say, the prestigious journals dominating the humanities and social sciences fields of the English-language academic community have their academic preferences, "*problématiques*" or at least their preferred basic "methodology" or "epistemology." These preferences in *problématique*, methodology or epistemology are all rooted in the academic traditions and cultural backgrounds of Western Europe or North America, and are typically quite far removed from the indigenous academic or cultural traditions of the non-English-speaking regions of Asia, Africa and Latin America. However, in recent years Taiwan has gone too far in giving preference to papers published in SSCI- and A&HCI-listed journals, and as a result scholars in Taiwan have gradually become estranged from their own Chinese academic tradition. In extreme cases, they can easily slip into the tragedy of "academic self-colonization"! Third, in the academic community of the humanities and social sciences, to stress excessively the number of papers published encourages scholars to put their efforts into shallow and narrowly specialized research, leaving them with nothing to spare for research on more worthwhile projects that require long-term accumulation of data and sustained reflection. Indeed, this emphasis on journal articles makes it more and more unlikely that twenty-first-century academia will produce any great scholars of the magnitude of an Immanuel Kant (1724–1804), Georg Wilhelm Friedrich Hegel (1770–1831) or even another Karl Marx (1818–83).

The turn of evaluation for the humanities and social sciences

Regarding the above-mentioned drawbacks to taking the number of papers published in SSCI- and A&HCI-listed periodicals as the sole index for evaluating research results in the humanities and social sciences, I would like to propose the following, the "turn of evaluation."

1 Shift of the principle of evaluation from "formalism" to "substantialism." I suggest turning attention away from the number of publications in SSCI- and A&HCI-listed journals and emphasizing the recognition of specialized books published by publishers with review systems in place. The evaluation should consider the new "theses" and "arguments" presented in the book, as well as questions like the book's findings and contributions to the field.
2 Three items to be included in the evaluation criteria:
   a cognitive creativity or innovativeness of the research work;
   b insights of the research work that might stimulate readers' value outlook and world outlook;
   c contribution or impact of the research work to the society and culture.

Item (a) could be carried out in a relatively short period of time as a purely academic measure for conducting evaluations. Items (b) and (c) would need more time to be installed as evaluation measures. By applying these, we can observe the biggest difference between research conducted in the humanities and social sciences and that in the natural sciences. Most research results in the natural sciences can be verified or falsified through standard verification procedures, usually in a relatively short time; but research results in the humanities and social sciences usually take longer to be certified.

Conclusion

In 1994, the former vice-president of Academia Sinica, Taipei, Chang Kwang-chih 張光直 (1931–2001), said, "Every Chinese has the basic ability to undertake research in the humanities and social sciences. The research materials are contained in the *Twenty-Four Histories*. From the 1950s, Professor Mary C. Wright introduced this richest treasure in the world, a treasure house of all kinds of rules of conduct from the study of human history. Why is it that in twentieth-century scholarship, China has shown no potential to make any contribution in the humanities and the social sciences?"[6] Chang Kwang-chih's question really merits deep reflection.

The reasons why the humanities and social sciences have not rooted firmly in the Chinese-language academic community are rather complex. The first and most crucial factor is that the Chinese intellectuals of the twentieth century fetishized scientism.[7] Under the new religion of scientism, the *modus operandi* of research conducted in the humanities and the social sciences came under the sway of the *modus operandi* of scientific research. Using the number of articles published in SSCI- and A&HCI-listed periodicals as a way to calculate and measure research results in the humanities and social sciences is a manifestation of control of the procedures followed by the natural sciences. Under the sway of the *modus operandi* of the natural sciences, any questions or problems that cannot be "quantified," "specified" or "standardized" are marginalized or regarded as pseudo-questions or pseudo-problems.

The second reason is that in the twentieth century many writers in the Chinese academic community used the Western experience to serve as a frame of reference when they did research. That is, to use the East Asian experience to confirm Western academic theories in effect. For example, a famous intellectual historian of the twentieth century, Hou Wailu 侯外廬 (1903–87), announced that he, "advocate[d] combining the scattered raw materials from ancient China with historiography's principles of development in antiquity in order to conduct well-organized research properly. In effect, this is the Sinicization of historiography's principles of development. In an extended sense, [my book] is the Chinese version of [Engel's] work on the ethnic group, wealth production and nation state."[8] Hou Wailu's *Zhong'guo gudai shehui shi* 中國古代社會史 (History of Ancient Chinese Society) was really intended to use China's historical experience to serve as an Asian footnote to the theories of Karl Marx and Friedrich Engels (1820–95). In the Chinese academic community, the *problématiques* – not to mention the methodologies and epistemologies – selected for research always fall under the sway of the Western academic community. Now, the requirement to publish papers in the English-language journals listed in SSCI and A&HCI as the evaluation standard further subjugates the Chinese academic community, so it will be even more difficult for later scholars to "baptize" themselves into their own cultural and academic tradition. Moreover, it will be yet more difficult for research and innovation to have academic themes and approaches that reflect specifically Asian cultures and civilizations.

In light of the foregoing discussion, the problem pointed out by Chang Kuang-chih really is a problem involving many complex factors and historical backgrounds. I hope that in the twenty-first century Chinese humanities and social sciences studies will break free of the bonds of scientism and experience a healthy development; going beyond the evaluation criteria of publishing English-language papers in SSCI- or A&HCI-listed journals would be the thing to start with. By just going beyond the evaluation criteria of quantification, specificity and standardization, we would be able to turn from shallow "formalism" to solid "substantialism." We could then turn to use specialized books to serve as the new academic evaluation criteria in the humanities and the social sciences and head for a new advanced level of research and innovation in Chinese humanities and social sciences.

Notes

1 See Kauko Hamalaine, "Common Standards for Programme Evaluations and Accreditation?" *European Journal of Education*, 38(3) (2003): 291–300.
2 See Lee Harvey, "The Power of Accreditation: Views of Academics." *Journal of Higher Education Policy and Management*, 26(2) (July 2004): 207–23.
3 In 1947, Max Horkheimer (1895–1973) and Theodor W. Adorno (1903–69) of the Frankfurt School analyzed the self-destructive nature of Enlightenment civilization. They critiqued the Enlightenment's destructive industrial civilization's maladies of "quantification," "standardization" and "commodification." See Max Horkheimer and Theodor W. Adorno, *Dialectics of Enlightenment* (New York: Continuum Press, 1982). The three great maladies of Enlightenment industrial civilization as criticized some 60 years ago are clearly and evidently present in contemporary universities around the world.
4 Chu Ching-yi, "Wu nian wu bai yi mai motou shibushi hao touze?" 五年五佰億買魔豆是不是好投資 [Is Purchasing a Magic Bean for NT$50 Billion over Five Years a Good Investment?]. *Zhong'guo shibao* 中國時報 [*China Times*], December 11, 2006, p. A4.
5 Cai Yuanpei 蔡元培, *Cai Yuanpei quanji* 蔡元培全集 [Collected Works of Cai Yuanpei] (Zhejiang: Zhenjiang jiaoyu chubanshe, 1997), vol. 3, p. 58.
6 Chang Kwang-chih, "China's Humanities and Social Sciences Should Join the World Mainstream" [中國人文社會科學該躋身世界主流]. *Asiaweek* (亞洲週刊), Hong Kong, July 10, 1994.
7 See Daniel W. Y. Kwok, *Scientism in Chinese Thought, 1900–1950* (New Haven: Yale University Press, 1965).
8 Hou Wailu, *Zhong'guo gudai shehui shi* [History of Ancient Chinese Society] (Shanghai: Zhong'guo xueshu yanjiusuo, 1948), "Zixu" 自序 (Preface).

14 Learning outcomes of general education courses with a service-learning component

A case for academic and student affairs collaboration in Hong Kong

Lai Kwok Hung and Xu Hui Xuan

Introduction

Among educators in higher education institutions, collaboration connotes relationships of somewhat greater intensity than does the word "cooperation," and it generally implies a relationship among equals pursuing a goal of mutual interest or defined outcomes in student learning. To facilitate a seamless learning environment, the General Education Office (GEO) and the Student Affairs Office (SAO) of the Hong Kong Institute of Education (HKIEd) work collaboratively to launch pilot credit-bearing courses that incorporated a service-learning component in general education. This attempt tries to make service-learning a credit-bearing educational experience in which students participate in an organized service activity that meets identified community needs and reflect on the service activity in such a way as to gain further understanding of the course content, a broader appreciation of the discipline and an enhanced sense of civic responsibility. The aim of this chapter[1] is to explore what students have experienced and reflected on and the learning outcomes gained after being involved in service-learning, especially in terms of their generic skills competency and knowledge integration abilities, through the use of documentary analysis and quantitative survey. In addition, focus interviews and observations are used to evaluate how students perceive their own learning and provide further feedback on how such courses should be conducted. The implications on how a service-learning component can be integrated into academic learning and the building of collaborative relationships between academic faculty and student affairs are discussed.

Educational outcomes of service-learning

Community service is always regarded as an extra-curricular or co-curricular activity. Through serving the community in the form of volunteer service projects, the SAO of HKIEd provides an experiential learning environment for students to actualize what they have learned in class and complement what is not taught in the formal curriculum (Lai, 2009b). However, it is believed that service-learning goes beyond community service because the former experiences "connect students to their communities, enrich students' learning, and help them develop personally, socially, and academically" (Kinsley and McPherson, 1995, p. 1). The National Service-Learning Clearinghouse (2011) defined service-learning as a "teaching and learning strategy that integrates meaningful community service with instruction and reflection to enrich the learning experience, teach civic responsibility, and strengthen communities."

In this sense, service-learning is a form of experiential learning based on the well-established educational and cognitive theories of constructivism, pragmatism, progressivism and experiential education (Brunner, 1960; Dewey, 1938; Freire, 1970; Gardner, 1984; Kohlberg, 1984; Kolb, 1984; Lave, 1988; Piaget, 1954) in which students engage in activities that address human and community needs together with structured opportunities intentionally designed to promote student learning and development (Jacoby, 1996; Lai and Chan, 2004). It is an "academically rich form of service-based experiential education" (Furco, 2002) developed as an evolving pedagogy that incorporates student volunteering into the dynamics of experiential learning and the rigors and structure of an academic curriculum (Hink and Brandell, 2000) to encompass students' intellectual, social, personal, civic, moral and vocational development (Boud, Cohen and Walker, 1993; Dewey, 1938; Kolb, 1984; Lai, 2009b; Perry, 1970).

Through service-learning activities, students are believed to attain various personal, social, academic and career goals, such as stimulating academic performance, increasing campus engagement, enhancing leadership capabilities and multi-cultural competency, improving the environment for making ethical decisions and enhanced moral reasoning, promoting critical-thinking and problem-solving skills, increasing awareness of community problems and challenging social inequalities, becoming involved in the social problems facing their communities and heightening the connection of theory to practice (Astin and Sax, 1998; Baldwin and Buckanan, 2007; Bringle and Kremer, 1993; Cohen and Kinsey, 1994; Cutforth, 2000; Eyler and Giles, 1999; Eyler, Giles and Schmiede, 1996; Gray, Ondaatje, and Zakaras, 1999; Lai, 2009b; Lai and Leung, 2010; Meaney *et al.*, 2008; Pinzon and Arceo, 2006; Simons and Cleary, 2006). Furthermore, a multi-year investigation of student learning through independent assessment of student products within and across a sequence of service-learning enhanced courses further demonstrates that instructional methods intentionally designed to build on earlier service-learning-enhanced courses do lead to higher-order thinking and progressively more sophisticated understanding of course material (Jameson, Clayton and Bringle, 2008). In brief, it integrates community service with experiential learning – an effort to develop leadership and organizational abilities, enhance professional knowledge and promote social justice (Lai, 2009a).

For pre-service teachers, service-learning also enhances self-esteem, self-efficacy, positive views of diverse others, an ethic of caring (Donahue, Bowyer and Rosenberg, 2003; Freeman and Swick, 2001; Root, Callahan and Sepanski, 2002a; Root and Furco, 2001; Tellez *et al.*, 1995; Wade and Yarbrough, 1997), contributes to professional enhancement through increasing students' understanding of students and perceived competence as instructors (LaMaster, 2001;

Harwood, Fliss and Gaulding, 2006), improves teaching skills and increasing use of varied instructional strategies (Kahan, 1998; Watson *et al.*, 2002; Freeman and Swick, 2001; Verducci and Pope, 2001; Lake and Jones, 2008; Lai, 2009b) and increases their intent to incorporate service-learning in their future classrooms (Root, Callahan and Sepanski, 2002b).

A related theme of service-learning outcomes explored is program characteristics, that is, how the elements in the design of a service-learning program contribute to student learning gains and achievements. Reflection has been almost the most important element in previous studies as a key moderator to facilitate successful service-learning (Eyler and Giles, 1999; Eyler *et al.*, 2001). An effective reflection design is believed to give consideration to the following characteristics: scope (Blyth, Saito and Berkas, 1997), weekly, systematic and directed features (Conrad and Hedin, 1990), structure and regularity and to clarify values (Hatcher, Bringle and Muthiah, 2004).

Duration and intensity of service activities are raised in several studies as essential factors (Eyler *et al.*, 2001). Some studies reveal that longer, more intense programs produce better academic achievement and social impact (Conrad and Hedin, 1990; Blyth, Saito and Berkas, 1997), while others contrariwise indicate that the number of service hours and the number of weeks of service have no significant influence (Conway, Amel and Gerwien, 2009). However, placement quality is raised by Eyler and Giles (1999) as one of key influencing factors, and similarly, the involvement with service users and agency support are strong predictors of learning outcomes in the same way (Ngai, 2006). In the study by Astin *et al.* (2000), the involvement of faculty with reflective discussion in class is another key factor to facilitate successful learning. Ngai (2006) uses class experience to describe the role and responsibility that academic staff should take during the course offering.

The characteristics summarized above are applied in this study to analyze learning outcomes achieved and to discuss the problems we encountered.

General education in the HKIEd context

The concept of general education originated from liberal education in ancient Greece, when education was only provided for freemen and focused on the cultivation of good citizens. Since the beginning of the twentieth century, general education has been regarded as a form of curriculum and a balance to the increasing specialization in higher education. Reflecting different theoretical backgrounds, a variety of general education curricula have been developed, whether described as a general education curriculum within a liberal education tradition, intellectual essentialism and progressivism, or a combination of the above perspectives, to respond to the mission of individual higher education institutions (Xu, 2008).

In their study, Boyer and Levine (1988) reviewed the purposes of general education in three periods in the United States, 1918–30, 1943–55 and 1971–81, and over 50 different statements were listed. They found that there were two different orientations of the purposes of general education – promoting social integration and reducing the chances of disuniting society. The common purposes across the three periods included protecting a democratic society, social responsibility, morality, global perspectives and integrating different people into society. Smith (1993) reviewed the purposes of general education in different higher education institutions in the early 1990s and summarized six different views, including focusing on heritage, counterpoint to specialization, instrumental skills, student development or empowerment, social agenda or valuing.

In the Hong Kong Institute of Education, the overarching purpose of the existing general education curriculum is "to enrich the Bachelor of Education student's intellectual nutrition with a balanced diet of modules from different academic disciplines, which relate to the life of the student as a highly educated and cultured citizen of Hong Kong" (General Education Office, 2005). It recognizes the broadening of knowledge and its relation to student life, and adopts an intellectual and academic orientation. Students are required to take a minimum of six courses during their years of study and they need to take at least one course from each of the four areas, and no more than two courses from each area. These four areas are (1) philosophical and spiritual; (2) literary and artistic; (3) social and historical; and (4) scientific and technological.[2]

In HKIEd, general education courses offer serious academic study of a topic within one or more academic discipline(s), and include knowledge of the concepts, facts, theories and methods of the discipline(s) at an intellectual level. These courses usually focus on life-oriented issues, accompanied by engaging students' life experiences through an active reflection of theoretical concepts and knowledge gained in class (General Education Office and Student Affairs Office, 2008). The Institute offers these courses to expand the scope of knowledge of students outside the teacher education curriculum (Lai, 2010).

General education courses with service-learning component

The commonality of general education and service-learning in the context of HKIEd lies in the concept of relating learning to life, which means employing both the general education curriculum and service-learning to help students construct meanings and connections between academic study and actual life. On the general education side, students are expected to get a full spectrum of the understanding of the person, society and nature through looking into a life-related theme, topic, problem or issue, while on the service-learning side, experience gained from real life is one of the most valuable learning materials for constructing knowledge.

Students are expected to achieve various objectives and gain learning outcomes after completing the general education courses with a service-learning component. They include: (1) critically reflect, integrate, apply and re-examine the concepts and knowledge that they have learned in class to real-life situations in which service is involved; (2) develop active citizenship, such as becoming more aware of civic responsibility and involving themselves in concrete action that may address social justice issues and activating social change; (3) enhance personal growth via learning about oneself and one's relationship with the world and community, for example, developing skills and attitudes to become community builders in a rapidly changing and diverse world; and (4) benefit the community.

Thus, it is expected that such an initiative to incorporate a service-learning component in academic general education courses engages students in an educational process that maximizes student learning and personal development. Through serving the local and overseas communities, the Institute provides an experiential learning environment for students to actualize what they have learned in class. It encourages a natural partnership between the Institute and the community, providing students with experiences that combine real community needs with intentional learning goals, conscious reflections and critical analysis. Besides serving the population, service-learning can further build authentic partnerships and enhance collaboration with NGOs, schools, local, national as well as international organizations for the Institute.

Academic–student affairs collaboration

Student affairs practitioners usually lament the lack of relationships with their academic colleagues, while at the same time focusing their work on the out-of-class aspects, sometimes even competing with academics for their students' studying time. On the other hand, as a result of the high degree of autonomy afforded faculty and the fragmented organizational structure characteristic of the Institute, academicians are hardly aware of the existence of student affairs counterparts on campus and tend to view their functions as separate and unequal. Stereotypically, the norm of teacher education is professional training which lies in the hands of academics, with an emphasis on students' cognitive and teaching skills development, while the student affairs staff minister to the affective growth and the enhancement of generic skills of students and attend to their out-of-class experience or simply the "non-cognitive" part in the whole education of students. Such a division is arbitrary. Students may perceive these learning experiences as disjointed and unconnected. In order to create an educational environment in which students may extend their learning from one domain to a full development, academics and student affairs professionals should work together to bridge organizational boundaries for the benefit of students (Lai, 2010). From time to time, both academics and student affairs professionals become aware that students' learning should be regarded as integrated towards a total learning experience that exists both in the classroom and out-of-class environments.

Donaldson and Kozoll (1999) identified that a collaborative relationship followed a process that involved four stages, namely, emergence, evolution, implementation and transformation. Based on such a framework, Lai and Chan (2004) analyzed a collaborative partnership forged between an academic department and student affairs to launch peer mentorship and service-learning projects to improve freshmen's adjustment and sense of belonging on campus and to widen their exposure and involvement in the community through adopting the reciprocal skills of each stakeholder to achieve program goals.

To facilitate the collaboration between student affairs professionals and academics and to introduce a service-learning component into the general education curriculum, a Task Force on Service Learning in General Education was formed in 2008 to develop general education courses, adjust and formulate course content, make proposals on the necessary roles and responsibilities of the parties concerned, solicit for additional resources, suggest appropriate assessment guidelines for the courses and conduct briefing sessions for staff and students on this new initiative. These initiatives aim to further broaden students' learning from classroom study to get rich and direct experiences by providing service in communities, and at the end, integrate academic study with service experiences and enhance both learning and community. To capitalize on the expertise of academics and student affairs practitioners for the greatest benefit of students, the GEO and SAO invited lecturers from departments to offer courses to incorporate a service-learning component in credit-bearing general education courses from January 2009.[3]

Design of general education courses with a service-learning component

Academic and student affairs collaboration is an initiative new not only to the Institute but also in Hong Kong. The service-learning component of the general education courses takes the form of community service or work attachment, in either concurrent or block mode, and in local or overseas placements. Four stakeholders are engaged in these pilot courses. The course lecturers provide theoretical elements to students in classes and help them to integrate and re-examine concepts and knowledge acquired with their service experiences. Student affairs practitioners act as field instructors, providing guidance and support to students during the practicum, while liaising and coordinating with respective service agencies to foster students' learning experiences in accordance with the educational goals of the courses. They also attend lectures in these courses alongside students to enrich their knowledge base. Service agency supervisors from organizations or community groups provide diversified but intentionally designed learning opportunities for students. As service-learning is a kind of experiential education and the focus of learning is on what the learner will experience, reflect on and integrate in a course, the three parties above think carefully about the kind of academic study and practicum for inclusion that would be most appropriate. The relationship between course lecturer, field instructor, service agency supervisor and student and the learning components involved are shown in Figure 14.1.

For credit-bearing service-learning courses, students are required to connect the service experiences with some overriding context – a constant effort to derive meaning from the experiences gained in the service agency and in the classroom. The context is created primarily by the course lecturer and subject matter of the course. Each service activity needs to be understood in terms of the subject being taught. As students expect to earn credit in their general education courses, their learning objectives and activities at the service agencies must be connected to the intended course learning outcomes.

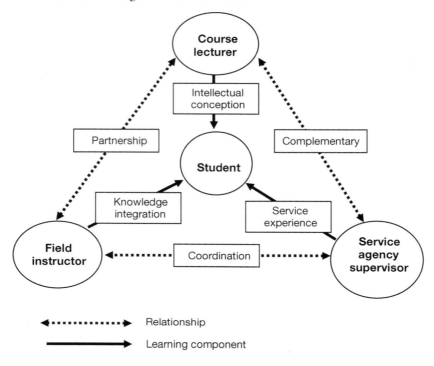

Source: Lai (2010).

Figure 14.1 Service-learning model.

After the course registration period, 25 students had enrolled for the 3 pilot service-learning general education courses for the second semester of the academic year 2008–9. They were Understanding Human Rights (GEC 1008), Christianity and Social Concern (GEA 1014) and Humanitarian Services for Developing Countries in a Globalized World (GEC 1020). Students enrolled for the former two courses were involved in concurrent placements in various local service agencies or NGOs, and the latter course offered an 11-day block placement in Vietnam. For the concurrent mode, lectures and service-learning practicum ran parallel to each other, and the latter was conducted between the third and ninth week of the second semester. In the block mode, the service-learning practicum was conducted during the Easter holidays after all lecture sessions were completed.

Before the service-learning practicum commences, students are informed about the advantages of service-learning, liability and responsibility issues and how they should approach the learning experience. They are encouraged to adopt the attitude that both the learners and the service recipients are the true beneficiaries of the service rather than the students perceiving themselves as knowledgeable individuals who come to help those that are disadvantaged. In other words, service and learning are of equal importance throughout the practicum period and students are encouraged to approach the learning experience with an open mind and an open heart, together with a desire to serve. Further, a training workshop is conducted by student affairs practitioners before the service-learning practicum for enrolled students to equip them with basic generic skills for the service-learning environment and to gain better understanding of the requirement and arrangement of different service agencies.

The field instructors facilitate the flow of information between course lecturers and service agencies. Service agencies are selected for their applicability to the subject matter of the course. A key consideration is whether the agency is a setting where service-learners will have chance to employ the subject matter of their respective courses. Students can indicate their preferences for which service agency they want to serve after an orientation by the field instructors or sometimes even by the service agency supervisors. Students are required to complete a minimum of 40 hours of service, which occupies at least 40 percent of the course time. This includes an orientation to the partnership organizations, direct services to the community and meetings with service agency supervisor and field instructor.

Before the course begins, students are matched with and allocated to service agencies. The course starts with a few lectures conducted by the course lecturer to introduce the basic knowledge and theory in respect of the course objectives. Students usually start their service-learning practicum from the third teaching week of the course. In other words, lectures and service-learning experiences run parallel to each other and the number of service-learning visits depends on the agreement between the service agency supervisor, field instructor and the students concerned. At the last lesson of the course, students conduct group presentations reflecting on their learning experiences in their service-learning placements.

Learning components of service-learning

Learning journal and service-learning agreement

Students are required to keep a learning journal. Journaling is an informal and expressive form of writing, and a way to actively engage students and promote learning (Connor-Greene, 2002). It provides students with the opportunity for reflection, self- and subject matter exploration and most importantly for making links between the service, theoretical concepts and personal experiences. Students need to complete a journal entry for each visit to their service sites. Each entry is required to include four components: a description of service activities; major accomplishments; discussion on the linkage of the day's events to course concepts, perspectives or reading; and suggestions for better performance. During the first two visits, students need to complete a service-learning agreement attached in the journal, specifying learning objectives under generic skills, theory integration and performance, after discussing with their respective field instructors. Besides day logs, the learning journal includes a critical reflection on learning experiences, unexpected issues arising and suggestions to improve learner's performance and the service quality of the respective agencies, implications of such learning experience for the individual and, finally, a plan for self-advancement after the service-learning practicum.

Service observation

The field instructors conduct service observation to support and provide necessary assistance to students during the service-learning practicum. On the one hand, the field instructor can understand more of the interaction between the students and service recipients during the process. On the other hand, the field instructor can monitor whether the service agencies can provide sufficient and appropriate service-learning opportunities to students.

Service-learning practicum meetings

For each service agency or the practicum site, the field instructors initiate meetings that involve students with a service-learning practicum in the same service agency and their supervisors. This provides a platform for the three parties to share their ideas and feelings about the practicum as well as allowing the service agency supervisor and students to have direct communication and responses to comments after the service-learning practicum. The field instructor can better understand the problems and difficulties encountered in the service-learning practicum.

The practices above are assessed by field instructors and service agency supervisors and 30 percent of the overall course grade is based on their feedback.

Class discussion and presentation

Students are asked to conduct a class presentation individually or in a group, depending on the number of students placed at that specific service site, to share and reflect on their learning experiences. Their performance during class discussion and presentation as a reflection of their integration of academic knowledge and service-learning experiences are assessed by the course lecturer. This constitutes 20 percent of the overall course grade.

Reflective essay

The assignment requires students to wrap up the learning experiences, to reflect upon them, to integrate them with the course material and personal values, to explore the impact of the service experience upon themselves and to demonstrate their ability to integrate theories and concepts with the practicum experience. In other words, it is a reflective essay and it constitutes up to 50 percent of the overall grade as proposed by the lecturer.

Enhancing knowledge integration through reflection

Kolb (1984) defined learning as "the process whereby knowledge is created through the transformation of experience" (p. 38). In order to transform the service experience into a learning process, learners must be provided with sufficient opportunities, space and guidance to reflect upon the service experience. In other words, the key pedagogical ingredient for service-learning is thoughtful reflection, whereas the goal of reflection is for students to construct meaning out of their experiences (Bringle and Hatcher, 1999; Conrad and Hedin, 1990; Eyler and Giles, 1999; Eyler, Giles and Schmiede, 1996; Hatcher and Bringle, 1997; Horwood, 1995, p. 227; Stanton, 1990) and transform their experience into learning (Schon, 1987). While the service-learning experience enables students to work with and apply course concepts and perspectives while stimulating acute feelings, they need distance to think analytically and critically about these feelings and experiences.

To facilitate such a learning process, individual consultative sessions or interviews are arranged between the students and their field instructors to negotiate the learning agreement and to provide the necessary guidance and support. In addition, consultation meetings are conducted before and during monitoring visits and after the completion of the service-learning practicum by the field instructors. Group discussion and reflection help students process their experiences while recognizing that their peers share similar experiences (Hilligoss, 1992). Student reflections on service-learning projects usually express satisfaction with their experience and the difference they have made in the community.

Becoming capable of integrating theory acquired in the academic program into real practice is one of the goals of incorporating a service-learning practicum in general education courses. Assessment is employed to establish whether students are able to integrate what they have learnt in class into the service-learning practicum. The structured reflection activities involved in these general education courses are learning agreement, learning journal, class presentation, three-party meetings among service agency supervisors, field instructors and students and reflective essay. Field instructors, who liaise and coordinate with respective service agencies and provide guidance and support to students during the practicum, are also assigned with the responsibility to help students make a connection. Field instructors try to capture their learning on this by reviewing their learning journals and conducting practicum observation as well as discussion with service agency supervisors and students.

Research methodology

Given the complex and idiosyncratic nature of the service-learning activities incorporated into an academic course, the authors adopt Bloom's taxonomy as a framework to identify the three overlapping learning domains in the analysis – cognitive, affective and psychomotor, representing the acquisition of knowledge, values and skills. The *cognitive* domain contains six major levels – knowledge, comprehension, application, analysis, synthesis and evaluation (Bloom and Krathwohl, 1956). Recently, this has been revised as to remember, understand, apply, analyze, evaluate and create (Krathwohl, 2002). Each of the higher levels incorporates the previous level as a subset of it. The values or *affective* domain consists of such behaviors as awareness, interest, attention, concern and responsibility, relating to emotions, values, attitudes and the like (Krathwohl, Bloom and Masia, 1964). Others are left to develop the *psychomotor* or skill domain, which may consist of six levels, namely, fundamental movement, perceptual abilities, physical abilities, skilled movement and non-discursive communication (Harrow, 1972; Kearsley, 2011). The authors suggest that only the cognitive and affective learning domains are included in the study as they are more relevant to service-learning educational objectives.

The authors sought to collect a wide range of data from a variety of data sources and adopt both quantitative and qualitative approaches to analyze the impacts of service-learning on students attaining the intended course learning outcomes within the framework of the two learning domains. Along with collecting pre- and post-experience survey data on students' self-perceived generic skills capabilities and performance evaluation questionnaires submitted by service agency supervisors for quantitative analysis, data were also collected through observations, focus interviews, analyzing samples of student work and the content of completed learning journals qualitatively. Each of these sets of data provided the authors with information about the various aspects of the students' service-learning experiences and served the purpose of triangulation to verify the quantitative data collected.

Observations and focus interviews

Three courses offered in the academic year 2008–9, Humanitarian Services in Developing Countries (GEC 1020), Christianity and Social Concern (GEC 1004) and Understanding Human Rights (GEC 1008) are our research targets and researchers conducted class observations, observations on meetings, individual interviews focusing on the design and implementation of the reflection components and analysis of sample reflective essays submitted by students of the three courses.

Observations are conducted during class presentation sessions and four group discussion sessions, participated in by students, field instructor and service agency supervisors. As an outsider, the author tries to find out how students reflect. Focus interviews with students, course lecturers, field instructors and service agency supervisors are conducted from the middle of the course to the end. Students are interviewed twice, either in a group or as individuals, and others are interviewed at the end of the course. Questions are semi-structured, and interviewees' actions, observations, perceptions and evaluations of the reflection activities are studied. These interview sessions are digitally recorded and the content is transcribed word by word.

Personal abilities self-evaluation questionnaire

In line with the curriculum development for Hong Kong schools, the service-learning practicum also aims to facilitate students to develop their generic skills through learning and teaching in the contexts of different subjects and are transferable to different learning situations. Generic skills are demanded in the Hong Kong school curriculum reform as key values that ought to be promoted through planned activities (Curriculum Development Council, 2000, 2001). Out of the nine generic skills outlined in the school curriculum, the authors select only five that receive more emphasis and are expected to be acquired through service-learning practicum. They are collaboration, communication, self-management, critical thinking and problem-solving. The first three provide the basis for affective skills learning, while the latter two constitute the cognitive abilities.

During the generic skills training workshop held before the service-learning practicum and after the final group discussion sessions when the practicum has been completed, students have to complete a Personal Abilities Self-Evaluation Questionnaire to assess their present self-perceived generic skills capabilities. Students are informed of the study's purpose and assured that their participation in the study will have no direct bearing on their course grade. After informed consent is provided, the participants complete questionnaires that measure generic skills capabilities. The questionnaire consists of 25 statements employing a Likert scale. These statements are grouped into five categories of generic skills as described above. Since this questionnaire is also used for students involved in service-learning as a co-curricular activity, the items created do not include aspects related to knowledge integration and perceptions on attainment of intended course learning outcomes. This can be regarded as one of the limitations in the survey design.

Content analysis of learning journals

Content analysis is conducted on the learning journals. Since the sample size is only 25, the authors decided not to employ a systematic data-coding procedure to develop themes and abandon the counting of frequencies and calculating the percentages in categories. The text is simply analyzed and interpreted mainly from the two learning domains as suggested by the authors. The focus of the analysis is on how these two domains are developed, and the process of change is the essence of what the data reveal. Through searching and examining the content of the students' writings, it is hoped that the study can reveal how fruitful learning experiences are gained through these general education courses.

Service-learning practicum student performance evaluation form

To acquire a better understanding of students' involvement and commitment to service, their performances at practicum sites are also being assessed. A service-learning practicum student performance evaluation form is given to the service agency supervisor for completion. Assessment items in the feedback form include language skills, generic skills, work-related qualities, and so on. With this completed form, the field instructor can obtain more information to assess general performance, such as work attitudes and generic skills of the students, and it can serve as a reference for proposing marks for the service-learning practicum.

Apart from service observation, group discussion with supervisor and supervisor feedback form, field instructors also discuss the learning agreement with each student so that they can better understand students' performance and the learning process involved in the service-learning practicum. In addition, validity and reliability are also considered during the study. Though there is no consensus on the application of the concepts of validity and reliability in qualitative research, scholars make use of various methods to avoid validity threat in a qualitative study and evaluate the consistency between research results and real situation, instead of focusing on the evaluation of research instruments (Chen, 2000). Two methods are used in the current study to ensure validity: (1) examining personal notes and seeing how the data have come from initial assumptions and (2) using triangulation, that is, comparing data obtained from focus interviews, observations, group discussions and learning journals.

Learning outcomes under the educational assessment framework

Since the total number of respondents is too small, there is no statistical significance when the students' mean values for overall or respective generic skills are analyzed before and after the service-learning practicum using t-test. For those 25 students, when they are asked to indicate if there are changes in their generic skills before and after the service-learning practicum by choosing within a range from "highly improved" to "highly regressed" and give reasons for their choice, all report that they have either "improved" or "highly improved" in collaboration and communication, whereas 84 percent of the respondents report improvement in critical thinking, problem-solving and self-management. Service agency supervisors are also requested to rate the level of generic skills attained by the students. All feedback forms completed by service agency supervisors reflect that students experience a positive gain throughout the service-learning experience.

Developing affective skills through mutual support and interaction

Collaboration skills are mentioned by many students, for they have rarely worked with colleagues in agencies or with their classmates before. Three students collaborated to produce a video about different people's views on asylum seekers, two students worked with a social worker to visit elderly people and women in their community, a group of three to four students taught a group of disabled children: these are examples of collaborative tasks they were involved in.

Many students also perceive a great improvement in communication skills, especially in the ability to communicate with people from different backgrounds. At the beginning of the practicum, many students do not know how to start a conversation with service recipients, such as communicating with a sex worker, an old man, adult women or even a child; but at the end of the practicum, most students report an increase in confidence in communicating fluently with such service recipients.

After analyzing the content of learning journals, it is clear that self-confidence, communication abilities and other generic skills are developed through interaction and reciprocal influence among members of the practicum unit when students become increasingly engaged in a process and develop confidence in their ability to experiment with new ideas, improve their skills and, consequently, speak out on issues that influence the achievement of learning goals.

A group of students were involved in a community organization serving a disadvantaged group as a service-learning experience for the course on understanding human rights. From a student's description in a learning journal, the authors realize that she was able to establish the necessary rapport and was being trusted through genuine relationship-building. In fact, the student was not trained as a counselor, but she claimed to have gained the skills through being involved in interaction with clients. For instance, she reflected on how she could improve and explains: "To learn and know more about sickness related to sex workers can help to develop chat topics."

Again, after preparing the roadshow and exhibition, a student reflected that besides knowing more about the concept of discrimination, he also realized how promotional materials could be more effective in educating the public on respecting human rights. In addition, he claims to have improved his communication skills through serving as a promoter of educational exhibits.

One student who works in an NGO serving women says, "I developed cooperation skills with volunteers." Another adds, "I learned that women can be very open-minded. They are willing to learn and they have their own ways and thoughts." The service-learning practicum clearly provides opportunities for students to get in touch with different target groups in society and to go beyond their limited contacts within the school setting in traditional teaching practice experiences.

From workshop to personal consultation, from individual contact to group discussion, field instructors have demonstrated their professional knowledge and competencies in helping students to adopt appropriate approaches to improve their generic skills.

Enhancing cognitive learning through knowledge integration and reflection

Among other cognitive outcomes, a better understanding of social groups is reported by many students, as service-learning provides opportunities to contact social groups such as women, the elderly, sex workers, asylum seekers, problem gamblers, disabled children, orphans, and so on, whom they would not encounter in their daily life.

Some students reflect on a better recognition of the institutions of Hong Kong society. Before taking the course, most students obtained their knowledge of Hong Kong from textbooks and the media, and there is a large gap between the macro society and students' personal life. The world is just out there. Through these courses, students have had an opportunity to know more about social issues, social, political and economic institutions through their own first-hand experiences.

One student who enrolled for the understanding human rights course and was placed in an NGO serving sex workers, explains:

> Through this service-learning practicum, I learned to think and consider more about the feeling and situation of the client ... I have objectively rethought the stereotypes of sex workers ... they are facing serious problems and discrimination and I think no human being deserves to have this ... There is no law protecting sex workers' rights ... their education level is low so that they don't know they can fight for their own rights ... so, education is very important.

She continues:

> A newcomer says she is working for her school fees as a law student, but she doesn't know much about Hong Kong law related to her job ... I try my best to explain what I know to her ... Another client says that she is told about the death of her friend who is also a sex worker ... she is very angry and concerned about how unsafe the workplace is and queries how far she could be protected by society.

After joining the discussion on "How does the financial tsunami affect women?", a student claims to realize that the government does nothing to help women facing financial problems. He further shares why women need to develop a critical perspective before they can develop their awareness of their own rights in retraining, employment and retirement protection, even if they are housewives.

Further, a student suggests that to build up women's awareness of their own rights, they first need to develop their political attitudes, because striking for human rights improvement itself is a political issue. These reflections demonstrate that students have deduced what they have realized and observed from daily interactions. But it seems there is still a lack of a more in-depth discussion on the theoretical aspects concerned.

A male student placed in the agency serving sex workers writes:

> I understand how an NGO operates and the importance of team work to overcome difficulties. I also deeply feel how sex workers are being discriminated against, which affects their normal social life and develops feelings of alienation towards society. In spite of such an adverse situation, sex workers take their jobs seriously and want to perform well. With such a good working

attitude, they should not be discriminated against. Those who have power simply take advantage of this minority group, suppressing or treating them as a commodity or a political tool to build up their own reputation. This issue should be further examined. Whereas, what the NGO concentrates on relates to safe sex education instead of adopting social action approaches to advocate for public recognition for their suppressed human rights. After the placement, I started to develop new perspectives towards issues relating to sex, especially sexual discrimination. This experience encourages me to adopt different perspectives in exploring our society.

Such reflections demonstrate that the student has developed fresh viewpoints after working with sex workers.

One student, after working with a group of asylum seekers from Africa, for the course on Christianity and social concern, suggests that descendants of Chinese refugees in Hong Kong should take responsibility for caring for them when they were in Hong Kong. Another student involved in an NGO with a Christian background is moved by the commitment of staff to strike for social justice for the ethnic minority population and the victims of the June 4 incident 20 years ago.

A student involved in the service-learning practicum in Vietnam for the course on humanitarian services for developing countries in a globalized world, expressed how conservation of traditional culture is important under conditions of rapid globalization. She is astonished to see advertisements for international brand products and imported goods everywhere, but most people cannot afford to buy such products. Another student realized that globalization implies inter-dependence and international cooperation through the production and diver-sification of goods. One student concluded that "globalization makes people closer" when she saw products from China everywhere and local shopkeepers speaking Chinese at tourist spots.

Problems arise as a result of rapid economic development. One of the most obvious problems students identified in a developing country like Vietnam is the great discrepancy between the rich and the poor. One student explained in her learning journal that "globalization enables the rich (producers) to export goods, but the poor (farmers) need to buy expensive imported products because the quality of local products is so bad." One student commented that Vietnamese education is vocationally oriented – to train skilled labor to meet societal needs – and generic skills and personal values are totally neglected.

In terms of technological development, another student commented that:

Society is inclined towards internet technology and ignores medicine and public health because the former has higher economic value. Water is polluted as corporations are attempting to trade-off industrial produc-tion against environmental conservation. Similarly, orphans do not have the right to study in public schools unless they are adopted. Social welfare systems lag behind. Corruption is seen everywhere, which creates unfair competition and exploitation. For instance, prices at supermarkets are not set at the "required" standard because government officials are corrupt and do not mount prosecutions.

Through such observations and daily interactions with local people, students know more about what problems developing countries have faced due to rapid economic development. This first-hand information is a valuable asset when they analyze globalization issues. However, from the learning journals, the authors discovered that students focus on describing what they have observed (such as international brands, imported food and poor people), with little in-depth discussion and reflection. Some write down a few questions as reflections, such as "How can WTO and the Vietnamese government help to reduce exploitation of foreign companies?" Others realize their own weaknesses in leadership abilities, communication, knowledge of Vietnamese culture, low adaptability to acute shortage of facilities, passiveness, and so on.

In general, students usually focus on how effective their practicum performance is (tasks accomplished) and overlook their role in dealing with a social phenomenon or the impact of their work on the identified social problems from a theoretical perspective (knowledge integration). Students usually report on an increase in their ability for self-reflection on their own personal values and life conditions during and after service activities. Though some students claim that they have experienced improvements to their critical thinking skills, their service agency supervisors and course lecturers have expressed different views. Students usually admit that they are able to understand an issue from different perspectives, but the respective agency supervisors and course lecturers continue to regard their students as unable to understand an issue based on reliable evidence and make logical and reasonable judgments.

Problems encountered and suggestions for overcoming them

Course duration and learning activities

When the field instructors negotiate for placements with service agencies, some difficulties are encountered. Some agencies wonder if pre-service teachers are capable of handling assigned tasks they are not trained for. It is found that both students and agencies reflect that some students lack the appropriate program and communication skills, especially in placements that need students to work with clients from different cultural backgrounds, such as asylum workers, sex workers and Vietnamese. Since the placement period is only 40 hours, agencies have difficulty assigning appropriate tasks for students, especially tasks that could enable students to incorporate learned theories, since agency supervisors have little idea of what specific theories students have learned in the course. Students also find it difficult to establish working relations within such a short time span. So, in order to purposefully synthesize service-learning activities with academic study, the planned service-learning experience must be more than just an add-on to an already full syllabus or an existing course.

One common concern raised by both field instructors and course lecturers is that the existing course design cannot provide students with sufficient academic preparation. Fewer class sessions are allocated for service-learning general education courses, and only six or seven class sessions are arranged in the ten-week system. Given this limitation, course lecturers have to cut down the coverage of course content, students do not have enough time to read recommended materials after class due to their busy schedule, and there is no tutorial period for different parties to discuss specific issues.

More demanding than traditional classroom learning

In general, students are very engaged in the educational process of the courses, and they are keen to participate and learn. They treasure the opportunity to widen their exposure outside the classroom. Integrating academic content and service in the community brings students a sense of connectedness between classroom learning and their personal lives and the lives of others within the larger community. Requiring students to become active participants in their community takes them away from the passive role of simply reading and taking notes. Being active in this capacity allows them to discover for themselves the link between subject matter and actual experience.

However, integrating service-learning into a course involves several trade-offs for the course lecturers, the field instructors and the students. The primary trade-off is the time required of these parties. Especially in the case of field instructors, they must spend time getting familiar with the service agencies, contacting the agency supervisors and visiting them at least once before or during the semester. The learning journals require a significant amount of time to read. In addition, both course lecturers and field instructors have more out-of-class discussions with students than in traditional classroom teaching courses, usually involving reactions to or concerns about the service-learning practicum. Students certainly find being involved in the service-learning practicum time-consuming, especially when traveling time to the practice site is required but does not count as part of the 40 hours. They find such arrangements much more demanding in terms of time input than other courses where they need only attend lectures. This trade-off is acceptable and expected, since the process helps students integrate their educational and "real-life" experiences.

Discrepancies in perception and expectation

Administrative work, described by the service agency supervisor as helping students understand the organization, such as counter duties, data entry and archiving files, is regarded as irrelevant to the course, boring and a waste of time by students. Few students have any interest in exploring or finding out relevant materials actively during the office work. This discrepancy between students and their respective service agencies is because students are not sure of the purpose of the administrative work or have different expectation of the service practicum.

In one agency, students are asked to attend talks delivered by other social service agencies and regard these talks as unrelated activities. From the agency's view, talks organized by other agencies to create awareness of the rights of minority groups are related to specific human rights issues. Students' perception of irrelevancy may be accounted for by their inability to relate abstract knowledge about human rights concepts to real-world situations. So, more debriefing after such talks or clarification of the objectives of field activities might be needed.

In order to match the agencies' missions and service-learning assignments, the course lecturer intentionally adds or drops some academic topics, and what students perceive is a weak relationship between the domain of topics and experience. What happens in the field is usually more diversified and hard to control. When the range of topics selected is narrow, it is more difficult to make connections.

When the course lecturer designs the course content, he considers only the relation between the topics offered and the mission of the collaborative agencies, and has not constructed a clear mapping between each academic concept and assigned service activities. This is because the course lecturer has a vague concept of what students are supposed to do and the service activities are mainly arranged by the service agency supervisor, who might have different perception on the nature and types of activities. So, to improve this, communications among the three parties should be enhanced in order to establish clear guidelines and expectations on assignments for students.

Integrating knowledge and synthesizing concepts

Students appreciate the harmonious working environment and culture in NGOs. They have gained a better knowledge in specific areas when dealing with new job assignments. They have reflected that they have become more resourceful and more mature after dealing with difficult cases, especially in terms of problem-solving abilities and self-management skills in a different cultural setting. However, from analyzing the content of the learning journals, it is clear that students' ability to synthesize theoretical concepts is quite weak. In order to help students connect academic study with service activities, more guiding questions in lectures and class discussions are necessary. The former are used to help sensitize students to the practicum experience, while class discussion would encourage students to synthesize concepts or theories learned in class with specific issues and experiences encountered in the field, and to interpret such experiences from the academic perspective. Identifying readings that link the service to specific topics would also be helpful.

At the focus interview sessions, students report difficulties in making connections between academic content and their field experience at different levels. Most students taking the understanding human rights course claim that it is hard to see the relevance of concepts such as human rights, discrimination and social justice to the service tasks they are currently involved with at the first interview. While some students have an opportunity to apply some key concepts they learned in the course while they are working in the field, others report that they do not have appropriate concepts or sufficient academic perspectives when they conduct observations for reflective thinking.

One group of students, assigned to conduct a survey for a service center for the elderly, reported positive connections at the second interview, and were able to explain in great detail how their work was related to human rights issues, particularly on the appropriate rights of the elderly, after analyzing the unfair situation and lack of policy support to alleviate poverty. They were engaged in certain social actions, such as demonstrations, to express the needs of the elderly. These experiences are good examples of gains in higher-level cognitive development, in which their conceptual knowledge functions at the level of evaluation and reframing.

Though some students clearly reported being able to integrate what they have learned in class when their service experiences are related clearly with academic content, a large number of others commented that their academic outcomes from course lecturers were not as positive as expected. Based on the reflective essays collected and performance in class presentation, students are perceived as not able to employ course concepts to explain specific issues they have encountered in the field or display a consistent understanding of an issue through linking materials with class lecture, readings and practical experience. Class presentation is more a chance to share service experience than a demonstration of cognitive abilities, such as raising important social issues, identifying the causes and problems, interpreting issues and events from an academic point of view, formulating personal explanation and making defensible judgments, and so on. As there is no explicit requirement in the assignment requirements that the connection should be addressed in one course, the reflective essay is used by students as a means to enhance their linkage and in-depth analysis.

Field instructor

In the original design, field instructors are expected to facilitate students in knowledge integration, but it turns out that field instructors are focusing more on students' personal development. This may be explained by the nature of the expertise of student affairs practitioners in developing students' generic skills through co-curricular activities. In addition, these field instructors do not have similar service-learning experience before or they are not trained specifically in this aspect.

Service agency supervisor

Whether the service agency supervisors can facilitate students in knowledge integration depends on work allocation for students and their academic background. When a service agency supervisor is a social worker, students would be more likely to get briefing or debriefing experience. However, service agency supervisors may not be very clear about the objectives and content of the course and they may not have expertise in teaching and delivery of a concept. They should not be expected to play a key role in facilitating students to make knowledge connections purposefully. Some service agency supervisors arrange briefing and debriefing before and after each service entry, some provide students with training at the beginning and then let students work by themselves, while others provide instruction to students randomly. Some supervisors relate service activities to course themes intentionally, while others just point out a direction with no detailed analysis for sharing.

Students are supervised by service agency supervisors in the practicum, who might adopt different perspectives to interpret social issues from those employed by course lecturers. For example, one group of students in the course on understanding human rights reports that their agency supervisors always explained and interpreted women's groups from the point of view of a social worker, while the course lecturer analyzed the issue from the legal perspective, which sometimes confused them.

Course lecturer

Course lecturers have relatively little knowledge of students' actual fieldwork experience and spend most of the time in the delivery of course content and are not involved much in helping students to reflect on and establish knowledge–experience integration. With a clear understanding of the academic content to be delivered, the course lecturer should take up a more central role in helping students achieve integrative learning, grasp social issues from an academic perspective and achieve better understanding of academic topics. As course lecturers are not able to spend a long time with students during their service-learning placements, classroom discussion is suggested as an alternative initiative to facilitate student integration. Students are asked to share what they have experienced and the questions and social issues they have identified in the field, and become involved in lecturer-led discussions with other learners on the possible perspectives and concepts for further exploration.

Learning components re-considered

Learning journal writing

Students adopt different ways to respond to the requirement of journal writing, such as writing the most important experience and inspiration, or filling the column as part of completing an assignment. Some students report positive effects of writing a learning journal, such as inspiring more reflection, identifying achievements every day and building on personal learning experiences. But others comment that it is not necessary to describe similar experiences every time they complete a journal entry and it is too structured to have to answer four questions for each journal entry, as some questions are not really necessary for each entry, such as "How can I be better?". They prefer more open-ended descriptions.

Service-learning agreement

Four questions are asked to guide students to set up their own objectives for learning in the practicum, but students have different views on it. Some regard the questions as totally beyond their experience on the practicum, questions are not very relevant and appropriate, though some agree that the learning agreement helps them a lot during the practicum.

Class presentation

Students are inclined to report what they have experienced in the field and provide general connection between the case they have met and the legal issues or the theoretical explanations behind it. If the presentation is regarded as a way to demonstrate students' understandings of social issues, more detailed guidelines may be required to make learning meaningful.

Reflective essay

Just from some of the essays submitted to the lecturer, the authors report that students work well on writing and with reference to basic literature as they are able to analyze issues by borrowing the concepts delivered and discussed in class. Service-learning experiences make students better able to finalize the paper because they feel more sensitized to both experiences and academic study.

Research limitations

These three pilot courses enabled the authors to examine what learning experiences are gained by students after engaging in a service-learning practicum. The qualitative analysis of the day-logs and learning journals demonstrates the knowledge and behaviors gained by these pre-service teachers, especially in communication and collaborative abilities, but the lack of a systematic assessment of the outcomes related to the course limits this investigation. As pilot courses, the total number of students involved is not large enough for a more quantitative analysis. Replicating and extending these findings to include perceived benefits and outcomes by the service recipients and the community would significantly contribute to the literature on courses with service-learning components.

Discussion

Integrating a service-learning component in general education

Service-learning, as pedagogy, has been used in various disciplines, and the existing study is an illustration that service-learning could be incorporated into general education courses effectively. However, though general education in HKIEd has a broad scope and includes the domains of the humanities, social sciences and science and technology, only courses in social sciences have been developed in the pilot round. This is because themes and issues in social sciences are more relevant to social life and more suitable for an experience-based approach, and students may learn a topic or concept through observing and participating in activities.

When agencies consider possible tasks to be allocated to students from HKIEd, the initial concern is usually the expertise and professional abilities of students. Interviews from agencies show that students are always regarded as being equipped with appropriate teaching abilities, and service activities such as designing a teaching kit or teaching children should be arranged. This consideration raises one of the difficulties of incorporating service-learning in general education. General education in HKIEd does not intend to cultivate students' expertise in a specialized area, but instead is planned to broaden students' horizons in various areas and most students are expected to complete their general education requirement in the first two years. Students are therefore not prepared to equip themselves with the required professional skills during a service practicum, such as providing a consultation service to women on legal issues or their own rights, conducting a workshop for or educating a group of gamblers from the perspective of Christianity, and so on. The lack of professional skills or adequate knowledge of specific aspects usually creates difficulties for students while completing their assignments, though such knowledge and skills are related to the course content.

Another limitation arises from the structure of the pilot general education courses. As only 40 percent of the course time is taken up by the practicum, equivalent to at least 40 hours of service experience, students always report that they have not fully equipped themselves with the necessary academic knowledge for a fruitful processing of their service-learning experiences. On the other hand, students need to devote more time to commit themselves in both academic study and service practicum when compared with peers who are assessed only on their coursework in other general education courses. Though students reflect a higher satisfaction gained from their own learning experience in both interviews and questionnaire survey, they complain at the higher demands of completing these pilot service-learning general education courses.

Another issue relates to the academic rigor and the design of the course. One alternative is to convert the three-credit-point course to a six credit-point-course and to extend the course duration to two semesters or convert it to a one-year course. In other words, students are expected to equip themselves with the necessary academic knowledge and theoretical concepts in the first semester, followed by the service-learning practicum, reflection and integration in the following semester or as a stand-alone course. In addition, there is also concern about the respective roles of course lecturer and field instructor in assisting students in broadening or deepening their knowledge base while processing their own learning experiences for knowledge integration through reflection.

Academic and student affairs collaboration

If collaborative efforts represent a real or perceived addition to people's normal work as assignments or appear to represent a more time-consuming approach to completing those assignments as mentioned previously, reluctance is inevitable. The SAO provides its support for the pilot courses through deploying its professional staff to serve as field instructors without demanding extra funding resources from respective faculties. However, in the long run, additional resources or a sharing of existing funds between faculties and the SAO may be required to support a collaborative effort, especially when resources are allocated according to the one-line budget principle. Though collaboration will result in more efficient use of time and money, few are likely to make that assumption in advance (Brown, 1990). So, commitment towards adopting an integrated approach or restructuring departmental barriers to facilitate students' seamless learning is needed.

Co-curricular activities and non-formal student activities have traditionally been considered as a supplement to the formal curriculum where the onus of education mainly lies. Without overthrowing the traditional values of classroom course-based learning, this approach of incorporating service-learning experience into credit-bearing general education courses allows for better synergy and seamless collaboration in which learning experiences gained from the classroom and out-of-class involvement could be integrated through involving academic and SAO colleagues as working partners. This helps to bring greater alignment and a more coordinated approach to achieving student development outcomes. This approach also encourages students to become actively engaged learners through increased emphasis on adopting experiential learning initiatives to holistic development and total learning. The reflection component on the service-learning experiences, so necessary for optimal experiential learning, could best be handled through classroom discussion and individual consultation at the service site. Both course lecturers and field instructors can find roles to play in this respect.

The results from this study add to a growing body of research documenting the impacts of service-learning experiences on knowledge integration in curriculum design and pedagogy. Most important, they shed light on how the curriculum and students' out-of-class learning experiences can be integrated. Sobania and Braskamp (2009) frame service-learning as part of a larger, more inclusive set of "study away" experiences that occur beyond the classroom and incorporate experiential learning techniques. Given their close proximity to students and the surrounding community, student affairs practitioners represent an important bridge in forging mutually beneficial study-away connections among students and the local community. Given their expertise in student development, student affairs practitioners are uniquely poised to take a more active or even leadership role in facilitating discussion with faculty about the connections between community engagement, service-learning, program innovation and curriculum design.

Conclusion

To build a seamless learning environment, academics and student affairs professionals should establish a truly collaborative effort to analyze, strategize, and implement programs to bridge organizational boundaries for the benefit of students. This collaborative initiative is clearly one way to offer expanded services to students at no additional expense, using the combined efforts of teaching staff and student affairs personnel (Lai, 2005). To enhance good collaboration, a shared vision and set of priorities about student learning that are congruent between academics and student affairs practitioners need to be developed. Mutual respect is the core element for success.

Notes

1   Part of this chapter is based on papers presented by Dr. K. H. Lai on "Developing Generic Skills and Enhancing Knowledge Integration through Service-Learning" and Dr. H. X. Xu on "Can Reflection Alone Facilitate Students to Integrate Academic Knowledge and Service Activities in an Academic Service Learning Course?" at the 2nd Asia-Pacific Regional Conference on Service-Learning held in Hong Kong in 2009; Dr. H. X. Xu on "Cognitive Learning Outcomes of Service-Learning Courses and Program Characteristics that Matter" at the 10th International Research Conference on Service-Learning and Community Engagement held in Indianapolis, USA in 2010. The authors want to express their sincere thanks to Ms. Loretta Leung, Mr. Tommy Law and Mr. Lin Chor, field instructors of the three pilot courses, for their contributions and suggestions to enrich the content of this chapter. In addition, during the planning and implementation of the pilot courses, Dr. Y. W. Leung, Mr. Y. K. Chong and Dr. Y. C. Lo, the course lecturers, shared their views on how this collaborative effort could be improved. Most important of all, we thank the 25 students who have been involved whole-heartedly in both local and overseas service placements and demonstrated how service-learning contributes to more fruitful learning experiences.

2   A new general education curriculum was launched in the academic year 2012/13. It is divided into three parts: (1) foundation; (2) breadth; and (3) consolidation. With an emphasis on integrative learning, students are expected to acquire a coherent learning experience that begins with a discussion about thinking skills in the context of disciplinary studies in their first year foundation course, extend their epistemic perspective through exploring the more focused topics across different fields within the breadth area and synthesize their disparate learning experiences into a meaningful whole for the consolidation course.

3   In the Hong Kong Institute of Education, the General Education Office is an administrative office and coordinates the daily administrative work. General education courses are provided and owned by academic departments. The design and quality assurance of the general education curriculum is monitored by an independent Committee on General Education.

References

Astin, A. W. and Sax, L. J. (1998). "How Undergraduates are Affected by Service Participation." *Journal of College Student Development*, 39: 251–63.

Astin, A. W., Vogelgesang, L. J., Ikeda, E. K. and Yee, J. A. (2000). *How Service Learning Affects Students* (Los Angeles: Higher Education Research Institute, UCLA).

Baldwin, S. C. and Buchanan, A. M. (2007). "What Teacher Candidates Learned about Diversity, Social Justice, and Themselves from Service-Learning Experiences." *Journal of Teacher Education*, 58: 315–27.

Bloom, B. S. and Krathwohl, D. R. (1956). *Taxonomy of Educational Objectives: The Classification of Educational Goals, by a Committee of College and University Examiners, Handbook I: Cognitive Domain* (New York: Longman Green).

Blyth, D., Saito, R. and Berkas, T. (1997). "A Quantitative Study of the Impact of Service-Learning Programs." In A. Waterman (ed.), *Service-Learning: Applications from the Research* (Mahwah, NJ: Erlbaum), pp. 39–55.

Boud, D., Cohen, R. and Walker, D. (1993). *Using Experience for Learning* (London: Society for Research into Higher Education).

Boyer, E. L. and Levine, A. (1988). *A Quest for Common Learning: The Aims of General Education* (Princeton: Princeton University Press).

Bringle, R. G. and Hatcher, J. A. (1999). "Reflection in Service Learning: Making Meaning of Experience." *Educational Horizons*, 77(4): 179–85.

Bringle, R. G. and Kremer, J. F. (1993). "An Evaluation of an Intergenerational Service-learning Project for Undergraduates." *Educational Gerontologist*, 19: 407–16.

Brown, S. S. (1990). "Strengthening Ties to Academic Affairs." In M. J. Barr, M. L. Upcraft and associates (eds.), *New Futures for Student Affairs: Building a Vision for Professional Leadership and Practice* (San Francisco: Jossey-Bass), pp. 239–69.

Bruner, J. S. (1960). *The Process of Education* (Cambridge, MA: Harvard University Press).

Chen, X. M. (2000). *Qualitative Research in Social Sciences* (Beijing: Educational Science Publishers).

Cohen, J. and Kinsey, D. (1994). "Doing Good and Scholarship: A Service Learning Study." *Journalism Educator*, 48: 4–14.

Connor-Greene, P. A. (2002). "Making Connections: Evaluating the Effectiveness of Journal Writing in Enhancing Student Learning." *Teaching Psychology*, 27: 44–46.

Conrad, D. and Hedin, D. (1990). "Learning from Service: Experience is the Best Teacher – Or Is It?" In J. Kendall and associates (eds.), *Combining Service and Learning, I* (Raleigh, NC: National Society for Internships and Experiential Education), pp. 87–98.

Conway, J. M., Amel, E. L. and Gerwien, D. P. (2009). "Teaching and Learning in the Social Context: A Meta-analysis of Service Learning's Effects on Academic, Personal, Social, and Citizenship Outcomes." *Teaching of Psychology*, 36: 233–45.

Curriculum Development Council (2000). *Learning to Learn: The Way Forward in Curriculum Development* (Hong Kong SAR: Government Printer).

Curriculum Development Council (2001). *Learning to Learn: Life-Long Learning and Whole-Person Development*. Hong Kong SAR: Government Printer.

Cutforth, N. J. (2000). "Connecting School Physical Education to the Community through Service-Learning." *Journal of Physical Education, Recreation and Dance*, 71: 39–45.

Dewey, J. (1938). *Education and Experience* (New York: Macmillan).

Donahue, D. J., Bowyer, J. and Rosenberg, D. (2003). "Learning with and Learning from: Reciprocity in Service Learning Teacher Education." *Equity and Excellence in Education*, 36(1): 15–27.

Donaldson, J. F. and Kozoll, C. F. (1999). *Collaborative Program Planning: Principles, Practices, and Strategies* (Malabar, FL: Krieger).

Eyler, J. and Giles, D. E., Jr. (1999). *Where's the Learning in Service-Learning?* (San Francisco: Jossey-Bass).

Eyler, J., Giles, D. E., Jr. and Schmiede, A. (1996). *A Practitioner's Guide to Reflection in Service-Learning: Student Voices and Reflections* (Nashville, TN: Vanderbilt University).

Eyler, J., Giles, D. E., Jr., Stenson, C. and Gray, C. (2001). *At a Glance: Summary and Annotated Bibliography of Recent Service-Learning Research in Higher Education*, 3rd edn. (Minneapolis, MN: Learn and Serve America National Service-Learning Clearinghouse).

Freeman, N. K. and Swick, K. (2001). "Early Childhood Teacher Education Students Strengthen their Caring and Competence through Service-Learning." In J. A. Anderson, K. J. Swick and J. Yff (eds.), *Service-Learning in Teacher Education: Enhancing the Growth of New Teachers, Their Students, and Communities* (Washington, DC: American Association of Colleges of Teacher Education), pp. 134–40.

Freire, P. (1970). *Pedagogy of the Oppressed* (New York: Continuum).

Furco, A. (2002). "Is Service-Learning Really Better than Community Service?" In A. Furco and S. H. Billig (eds.), *Service-Learning: The Essence of the Pedagogy* (Greenwich, CT: Information Age Publishing), pp. 23–50.

Gardner, J. W. (1984). *Excellence: Can We Be Equal and Excellent Too?* (New York: W. W. Norton).

General Edcuation Office (2005). Guidelines on General Education. Hong Kong: Hong Kong Institute of Education (unpublished).

General Education Office and Student Affairs Office (2008). Manual on Service-Learning in General Education. Hong Kong: Hong Kong Institute of Education (unpublished).

Gray, M. J., Ondaatje, E. H. and Zakaras, L. (1999). *Combining Service and Learning in Higher Education* (Washington, DC: Rand).

Harrow, A. J. (1972). *Taxonomy of the Psychomotor Domain: A Guide for Developing Behavioral Objectives* (New York: McKay).

Harwood, A. M., Fliss, D. and Gaulding, E. (2006). "Impacts of a Service-Learning Seminar and Practicum on Preservice Teachers' Understanding of Pedagogy, Community, and Themselves." In K. M. Casey, G. Davidson, S. H. Billig and N. C. Springer (eds.), *Advancing Knowledge in Service-Learning: Research to Transform the Field* (Greenwich, CT: Information Age Publishing), pp. 137–58.

Hatcher, J. A. and Bringle, R. G. (1997). "Reflection: Bridging the Gap between Service and Learning." *College Teaching*, 45(4): 153–58.

Hatcher, J. A., Bringle, R. G. and Muthiah, R. (2004). "Designing Effective Reflection: What Matters to Service Learning?" *Michigan Journal of Community Service Learning*, 11(1): 38–46.

Hilligoss, T. (1992). "Demystifying Classroom Chemistry: The Role of the Interactive Learning Model." *Teaching Sociology*, 20: 12–17.

Hink, S. S. and Brandell, M. E. (2000). "The Relationship between Institutional Support and Campus Acceptance of Academic Service Learning." *American Behavioral Scientist*, 43: 868–81.

Horwood, B. (1995). "Reflections on Reflection." In R. J. Kraft and J. Kielsmeier (eds.), *Experiential Learning in Schools and Higher Education* (Iowa: Kendall/Hunt), pp. 227–29.

Jacoby, B. (1996). "Service Learning in Today's Higher Education." In Jacoby (ed.), *Service Learning in Higher Education: Concepts and Practices* (San Francisco: Jossey-Bass), pp. 3–25.

Jameson, J. K., Clayton, P. H. and Bringle, R. G. (2008). "Investigating Student Learning within and across Linked Service-Learning Courses." In M. A. Bowdon,

S. H. Billig and B. A. Holland (eds.), *Scholarship for Sustaining Service-Learning and Civic Engagement* (Charlotte, NC: Information Age Publishing), pp. 3–27.

Kahan, D. (1998). "When Everyone Gets What They Want: A Description of a Physical Education-Teacher Education Service-Learning Project." *Action in Teacher Education*, 19: 43–60.

Kearsley, G. (2011). "Taxonomies." In the Theory into Practice Database. Online. Available HTTP: <http://tip.psychology.org/taxonomy.html>, accessed April 15, 2011.

Kingsley, C. W. and McPherson, K. (1995). *Enriching the Curriculum through Service-Learning* (Alexandria, VA: Association for Supervision and Curriculum Development).

Kohlberg, L. (1984). *Essays on Moral Development*, vol. 2, *The Psychology of Moral Development* (Englewood Cliffs, NJ: Prentice-Hall).

Kolb, D. A. (1984). *Experiential Learning: Experience as the Source of Learning and Development* (Englewood Cliffs, NJ: Prentice-Hall).

Krathwohl, D. R. (2002). "A Revision of Bloom's Taxonomy." *Theory in Practice*, 41(4): 212–18.

Krathwohl, D. R., Bloom, B. S. and Masia, B. B. (1964). *Taxonomy of Educational Objectives: The Classification of Educational Goals, Handbook II: Affective Domain*. New York: David McKay Co. Inc.

Lai, K. H. (2005). "New Student Orientation: Tri-party Collaboration Experience." In Asia-Pacific Student Services Association (ed.), *A Collection of Papers by Members of the APSSA and International Guest Participants at the International Symposium on Student Affairs in Higher Education* (Wuhan: Huazhong University of Science and Technology), pp. 11–23.

Lai, K. H. (2009a). "The Tri-values of Service-Learning." *Spring Breeze*, 1: 2 (Hong Kong SAR: HKIEd).

Lai, K. H. (2009b). "Developing Leadership and Cultural Competency through Service Exposure Attachment Program." *New Horizons in Education*, Special Issue, 57(3): 105–18.

Lai, K. H. (2010). "Building Students' Total Learning Experience through Integrating Service-Learning into the Teacher Education Curriculum." In Jun Xing and Carol Ma (eds.), *Service Learning in Asia: Curricular Models and Practices* (Hong Kong: Hong Kong University Press), pp. 47–61.

Lai, K. H. and Chan, T. (2004). "A Collaborative Student Affairs and Department Peer Mentorship and Service Learning Initiatives." *Proceedings of the 9th Asia Pacific Student Services Association Conference* (Bangkok: APSSA Conference Organizing Committee), pp. 181–87.

Lai, K. H. and Leung, H. Y. Phoebe (2010). "Change in Generic Skills Competencies after Participating in Service Education Projects." Paper presented at the 12th Asia Pacific Student Services Association International Conference, Brisbane, Australia.

Lake, V. E. and Jones, I. (2008). "Service-Learning in Early Childhood Teacher Education: Using Service to Put Meaning Back into Learning." *Teaching and Teacher Education*, 24: 2146–56.

LaMaster, K. J. (2001). "Enhancing Preservice Teachers Field Experiences through the Addition of a Service-learning Component." *Journal of Experiential Education*, 24: 27–33.

Lave, J. (1988). *Cognition in Practice: Mind, Mathematics and Culture in Everyday Life* (Cambridge: Cambridge University Press).

Meaney, K. S., Bohler, H. R., Kopf, K., Hernandez, L. and Scott, L. S. (2008). "Service-Learning and Pre-Service Educators' Cultural Competence for Teaching: An Exploratory Study." *Journal of Experiential Education*, 31(2): 189–208.

National Service-Learning Clearinghouse (2011). *What Is Service-Learning?* Online. Available HTTP: <http://www.servicelearning.org/what_is_service-learning/>, accessed January 18, 2011.

Ngai, S. S. Y. (2006). "Service-Learning, Personal Development and Social Commitment: A Case Study of University Students in Hong Kong." *Adolescence*, 41: 165–76.

Perry, W. G. (1970). *Forms of Intellectual and Ethical Development in the College Years: A Scheme* (Troy, MO: Holt, Rinehart and Winston).

Piaget, J. (1954). *The Construction of Reality in the Child* (New York: Ballantine Books).

Pinzon, D. P. and Arceo, F. D. B. (2006). "Critical Thinking in a Higher Education Service-Learning Program." In K. M. Casey, G. Davidson, S. H. Billig and N. C. Springer (eds.), *Advancing Knowledge in Service-Learning: Research to Transform the Field* (Greenwich, CT: Information Age Publishing), pp. 89–110.

Root, S. and Furco, A. (2001). "A Review of Research on Service-Learning in Preservice Teacher Education." In J. A. Anderson, K. J. Swick and J. Yff (eds.), *Service-Learning in Teacher Education: Enhancing the Growth of New Teachers, Their Students, and Communities* (Washington, DC: American Association of Colleges of Teacher Education), pp. 86–101.

Root, S., Callahan, J. and Sepanski, J. (2002a). "Service-Learning in Teacher Education: A Consideration of Qualitative and Quantitative Outcomes." In A. Furco and S. H. Billig (eds.), *Service-Learning: The Essence of the Pedagogy* (Greenwich, CT: Information Age Publishing), pp. 223–43.

Root, S., Callahan, J. and Sepanski, J. (2002b). "Building Teaching Dispositions and Service-Learning Practice: A Multi-site Study." *Michigan Journal of Community Service Learning*, 8(2): 50–60.

Schon, D. A. (1987). *Educating the Reflective Practitioner* (San Francisco: Jossey-Bass).

Simons, L. and Cleary, B. (2006). "An Evaluation of Academic Service-Learning." In K. M. Casey, G. Davidson, S. H. Billig and N. C. Springer (eds.), *Advancing Knowledge in Service-Learning: Research to Transform the Field* (Greenwich, CT: Information Age Publishing), pp. 113–35.

Smith, V. (1993). "New Dimensions for General Education." In A. Levine (ed.), *Higher Learning in American 1980–2000* (Baltimore, MD: Johns Hopkins University Press), pp. 243–58.

Sobania, N. and Braskamp, L. A. (2009). "Study Abroad or Study Away: It's not Merely Semantics." *Peer Review*, 11(4): 17–20.

Stanton, T. K. (1990). "Liberal Arts, Experiential Learning and Public Service: Necessary Ingredients for Socially Responsible Undergraduate Education." In J. Kendall and Associates (eds.), *Combining Service and Learning, I* (Raleigh, NC: National Society for Internships and Experiential Education), pp. 175–89.

Tellez, K., Hlebowitsh, P. S., Cohen, M. and Norwood, P. (1995). "Social Service Field Experiences and Teacher Education." In J. M. Larkin and C. E. Sleeter (eds.), *Developing Multicultural Teacher Education Curricula* (Albany: State University of New York Press), pp. 65–78.

Verducci, S. and Pope, D. (2001). "Rationales for Integrating Service-Learning in Teacher Education." In J. B. Anderson, K. J. Swick and J. Yff (eds.),

Service-Learning in Teacher Education: Enhancing the Growth of New Teachers, Their Students, and Communities (Washington, DC: American Association of Colleges of Teacher Education), pp. 2–18.

Wade, R. C. and Yarbrough, D. B. (1997). "Community Service-Learning in Student Teaching: Torward the Development of an Active Citizenry." *Michigan Journal of Community Service Learning*, 4: 42–55.

Watson, D. L., Crandall, J., Hueglin, S. and Eisenman, P. (2002). "Incorporating Service-Learning into Physical Education Teacher Education Programs." *Journal of Physical Education, Recreation, and Dance*, 73: 50–54.

Xu, H. X. (2008). "Historical Development of the General Education Curriculum Content in the United States and its Implications." *University General Education Bulletin*, 4: 107–28.

15 Current status of general education outcome assessment and the establishment of an assessment system in mainland China

Feng Huimin

Over the twentieth century, with rapid social development and globalization, countries all over the world have made a commitment to reforming their higher education systems. This trend is propelling university general education (GE), fostering individual talents who can adapt to the rapidly changing world. Thus, GE has become an important part of education reform and development in higher education across the globe.

General education has been widely adopted across colleges and universities in Taiwan, Hong Kong and mainland China. In the late twentieth century, universities and colleges in the three places engaged in extensive and in-depth discussion on the content and objectives of GE, initiated a series of GE courses and developed a large number of GE activities. Despite its grand scope and scale, so far there is little attention being paid to GE impact and quality. Assessment and quality control have not been taken seriously, either.

Quality is the lifeline of a university. Quality control contributes to the achievement of the intended GE objectives, as well as the overall quality of college graduates. In turn, GE quality depends on outcome evaluation, which offers assessment and future directions. Indeed, the enhancement of GE quality cannot be achieved without assessment, which provides both a foundation and a future direction. GE assessment plays an irreplaceable role in improving its quality. GE implementation will be clueless and ineffective if a well-designed assessment system is not in place.

Since the 1990s, many American universities have been paying attention to the real outcome of GE. Many of them set up GE assessment committees or specialized agencies under university-wide assessment committees to evaluate GE and plan new GE assessment schemes. These universities have used a variety of direct and indirect assessment methods and tools on and off campus to evaluate GE outcome. Data are collected for the committee in planning and improving the curriculum. Likewise, Taiwan has organized two large-scale GE assessments and developed a distinctive GE assessment system there. What, then, is the situation of GE assessment in mainland China?

Current status of GE assessment in mainland China

At present, assessment of GE has just started in mainland Chinese colleges, with no mature theories or methodologies. There are several major problems in GE assessment on Chinese university campuses.

1   There is no widely acknowledged, scientific and systematic GE assessment system. Over recent years, with the further development of GE, its assessment has become a part of the working agenda for mainland Chinese universities. However, currently, for the majority of them, there are no specific standards for GE assessment. Instead, they have been using the same benchmarks for evaluating specialized courses. Only a few campuses have set up specific GE evaluation standards, but the standards are often messy, confusing and ambiguous, and most of them are highly abstract, general, random and subjective, with little scientific basis or theoretical grounding. Also, the standards vary from school to school with little regularity. There is no widely acknowledged, scientific and systematic GE assessment system.

2   The objectives for GE assessment are not clearly defined and its content is not comprehensive. Without clearly defined GE learning outcomes, Chinese universities have not been able to establish objectives for GE assessment. Assessment conducted by many universities focuses on the popularity of GE courses among students. Due to the ambiguity of evaluation objectives, many universities have focused on GE teachers' attitude, language fluency, clarity of thinking and student behavior in the classroom as the main benchmarks of GE assessment. In fact systematic GE assessment should focus on the evaluation for teaching and learning objectives, content, mode of delivery, methodology and effects. Moreover, every focus area should have its own evaluation indexes, which need to be scientific, specific, detailed and reliable.

3   The benchmarks of GE do not reflect unique GE features. On most mainland university campuses, GE assessment is primarily included in the general assessment schemes of undergraduate education. Since undergraduate assessment covers all courses, the standards for evaluation are often broadly based, unspecific, and cannot reflect the unique GE features. Indeed, GE has its own unique features:

  • Foundational. GE requires that students gain foundational knowledge in broad areas of human knowledge, i.e. to understand and master the basic content of each discipline and its methodology in order to get basic knowledge and skills, laying an extensive foundation for future professional and personal development.
  • Interdisciplinary. GE is interdisciplinary in nature, which means equipping students with creativity in their interdisciplinary studies.
  • In-depth. GE not only helps students gain knowledge of different fields, but, more importantly, helps students develop critical thinking skills, build their character and nurture their soul, which contribute to the development of a harmonious human world. In view of these special

features, GE should have its own evaluation standards highlighting its unique features.

4   The evaluation method of GE is monolithic. Chinese universities have adopted different evaluation methods for GE programs. For example, Peking University primarily takes student evaluation plus peer reviews by senior professors, university administrators, deans and department heads. Fudan University in Shanghai relies mostly on online student evaluations, complemented by instructor self-evaluation and class visits by specialists/ advisors. Wuhan University takes the student rating, GE project initiation, inspection and acceptance, handled by the office of academic affairs, as its main method, and the evaluation by a faculty steering committee as a supplement. Although the universities have used different approaches, the methodologies they have adopted tend to be monolithic. In most cases, surveys or questionnaires are used to collect student and faculty feedback on GE while other methods are rarely considered.

In fact, GE assessment calls for a diversity of methodologies. GE is different from professional education. It is not only about the learning of knowledge, but also the nurturing of student emotions, capability, morality and personalities. Knowledge acquisition can be measured by the assessment methods of specialized disciplines, but the degree and stages of the development in emotions and abilities demand different benchmarks for evaluation. No single method is perfect or capable of measuring the full range of educational goals, especially with regard to student skills and abilities, behavior and attitude, which must be measured by a combination of different methodologies.

There are many categories of evaluation methods. In the United States, they are often classified as direct methods and indirect methods. Direct methods in higher education mainly include external and internal standard tests and various portfolios. Indirect methods mostly refer to various questionnaires, research indexes such as course enrollment rates, grade distribution and graduation rates as well as reports by relevant staff and departments. Each university chooses its own methodology based on the specific objectives of their GE program. In addition to the course-specific learning outcome assessment, some universities also implement comprehensive assessment of the entire GE program. For example, longitudinal studies are undertaken to compare pre-learning test results with post-learning test results, and to compare student on-campus self-evaluation with employer evaluations. All these methodologies can serve as good models.

5   Faculty and students are not actively participating in the process of GE assessment. At present, for most mainland Chinese universities it is often the office of academic affairs that oversees and administers GE assessment. Even at universities such as Beijing University and Fudan University, where they have established Yuan Pei College and Fudan College as independent GE units, it is also the office of academic affairs instead of those independent units that administers GE assessment. The office of academic affairs decides on the timing of assessment, the questionnaires, class visits and the design,

inspection and acceptance of GE courses. In theory, faculty and students, as the main GE stakeholders, should have the primary responsibilities, but in reality, they are often excluded from the assessment process. As a result, faculty members have become outsiders or bystanders to the process. While they often end up as the main objectives of evaluation, they are rarely able to participate in the process of subject evaluation. As for students, they are also passive receivers of various course evaluations and questionnaires on the GE curriculum. Indeed, GE assessment cannot play a guiding role effectively without the active participation of faculty and students. Teachers and their students are the backbone of any curricular program; they are involved in the practice and know exactly what goes wrong in the implementation of theories. Their participation makes the assessment process more authentic, situational, more credible and effective. For so-called "embedded assessment," a popular model among American universities, faculty play an important role in its implementation. This method not only allows the instructors to understand the overall GE objectives on campus so that they can align their course learning outcomes, but also to measure the results of individual student learning outcomes against specific course objectives. Finally, they need to reflect upon the outcomes and make improvement plans accordingly. Although this arrangement represents a challenge for the faculty, they should feel that they pride themselves as the key players in the implementation of GE on campus. In turn they feel inspired to help further promote and achieve GE objectives.

6   Insufficient emphasis on and commitment to GE teaching quality assessment by administrative departments. Many university administrators do not take GE assessment seriously, and they often lump it together with the assessment work of disciplinary courses. They do not think it is necessary to distinguish GE assessment from other assessment work. Therefore, little investment is made in time, funding, staffing and resources for GE assessment. This lack of investment is due to neglect by administrators, but even more importantly, it is because there is not a scientific and working system of GE assessment in place, so they do not know how to conduct the assessment in a scientific and effective way.

The problems listed above indicate that it is imperative to establish a scientific and operational GE assessment system to improve the quality of GE and achieve its intended objectives.

The theoretical foundation of GE assessment: Bloom's taxonomy

Bloom's taxonomy

Toward the middle and latter part of the twentieth century, Bloom's "taxonomy of educational objectives" became widely known. Bloom's taxonomy divides educational objectives into three "domains," namely, cognitive, affective and psychomotor, and sets educational goals and educational processes accordingly. The objectives of the cognitive domain refer to knowledge acquisition, including knowledge, understanding, application, analysis, synthesis and evaluation. The objectives of the affective domain cover receiving, responding, developing, organizing value systems and their characterization. The objectives of the psychomotor domain refer to perception, guided response, mechanism, complex overt response, adaption and originality. In 2000, as a result of the joint efforts by many psychologists and experienced educators, *A Taxonomy for Learning, Teaching, and Assessing: A Revision of Bloom's Taxonomy of Educational Objectives, Abridged Edition* was published. This updated version of Bloom's taxonomy has revised the cognitive domain, adopting a new two-dimensional approach to cognitive objectives, focusing on both knowledge and process.

The knowledge dimension divides knowledge into factual knowledge, conceptual knowledge, procedural knowledge and metacognitive knowledge. Factual knowledge represents the essential elements any student must know to specialize in a discipline or solve a specific problem. Conceptual knowledge is the knowledge of classifications, principles, generalizations, theories, models or structures pertinent to a particular disciplinary area. Procedural knowledge is the "knowledge of how to do things" and refers to information or knowledge that helps students to do something specific within a discipline, subject or area of study. Metacognitive knowledge is the knowledge of one's own cognition and general cognition.

The knowledge dimension helps instructors to decide what to teach, while the cognitive process dimension assists them to make clear the process of mastering and applying the knowledge to the students, i.e. it is for the teachers to judge the students' levels of mastery and application of factual knowledge, conceptual knowledge, procedural knowledge and metacognitive knowledge. The cognitive process dimension of Bloom's taxonomy consists of six levels that are defined as memory, understanding, application, analysis, evaluation and creativity. As the main axis, knowledge and cognitive processes has formed a two-dimensional classification table. Curricular objectives, processes, activities and assessment are designed and placed in the corresponding cells of the table.

Bloom's taxonomy is the first theory that classifies the educational objectives as well as educational processes aimed at guiding teaching assessment. Through this taxonomy, for "the first time educators can evaluate student learning systematically."[1] It explains each single objective in a concrete, explicit, feasible way, creating conditions for evaluation and feedback. It is important to note that the teaching evaluation itself is an ongoing and dynamic process. Therefore, in this sense, Bloom's taxonomy is compatible with teaching assessment. Its worldwide impact and long-time practice over the years has further proved that Bloom's taxonomy can become the undisputable guide for teaching and learning outcome assessment.

Bloom's taxonomy has not only served as the first set of guiding principles based on classification of educational objectives for teaching assessment, but also, consistent with its taxonomy, offered more integrated viewpoints on psychology. To establish an innovative framework of educational theory is by no means the simple application and extension of existing psychological theory, but a kind of theoretical recreation. Psychologists Rohwer and Sloan once each used five different psychological theories, behaviorism, new behaviorism, information processing, cognitive development and cognitive science, to analyze Bloom's taxonomy. They both concluded that the psychological viewpoints embodied in the taxonomy could not be explained by any single school of psychological theory. Bloom created the taxonomy at a time when behavioral psychology and neo-behavioral psychology were at the peak of their dominating influence. However, Bloom's psychological ideas were not limited to the two schools, but were amazingly compatible with many of the viewpoints proposed by cognitive psychology, which was developed later. This has proved the scientific nature of Bloom's taxonomy from a different perspective.

Bloom's taxonomy has become an important guiding principle for teaching. It allows teachers to refine their course objectives, organize curricular activities and outcome assessment according to their teaching objectives. By applying Bloom's taxonomy to general education assessment, it should be able to help resolve the ambiguity of assessment objectives caused by confusions in setting up GE learning outcomes. Bloom's taxonomy offers important theoretical foundations for GE design, learning outcome classification and assessment.

The classification of GE learning outcomes

Objectives are the expected learning outcomes for students. An objective is an expectation that can be foreseen before action; it could also be a stimulus for outcomes with action. Setting up appropriate objectives can motivate, guide and inspire people. Objectives serve as guides and a theoretical basis for assessment. Without objectives, teaching loses direction and assessment lacks benchmarks. GE assessment follows closely the intended learning outcomes, and learning outcomes are an integral part of GE assessment. Clear, well-defined and workable objectives form the core of GE assessment in higher education. Taxonomy helps assessment activities remain focused on the learning outcomes, and become important trademarks of achieving educational goals. The lack of a scientific, clearly defined and workable taxonomy for GE will cause ambiguities in designing GE learning outcomes and make assessment activities difficult.

At present, there are divergent views on the learning domains of GE where there is no widely accepted system of learning outcomes classification. In the United States for example, the Commission on Higher Education has classified GE objectives into the following categories: promoting the code of conduct based on ethical principles; training knowledgeable and responsible citizens; understanding others' perspectives, expressing one's ideas effectively; and acquiring critical thinking skills and habits. The American Council on Education and educators from California have conducted a joint research project on GE objectives, where they classified the goals into twelve domains, including cultivation of students' abilities in exercising citizen rights and obligations in a democratic society; nurturing moral and spiritual development;

development of skills in expression; and acquisition of mathematical and mechanical skills.

At Tsinghua University in Taiwan, GE has the following objectives: broad and balanced knowledge background; critical reflection and heuristic reasoning; and global and local perspectives and empathy. For National Changhua University of Education in Taiwan, GE objectives are defined as: broad cultural literacy and artistic expression; effective participation in communications at various levels (local, national and global); deep understanding of the basic laws and principles in system operation in both the material world and life sciences.

Among mainland Chinese universities, Peking University has grouped GE objectives into eight categories: to help students master ideas and methods to understand and transform the world through basic knowledge acquisition; to develop students' critical thinking skills; to grasp the basic spirit of classic texts from a comprehensive perspective and provide enlightenment, and so on. For Zhejiang University, its GE objectives cover four dimensions: to improve student independent thinking and critical learning skills and to provide students with diverse perspectives and broaden their vision for the world.

Inconsistencies in classifying GE learning outcomes have made its assessment even more difficult. As a matter of fact, despite the variety of objective classifications, we might follow Bloom's taxonomy and group GE indexes into three broad categories, as follows:

- Objectives in the domain of knowledge – to improve student GE proficiency by teaching them knowledge and skills; to inform students of the relationship between this knowledge and skills and disciplinary knowledge, to equip students with multiple perspectives and a broad education to understand history, society and the world while forming a broad and balanced knowledge structure.
- Objectives in the domain of skills – to help students master disciplinary thinking, methodology and basic skills; to teach students how to use disciplinary knowledge in analyzing problems from other disciplines and to train student skills in thinking, critique and creativity; to raise student capabilities in lifelong learning; and to enable students to grasp basic skills in mathematics.
- Objectives in the domain of emotions – to guide students in developing particular interests, attitudes and values; to have a correct understanding of social phenomena and to live in harmony with nature, society and other people.

Corresponding to the three domains of learning outcomes listed above, the teaching objectives of GE can also be divided into objectives of knowledge, abilities and emotions. The three objectives can be further broken down into several sub-objectives. GE outcome assessment should benchmark these sub-objectives under these broad domains to avoid abstraction, generalization or ambiguity.

The establishment of a GE assessment system in higher education

Education quality evaluation is an assessment that evaluates the teaching process and outcomes. There are multiple important variables in assessing teaching quality, including teachers, students, curricular objectives, content, pedagogy and effectiveness. However, the teaching process and student learning outcomes are the primary areas for evaluation. Teaching process is evaluated mostly through teaching reviews, while learning outcome is often assessed through exams and tests. There are various means of assessment, but quantitative and qualitative reviews constitute the two major forms. Teaching quality evaluation is the way to "improve the teaching and learning process"; it aims to improve and optimize the teaching process. Through assessment, information and the basis of judgment can be made available for optimizing the learning process and improving teaching quality.

A university GE assessment index system should include the following categories: objectives, objects, methodology and contents. The specific indexes are as follows:

A   Objectives of assessment
Teaching objectives of a GE curriculum:
To what extent do the learning outcomes of a GE curriculum agree with the three broad domains of learning in GE?
Teaching content: does the teaching content match the three broad domains of learning in GE?
Teaching formats and approaches: are the teaching formats and approach conducive to the implementation of the three broad domains of learning in GE?
Teaching effect: does the teaching effect meet the learning outcomes as outlined in the three broad domains of GE?

B   Objects of assessment
Teachers: have they achieved their teaching objectives? It is mainly the assessment of the teachers of a specific course or a set of courses.
Students: have they achieved the learning objectives?

C   Methods of assessment
Portfolio evaluation, psychological scale test (tests conducted both before and after teaching to see whether and to what extent certain student skills are improved), standardized tests, questionnaires, course-embedded assessment, student on-campus self-evaluation and after-graduation employer evaluations, and so on.

D   Content of assessment
Teaching objectives (secondary): is the description of course objectives clear, specific and comprehensive (tertiary)? Are the objectives well defined and

structured (tertiary)? To what extent do the teaching objectives agree with the main domains of GE (tertiary); is the feasibility of educational activities fully taken into account in the implementation of objectives (tertiary), and do the objectives reflect student individual characteristics (tertiary)?

Teaching content (secondary): relevance (tertiary): relevance refers to the question whether the index is able to reflect GE teaching objectives. In line with the overall objectives of GE, the curricular goals of GE courses can also be divided into the cognitive, affective and psychomotor areas. For the cognitive, course content covers factual knowledge, conceptual knowledge and procedural knowledge. Factual knowledge introduces to students some of the basic information in the discipline, including case studies. Conceptual knowledge enables students not only to understand relevant concepts and knowledge, but also the essence, the spirit and the unique research perspectives and methodology presented in the course. Moreover, students not only need to know the relationship between those concepts and principles and their own discipline, but also their relationship with other disciplines. Procedural knowledge allows students not only to grasp basic disciplinary knowledge, but also learn how to apply that knowledge to solve other disciplinary or social problems. Inclusion of those three areas of knowledge in the course content becomes the major benchmark to measure if the cognitive objective is achieved. For the psychomotor, course learning outcome should include social skills, language skills, analytical and problem-solving skills, value judgment and aesthetics skills. Knowledge acquisition leads to skills development in the humanities, social and natural sciences. Focusing on those skills in designing course content is one of the major benchmarks for achieving the psychomotor objectives. For the affective, teaching content should include the cultivation of a rigorous attitude towards scholarship and life for mathematics and science subjects; teaching an objective and tolerant viewpoint on other cultures and histories for humanities subjects; developing a diverse perspective on ethical, social and political issues and value judgments for social science subjects. These elements in the curriculum serve as an important benchmark for achieving the psychomotor objective.

Scientific (tertiary): does the curriculum cover the foundational and core knowledge of the discipline? Does it present different schools of thoughts and various approaches? Does course content have a strong theoretical and ideological basis? Cutting-edge (tertiary): does course content bring students to the forefront of the discipline with new products, new trends, new information and their impact on future social development? Relational (tertiary): do factual knowledge and conceptual knowledge relate well to each other and prove and explain key points? Balanced (tertiary): does course content reflect a balanced representation between the breadth and depth of knowledge?

Pedagogy (secondary): does course content emphasize the teaching of methodology and critical thinking (tertiary); does it take a multidisciplinary approach, diverse perspectives and different ways of thinking (tertiary); does the teacher work with various teaching methods according to the unique characteristics of a particular course.

Teaching effect (secondary): namely, learning outcome assessment. The teaching effect needs to be measured by the student learning outcomes. Therefore, the evaluation should focus on the "student learning" instead of "instructor teaching." Outcome can be measured from the cognitive, the affective and the psychomotor domains. Evaluation can be designated as: fully achieved (tertiary); basically achieved (tertiary); and not achieved (tertiary). (A fourth-level index can be added based on the degree of the achievement in the cognitive, affective and psychomotor objectives.)

Conclusion

Assessment plays a very important role in educational activities. It guides, evaluates and supervises the objects under review. It also regulates and diagnoses educational activities to improve policy and the quality of education. A systematic and scientific GE assessment system is designed and based on overall GE objectives. Thus, it can serve as a road map for the implementation of the GE curriculum, for both "teaching" and "learning." When instructors design their GE curriculum based closely on the objectives and content of the system, their teaching will be more focused and this in turn makes it easier for them to achieve GE objectives. GE is an important part of higher education. With the improvement of GE, the overall quality of professional training will be strengthened. Therefore, a scientific, rational and effective GE assessment system carries real significance for the further reform of GE in higher education and improving the overall quality of talents training (in mainland China).

Note

1   Lorin W. Anderson and Lauren A. Sosniak, *Bloom's Taxonomy of Educational Objectives: A Forty-Year Retrospective* (New York: National Society for the Study of Education, 1994), p. 123.

Chapter 15 appendix (1)
Assessment indexes of theory courses, Peking University

I	Single choice a. Very satisfied b. Satisfied c. Neither d. Dissatisfied e. Very dissatisfied	a	b	c	d	e
	1. Instructor is dedicated, diligent and passionate about teaching 2. Instructor addresses our questions seriously and patiently in and after class 3. Instructor's presentation is clear, focused and well organized 4. Instructor can effectively adjust class schedule according to student feedback 5. Instructor's teaching is inspirational and arouses our curiosity 6. Instructor makes class dynamics lively and interesting 7. I believe the course has enhanced my knowledge and ability 8. Instructor makes good use of class time 9. Instructor is strict with us in every aspect 10. I think the instructor is an excellent teacher					

II	Multiple choices
	11. In studying for this course, you believe you still need:
	    A. To be provided with some suitable class materials, and given reading guidance
	    B. To get tutoring assistance (Q & A) not only before exams but also regularly outside class
	    C. Preferably a designated website for the course with discussion forums among the instructor and students
	    D. Guided in applying theories to practice with as many opportunities as possible (such as experiment, survey, design, etc.)
	12. As for attendance, do you often stay away from class?
	If not, your main reasons are:
	    A. This course is very important, and I can learn a lot from it
	    B. Excellent lectures
	    C. Strict attendance policy
	    D. The course is difficult, I am afraid of not keeping up with it
	If yes, your main reasons are:
	    A. The course is boring and useless; not interested
	    B. Ineffective teaching; I'd rather learn by myself
	    C. Instructor is lenient and I can pass the exam easily
	    D. The course it too easy; I can still keep up with it despite missing classes					

III	Short answer questions 13. What do you think is the instructor's most prominent strength? 14. What areas in the course do you think need urgent improvement?					

Chapter 15 appendix (2)
Assessment system design for new undergraduate curriculum, Fudan University

I	**Benchmarks for instructors** *[Basic questions]* 1. Instructor is serious and responsible in teaching, and is able to complete teaching tasks as planned 2. Instructor adopts excellent teaching materials or handouts, providing reference materials for student self study 3. Instructor is articulate and well organized 4. Instructor has good class management skills 5. Instructor communicates well with students, giving them ample opportunities to ask questions and express themselves *[Additional questions for seminar-type courses]* 1. The course adopts the seminar format, which can stimulate your research interest 2. Instructor can give advice before seminar and comments and summaries afterwards *[Platform for open comments]*
II	**Benchmarks for advisors** 1. You have easy access to the advisor when needed 2. Advisor can provide effective guidance when you encounter problems in learning 3. Advisor knows your academic performance and interest. 4. College and department solicit feedback from students about their advisors *[Platform for open comments]*
III	**Benchmarks for teaching assistants (TA)** 1. TA attends each class and fully understands course content 2. TA cares about student learning needs and provides student feedback to the instructor 3. TA gives timely and serious tutorials (such as helping with class exercises, experiments/practices, leading discussions, grading homework) 4. TA's tutorials are accurate and professional 5. TA conduct regular Q & A sessions outside class *[Platform for open comments]*

Chapter 15 appendix (3)
Class visit form, Wuhan University (for assessment experts)

General education classes					
Course name					
Instructor					
Offering unit					
Time	YY/MM/DD		Weekday		Period
Location					
Class discipline					
Total number of students enrolled:	Present		Late arrival:		Early departure:
Summary of class visit notes					
Instructor feedback					
Student feedback					
Evaluation of class teaching					
Indexes of evaluation					
Items	Main points of evaluation			Score value	Score
Teaching attitude	Fully prepared for class; start and finish class on time; maintain class discipline			10	
	Appropriate dress, agreeable manner, clear thinking, good lectures, and vivid language.			10	
Teaching content	Well-defined course objectives; matching course content.			10	
	Well-prepared lectures with key points and difficult issues highlighted			10	
	Very versed in course content with easy use			10	
	Course content reflects latest developments and trend of the field			10	
Teaching methods	Appropriate pedagogy, which is inspiring and artistic			10	
	Effective use of multimedia instruction			10	
Teaching effect	Motivates students and enlivens class dynamics			10	
	Distinctive teaching style and excellent delivery			10	
Total				100	
Overall evaluation	Excellent 100> x ≥85) [ ] Good (85> x ≥75)[ ] Pass (75> x ≥60) [ ] Fail (x <60) [ ]				
Comments and suggestions					
Made by Department of Academic Affairs 2009					

Chapter 15 appendix (4)
Student evaluation and feedback form for GE courses, Wuhan University

Time: YY/MM/DD			
Course name			
Instructor			
Offering unit			
Content of evaluation and score			

	Content of evaluation	Score value	Score
1	Starts and finishes class on time; maintains class discipline	10	
2	Enthusiastic, inspiring and engaging	10	
3	Helps students develop problem-finding, problem-analyzing and problem-solving skills	10	
4	Stimulates student mental development, nurtures artistic sensitivities and cultivates good character	10	
5	Informative, substantial and focused	10	
6	Reflects latest developments and trends in the field, and broadens perspectives	10	
7	Well-defined course objectives; matching course content.	10	
8	Effective use of multimedia instruction	10	
9	Motivates students and enlivens class dynamics	10	
10	Teaching materials and reference books available with homework assignments	10	
	Total	100	

Overall evaluation and feedback:

Designed by Steering Group

Afterword

As we advance into the knowledge society of the twenty-first century, universities across the globe are re-examining their mission and how best to respond to the new challenges coming along with globalization. There is also increasing awareness of the need to link the arts and sciences to cope with the more complex social, economic, political and ecological realities. In the midst of this growing awareness, the importance of general education is being emphasized as core to the undergraduate curriculum.

In Hong Kong, the value of general education and liberal studies is officially recognized as an essential ingredient of the educational experience. The New Senior Secondary (NSS) School Curriculum, implemented from 2009/10 at the secondary level, makes liberal studies a pre-requisite subject in the new Diploma of Secondary Education examination. With the adoption of a new four-year undergraduate curriculum from 2012/13 at universities along the lines of the North American model, the opportunity is taken to strengthen the breadth of tertiary education through added emphasis on general education.

There can be both a *minimalist* approach in that only lip-service is paid by both university educators and students in order to fulfill the "new" requirement imposed from above, or a *maximalist* approach by mainstreaming general education as part of liberal education in reinforcing the ideal of the university. Both approaches could be based on very pragmatic incentives. The world is fast changing into a "flat world" (according to Thomas Friedman's 2005 bestseller *The World is Flat*), where globalization has brought about both new opportunities and threats. In order to stay competitive, our young generation needs to be equipped with a broad knowledge base, adaptability, independent thinking and the ability for lifelong learning. However, education is not just about responding to globalization as such. It is, for all societies, more about nurturing citizenry and preserving and extending social traditions and values. It is also about character and identity formation, as well as grooming a "thinking" and "creative" community.

General education at present is very loosely and generally defined to the extent that its meaning varies according to academic context and strategy. Indeed it could be deemed a fuzzy concept. The minimalists and pragmatists may see general education as a kind of "pick what you want" option which helps get resources for teaching departments, and presents an easy way for students to get credits, especially when some general education courses are seen to involve less intensive teaching and assignments. For those educators who are serious about general education, it should exemplify a kind of liberal education through which students attain and practice virtue and wisdom, and develop a liberal and critical mind.

How *liberal* should general education be? What should general education be *freed from*?

To give these two critical questions a good answer, one has to look at the *modus operandi* of current higher education. Instead of achieving a broad intellectual and academic horizon of knowledge, higher education is becoming more and more narrow-based and discipline-based, in the name of specialization and professional/vocational preparation, so much so that students know very little beyond their own program area. General education should help free higher education from the "compartmentalization" of knowledge; it should help to halt the trend for knowledge to become "the discipline" which jealously guards its academic boundary and creates undue academic and territorial hurdles for cross-disciplinary intellectual pursuits. General education should be part of the academic "mainstream," not just a peripheral area or marginal to program teaching. It should not be casually construed as a host of "electives" that students choose in order to fulfill curriculum requirements, or as "secondary" courses that hand out credits easily in order to attract students and budget resources.

Over the past decade, higher education has also been undergoing a process of internationalization. The advent of globalization should have led to embracing more cross-national and cross-cultural diversities. Yet there are growing concerns about the risk in the loss of local identity and values of universities as institutions of higher learning. The obsession with international rankings and the commodification of higher education have together led many scholars to question if modern universities have already lost their purpose – "excellence without a soul," in the words of Harry Lewis, a former dean of Harvard College. Without underplaying the importance of modern universities in human-capital formation and in cultivating new knowledge to uplift human productivity, the point about nurturing the critical mind, cross-culturalism and true cosmopolitanism in a globalized world is beginning to become recognized in the current reflections on the future of higher education.

The new emphasis on general education and on multidisciplinary and alternative learning experiences arises not just from a concern about the narrowness of undergraduate education in many university settings, as universities are induced whether by government policy or market pressures to focus on specialization in professional and vocational education terms, at the expense of the broad-based liberal education which characterized the early universities. It also coincides with a growing awareness among university leaders of a looming crisis of university education. Ultimately, general education should reinforce the "ideal of the university" – to groom a free person and a good citizen. It should embrace diversity, and multidisciplinary and cross-disciplinary approaches to learning, facilitating students to relate to the past, the present and the future, and to relate to others (our society, our globe). With this in mind, there should be a proactive and purposeful strategy underpinning general education.

Against such a background, the publication of this book is most timely. The contributors cover a wide range of pertinent issues – conceptual debates and the philosophies and traditions of general education, curriculum designs and pedagogies, as well as the evaluation and assessment of educational outcomes. Their thoughts, observations and practical experiences will no doubt benefit academic and educational policy discussions, and make valuable contributions to the ongoing reflections on the direction and purpose of university education as a whole.

Professor Anthony B. L. Cheung
President
The Hong Kong Institute of Education
January 2008–June 2012

Index